SLICED BREAD

THE FOUR GOSPELS, ACTS AND REVELATION: THEIR LITERARY STRUCTURES

David G. Palmer

CERIDWEN PRESS, CARDIFF

Cover quotations are from correspondence with the author between July 1986 and May 1988.

Photgraphs by John Davies

British Library Cataloguing in Publication Data

Palmer, David G., 1948-
    Sliced Bread: (the Four Gospels, Acts &
    Revelation: their literary structures).
    1. Bible, NT — Critical Studies
    I. Title
    225.6

ISBN 0-9513661-0-6

Printed in Great Britain by Clifford Frost Limited, Lyon Road, Wimbledon SW19 2SE.

Published by Ceridwen Press, 17 Chargot Road, Victoria Park, Cardiff CF5 1EW.

Notes on the Author

Born in Hull in 1948, David Palmer later attended Hull Grammar School. After following a seven-year course in Architecture, based at University College London, he registered as an Architect in 1975. He has worked for the Hull City Architect's Department, Costain Construction Ltd., Yorke, Rosenberg, Mardall, and the Haringey Borough Architect's Service. In latter years, he has been a partner of the London-based Pickard and Palmer Partnership.

After a seven-year biblical, pastoral and theological training, he was ordained a Methodist Minister in 1983. He studied at All Nations Christian College, Ware, Hertfordshire and afterwards gained pastoral experience in a Lay Ministerial and Pre-collegiate appointment in Lower Holloway and Camden Town, North London, before continuing his studies at Wesley House and Fitzwilliam College, Cambridge.

His ministry since Ordination has been in the Methodist Circuit of Cardiff. His pastoral charges have included Loudoun Square and Christchurch, Fairwater. The Churches he serves at present are Clare Gardens, Conway Road and Wesley.

He and his wife, Susan, have four children: Gavin, Rosalind and Alice (on earth) and Anna (in heaven).

Dedicated to Sue, my wife,
who was born on St Luke's Day

and in memory of Anna, our fourth child,
who died on St Luke's Day, 1987,
aged 144 days.

Contents

Preface

TO THE WORK of investigating the literature of the four Gospels, the Acts of the Apostles and the Revelation to John, I have been able to bring the tools of two trades not normally associated. My training has been in both Architecture and Theology. In neither field can I consider myself an 'expert', but what I can claim to possess is a deep sense for 'design' and a passion for closely studying the scriptures.

For my part, I was attracted firstly to an examination of the Central Section of Luke's Gospel for 'order'. It formed a part of an undergraduate dissertation. Such a study proved to me that there was more 'design' to Luke's writings than had yet been discussed, or even discovered. It led me to an examination of the whole of the text of Luke's two-volume work and, in turn, to an examination of the other Gospels and the Book of Revelation. The work was begun in Cambridge during my time of preparation for ordination: in the setting of my ministry in the Methodist Church, in Cardiff, it has undergone much expansion and development.

The results of my investigations, it has to be said, have both surprised and startled me. I have hardly dared to believe that what has been uncovered has laid hidden to the eyes of Bible-students for so long. I have been caused, therefore, to read much more widely than ever I intended. Books and papers of scholarly analysis have been sifted as thoroughly as time has allowed. Some have given me inspiration. Others, for their lack of sound results of literary-analysis, and still others, particularly popularly-available commentaries, for their paucity of discussion on literary-composition, suggest to me that what I am sharing is a discovery of potentially major significance.

This book is a condensed and developed version of an earlier, unpublished work (or, unpublishable work?) of 350 pages of technical analysis and 27, A1-sized, charts. Much of the basic analysis is retained, but much detailed discussion is omitted. It may be that I will have opportunity to share this in other circumstances. Art-works and pictorial, educational-aids, based on the charts themselves are being prepared for production with church, college, school and home purposes in mind. Summary-only charts are presented in this book, in PART B. With its simplification and reduction of much detailed argument of analysis, it is hoped that this work will be useful to a wider readership than that of just academics.

My hope is that this book will stimulate fresh approaches towards a proper handling of these six New Testament documents, in all places where matters of Christian faith are primary. At times, I have despaired of what has seemed to be the ploughing of a lonely furrow, but now my work can be offered to the Church, to preachers, teachers, evangelists, expositors and, not least, its members. It is offered also to theologians, scholars, literature and bible students, bible editors and bible publishers, that through their further work the Church and its mission may benefit more.

My wife and my family have much supported me in my endeavours: without their forebearance and encouragement I could not have completed this project. I am most thankful to them. I owe a great debt also to the churches I have been serving as 'minister': they have tested with me my findings in sermons and bible-studies. I am grateful too to other churches, congregations, groups and authorities, for opportunities of examining these six New Testament documents with them: youth weekends (with teenagers and with some of younger years), Church weekends and broadcast services have given me much valuable experience. I am convinced, therefore, that this work can be shared widely and usefully.

David G. Palmer,
June 1988.

PART A

1 Introduction

'REJOICE with me,
for that which was lost is found.'

The purpose of this book is to reveal fascinatingly
new discoveries concerning the Four Gospels, the Acts of the Apostles
and the Revelation to John. For about two millenia, information which
would describe for us the compositional characteristics of their literary-
structures has lain deeply buried in the texts and therefore unexamined.
In this publication it is brought to the surface. In PART A, each of these six
New Testament Books is discussed. The Gospel of Luke and the Acts of
the Apostles are necessarily presented in tandem. What is given in each
chapter is the 'structural-shape' of each book and the primary features of
structural-analysis which support each presentation. The evidence for
literary-structural relationships between the books is also sifted. The last
chapter of PART A attempts a description of the agenda for further work
which, it is believed, is set by these findings. PART B comprises summary
charts which are intended to assist the reader in employing these
discoveries in his/her own reading and studying of the six books
themselves.

It would seem that these unearthed features of literary-design afford
new opportunities for appreciating the intentions and the endeavours of
the writers and, therefore, for understanding and enjoying the books
themselves. A greater unanimity in the interpretation and application of
their contents can be hoped for: previously because we have been
lacking this knowledge, a great many divisive theories have been
entertained. It may be that we all will have to be prepared to review the
positions we have taken and defended. At the very least, it seems that we
are promised a surer foundation for faith and, hence, a firmer basis for the
Church's continuing mission.

Of the twenty-seven, so-called 'books' of the New Testament canon,
twenty-one beg classification as 'letters'. Of the six which are properly
called 'books', it may be stated that four of them, 'the Gospels', describe
in their own particular ways the 'beginnings' of the 'Good News'. One of
the books, 'the Acts of the Apostles', presents 'continuations' in the telling

of the 'Good News'. The remaining one in the series of presentations, 'the Revelation to John', tells of 'completion' in respect to the 'Good News'. Approximately two-thirds of the contents of the New Testament are given over to these book presentations of 'Good News'. Such describes the scale of the work of this publication which is limited in its concern primarily to the form, the order and the design of these revelations, that is, the 'wholes' and the 'parts' which the literature of these six books comprises.

Justification, perhaps, for the enigmatic title of this book is warranted here. Old and New Testament passages link 'words' of the Lord and of eternal-life with what we call 'bread' (consider, for example, Deut. 8. 3 and Jn. 6. 30-69). But, 'Sliced Bread'? 'Sliced Bread' we might say is the 'best thing since'! For, in contrast to the loaves we enjoy today, which are 'sliced' in the 'slicer', each of the books here under scrutiny would seem to comprise sections, hence 'slices', which are carefully and individually hand-crafted, in each case. As a metaphor it at least builds on an old application. Its appeal as a title is stronger, certainly, than those of 'Decussate Literature', 'Six Book Structures', or 'Rhetoric Rediscovered'. 'The Works of Christendom's First Methodists', was considered as a title also: this was only rejected on the grounds that it might have provoked the charge of party spirit on the author's part.

Reading ancient texts:
The temptation with which we are faced, in reading the Middle-Eastern, first-century literature of New Testament faith, is to read it with the eyes and understanding of western, twentieth-century Christians . . . who possess an abundance of copy! We acknowledge readily that the first audiences of these works shared the thought-forms of the period of religious history as their writers: nowadays we work hard at recapturing the same, but we show little appreciation yet of the fact that few first-century Christians would have possessed 'bible' fragments to which they could turn in private devotion or in evangelistic work. We need to consider what features of literacy and methods of learning characterised the earliest Christian communities.

What the church learned in its first assemblies it would have learned by listening to eye-witnesses. In turn, it would have learned by listening to what was written down for reading aloud when the eye-witnesses were absent (either by their journeying or, later, by their deaths). The growing need in the developing church would have been for fuller accounts (and interpretations) of the past, present and future as it pertained to the Good News. There is indication that this is what gave the impetus to much literary effort.

This literature will have had to have been prepared primarily for 'un-bookish' though not necessarily illiterate communities. Christians from conscientious Jewish family backgrounds will have memorised the

Torah and other Scriptures and will have been educated, at least to that extent (consider Apollos, Acts 18. 24ff). We know that the Scriptures were being read aloud in the assemblies (1 Tim 4. 13): such was the practice of the synagogue (Lk. 4. 17; Acts 13. 15, 15. 21). By this means, the majority of Christians will have become acquainted with the Scriptures (of the Old Testament). The first followers of Jesus, themselves, though described as 'illiterate' (Acts 4. 13), need not have been without a good verbal (aural) education. Only the wealthy we might judge would have possessed their own copies of books (consider the Ethiopian eunuch, Acts 9. 30). Everywhere, therefore, there must have been a considerable degree of dependency on sheer memorising. Memorising what was heard read and understanding what was discussed in the assemblies will have been primary to personal growth and to the growth of Christendom.

Clearly, this literature that we enjoy today, as written and printed comparatively inexpensively and thereby possessed, likely functioned in a quite different way in the early years of the Church. That it was carefully designed not only to reveal the truths of faith (note Lk. 1. 4) but also to facilitate the systematic committing to memory of these truths is a distinct possibility. This might be what we need to know if we are to understand why it was so shaped. We marvel today how actors, trained and experienced in memorising large sections of script, have committed gospels to memory to deliver them word-perfect (and with dramatic presentation) to enraptured audiences. And this they have been able to do without the help of knowing their stuctures! We marvel, perhaps, at the followers of Islam who have committed to memory the whole of the Koran. Every true follower of Sikhism, even today, I am informed, knows at least a third of the Gurmat (the Gurus' Doctrine). The case could be made for Christians today to memorise, if not all the Scriptures, at least large sections of the Good News. That which is memorised can be shared. That which is memorised and stored for easy recall can 'direct our paths'.

The memorising of texts, by listening with the ear to what is read aloud, is assisted and enhanced by the rhythms of the words, sentences, 'paragraphs' and 'chapters' of revelation. Clearly, the human mind, today as in the past, can be trained to store accurately vast quantities of detail. Structured literature surely assists the process. Primary to the establishment of rhythm in literature, as in music, is the presence of order, of structure and of repetitions of theme and detail. Such qualities in the four Gospels, the Acts of the Apostles and the Revelation to John are there for our uncovering, it seems.

At the small scale, qualities of order have been much observed already: consider John 21. 15-17 (Jesus' commissioning of Peter) for a well-known example. It is the larger scale constructions that, for too long, have remained in obscurity. When it is considered that any book gains its clarity from its chapters, headings and paragraphs, that any story benefits from the way its episodes clearly differentiate and connect, then the implication is understood: any uncovering of a system, or systems, of composition of these six New Testament books would afford an opportunity for a better understanding and an easier memorising of what is written. Furthermore, such a discovery in this literature would allow a re-examination of the methods as well as of the results of scholarship pertaining to it.

Necessarily, in this introduction it seems, reference has to be made to details which will become clear only later in the book. It would appear to be the case that John's Gospel, in its earlier, shorter form (of prologue, seven linearly-arranged sections and epilogue), satisfactorily met the criteria for memorability. Its present, expanded form, expanded to include further kerygmatic and didactic material of the Apostle John (after his death? See Jn. 21. 23, 24), displays what might have been a synoptic influence, in this second stage use of chiasm (employed variously by Mark, Matthew and Luke, in turn). The decision to change the structure might have rested principally on arguments in favour of increasing the book's memorability: the purpose of the aesthetic of chiasm would seem indeed to be mnemonic. What is clear is that the book of John presently displays surprisingly clear dislocations and displacements of an earlier text. That these were acceptable in this fashion would seem to support the notion which sees as of the greatest importance the creating of documents schematically and structurally shaped for memorising.

Such a requirement will have demanded, during the processes of presentation and re-presentation of 'the Good News', *many sacrifices* of detail and/or sequence of the pieces of Christian tradition. Examples spring immediately to mind. John's placing of 'Jesus' clearing of the temple' (compared with that of the synoptics) and Luke's placing of 'the woman's anointing of Jesus' (compared with that of Matthew's and Mark's, and also of John's). Historical, sequential and theological data were, it seems, *sacrificeable* for reasons of structural necessity. The other functions of literature, of communicating correct details in correct order, of communicating by poetic presentation and so on, would seem to have been subordinated to the (more important) function, that of promoting and enabling the cerebral storage of what was written to be read aloud. One needs only to consider Matthew's genealogy or indeed Luke's rehandling of the incident (and the very point itself) of 'Jesus' anointing'. Is it not the case that Luke promised to write 'carefully in order' (Lk. 1. 3) in a literary sense?

Today, the Church on the whole mistakenly seeks a consistency of account, in historical and theological terms, as it reads these different books. But, the scriptures of the Early Church cannot do today what they were not intended to do then! Such a conclusion should prove salutary.

The above introduces the context for our considerations and demonstrates, be it at this stage pre-emptively, the far-reaching ramifications of the results of literary-structural analysis. Certainly, it has to be said that erstwhile sub-divisions of the documents (firstly, for lectionary purposes and secondly, by chapter and verse: a more modern characteristic by comparison with the early examples of the first) have assisted little in clarifying the literary- and thematic-structures of these books. If it is that these New Testament evangelists have ordered their works to structural and sub-structural principles, we simply want to know! Also, 'in what way?' and 'by how much?' and 'why?'.

What first-century, Christian literature, born in content at least in the Middle-East, did for the Early Church in fostering an understanding and a memorising of what was written to be read aloud, the same could do again for today's Church, which has the added advantage of print.

A summary of this book's basic propositions:

The results of my research and analysis are summarised here.

Mark's Gospel, it would appear, comprises a Prologue, Four Series of 'Seven Days' (by no means all consecutive, but set in chiasms) and an Epilogue. Few readers will readily accept that 16. 9-20 is original: but the case for it is strengthened by literary-analysis. The structure of the whole work can be described by:

Prologue; 1; C1; C1'; 1'; Epilogue

where for, reasons of structure, theme and detail, sections C1 and C1', 1 and 1', and Prologue and Epilogue can be said to correspond. Further, each primary book-element reveals a particular period in the life and ministry of Jesus. The book itself could be titled appropriately, 'Days in the Life of Jesus' or 'The Day(s) of the Lord'.

The Gospels of Matthew and Luke, it seems, are composed to the same basic structural framework. Each side of a central section are five balancing sections. By numbering these sections, the common book-structure can be described as:

1; 2; 3; 4; 5; C; 5'; 4'; 3'; 2'; 1'.

It would appear that the Acts of the Apostles enjoys the same structural scheme also. In its sections, on the Church, it parallels, section for section, in themes and in details, the sections on Jesus, in the Gospel of Luke. In his prologue to his Gospel, Luke promised order: it seems he more than kept his promise!

Matthew's Gospel alone displays independent linkages between the sections. The sections themselves break down into numerical listings of parts: the middle seven sections each consist of twelve parts; the two bordering sections consist of twelve, ten and twelve parts each; and the two peripheral sections consist of two sevens of parts. The main teaching-blocks number five and are found in sections 2, 4, C, 4', and 2'.

John's Gospel, it seems, constitutes a seven-section chiasm:

1; 2; 3; C; 3'; 2'; 1'.

The sections sub-divide into twelve parts each, as follows:

(1, 2, 3 : 1, 2, 3) : (1, 2, 3 : 1, 2, 3)

Couple these results with a consideration of already observed dislocations in the current text and the conclusion which is reached is that what we enjoy today is a re-arranged and enlarged version of an earlier book, with the likely title, 'The Book of the Seven Signs'. It can be argued that this earlier version comprised a Prologue, Seven Sections in linear-arrangement and an Epilogue.

The Book of the Revelation to John is structured similarly to the current version of John's Gospel. It is composed, it seems, of a Prologue, Seven Sections (each comprising seven parts, thematically) and an Epilogue, all of which is set in chiasm.

Order, structure, repetition of themes and details, rhythm, by whatever description, these qualities, it would appear, pervade the literature of these six books of the New Testament. The literary-aesthetic of symmetry and of symbolic numbering of parts (for example, three, four, seven, ten and twelve) are features of this literature which we cannot ignore.

Similarities in the structural-methodologies the writers employed beg us to consider also, in a hitherto totally fresh way, the possible relationships between these books. The priority of Mark seems assured. His material would seem to have been re-worked and added to by Matthew. Luke it seems then took these two compositions and re-worked them, adding material of his own to produce his first book. His second book gained its form and its pattern of contents most assuredly from the first. John's Gospel likely started life independently of the first three, but its final shaped would appear to suggest synoptic influence (in the use of chiasm). Lastly, the Book of Revelation may indeed have come from the same stable as that of the fourth Gospel.

The first question:

The first question which will be asked will be, 'Why have we been so unaware of such literary-structures for nearly two thousand years?' For the major part we can only conjecture. Linked to this is a second question. Are we to understand that the likely common practice of committing the scriptures to memory died out? It might be argued that it did, because of the growing profusion of available copy.

We consider the matter of copy. We know, from early manuscripts, that in the scribal transmission of New Testament literature the repre-senting of divisions and sub-divisions of the text relied mainly on edentations (protrusions of a single letter in the left-hand column). The leaves can be further described. The lines of text are tightly packed indeed. Where the end of a line is reached the remaining letters of an uncompleted word are simply carried over into the next line. Spaces between sentences or paragraphs are simply not shown. And examples abound where edentations are less that a full letter. The copying-process, the long-hand re-writing of texts, a tedious method much open to error, might account for much of the loss of evidence of the original divisions and sub-divisions. Another, alternative reason might be entertained, though it might be considered less likely: Goulder suggests that the margins of the early texts, which would have included the edentations, became worn and torn (1).

What did the first editions look like? We would like to know! We can only assume that the first editions, and maybe the earliest copies, demonstrated more clearly the sectional and sub-sectional characteristics of the writings than do those that we possess now. We properly observe that the features which have survived with clarity are the many small-scale balancings of pieces of text: they have been recognised through the centuries. It is they, if we would consider the matter carefully, that should have lent ready credence to the possibility of balancing, larger-scale constructions. It is they that should have spurred us on to seek, until we had found them.

The principles of literary order:

The structural principles which it seems have been employed in these six New Testament books are basically three-fold: they are: i) the numerical listing of parts; ii) simple parallelism; and iii) chiastic parallelism. Compounds of these are also employed. We examine them.

The numerical listing of parts is such where the parts that make up the wholes consistently and significantly number the same. Examples can be stated. Mark's Gospel gives evidence of four sections of seven parts. Matthew's Gospel would appear to contain seven (central) sections of twelve parts, parallel sections of composite listings of parts (twelve, ten and twelve), and parallel sections of paired listings of seven parts. John's Gospel exhibits a standard sectional usage of twelve parts. In its earlier form, series of threesomes of parts predominated. Numerical listing can be represented diagrammatically by:

$$i; ii; iii; iv; v; \ldots n.$$

Simple parallelism can be represented diagrammatically by:

$$i; i',$$

where i' is the balancing second part to i, the first part. In terms of protasis and apodosis, it is encountered in Luke's Prologue to his Gospel: what is set up in the first part (1. 1, 2) is completed in the second part (1. 3, 4). Or, on a larger scale, it is a repeating of the thematic content of the first part in the second part. Consider Section 3 in the Acts of the Apostles (2. 43-5. 42): the two parts (2. 43-4. 31 and 4. 32-5. 42) are similarly introduced; different incidents lead to similar opportunities for witnessing and, therefore, to the arrest, trial and judgement of apostles, in both cases.

Chiastic parallelism is simply an extension of the above, where i and i' are the balancing parts around a centre, c: it can be represented by:

$$i : c : i'.$$

Further developments of this are:

$$i : ci : ci' : i'$$

which is the major sectional arrangement of Mark's Gospel; and

$$i : ii : iii : iv : v : c : v' : iv' : iii' : ii' : i'$$

which is the sectional arrangement of the Gospels of Matthew and Luke and the Acts of the Apostles. The number of balancing parts are simply increased. At the smaller scale, the first example of this in Luke's Gospel is found in Section 3 (3. 1-4. 44). The genealogy (3. 23-38) is an eleven-part chiasm, with seven names per part, Joseph . . . Joseph, Mattathias . . . Mattathias, and so on. The term, 'chiastic' (note also the terms, 'chiasm' and 'chiasmus') derives from the Greek letter 'Chi', X.

Mark's and Matthew's Gospels give evidence of numerical listings of parts within chiastic structures. John's Gospel gives evidence of a chiastic arrangement of sections which sub-divide into simple parallelisms. A feature of Lucan construction is the frequent integration of simple and chiastic parallelism: a compound of the two can be expressed, for example, by:

$$i : (i : i') : c \, (i : c : i') : i' \, (i : i').$$

Sections 2 and 2' in both Luke's Gospel and the Acts of the Apostles are arranged in this way. Another example is:

$$i \, (i : c : i') : c \, (i : c : i') : i' \, (i : c : i').$$

Sections C, in both books, demonstrate extensions of this compound type.

Research into chiastic structures (2) has been with us, in modern times, since Bengal (in 1742). Goulder (3) appeals to rabbinical usage. Bailey (4) and Talbert (5) give many references to chiastic studies on Testamental and extra-canonical writings. Miesner (6) and Talbert (7) quote similar studies into other Middle Eastern literature, especially classical Greek. The repeated use of similar structure in Greek Architecture and Art, for parallel lines, aesthetic weight and balance, is similarly well attested (8). The probability is that all the writers of these six New Testament books knew and followed earlier examples of literary-structural organisation.

Literary criticism:
The work presented in this publication, properly understood, is primary to the study of Literary Criticism, which is the analysis of texts to establish their structure and composition, their possible use of sources (either oral, or written, or both), their integrity and their style. Literary works can be valued as aesthetic objects in themselves: it is the logic intrinsic in the form and structure of the writing which is sought for and assessed.

Some of the material we are handling is given its own category of Gospel-genre. Viewed by form-critics to be deposits of gospel pieces, the assessments of the Evangelists' role focussed on their arranging small independent units, bringing them together by devices characteristic of the process of tradition such as catchword association. The work of the Evangelists, as viewed by redaction critics, is much more compositional: no longer regarded as mere collectors, the Evangelists are acknowledged to have written with imaginative and purposeful control of their sources. What this book presents is the hard evidence of the truth of this.

What this book does not support, however, is what much redaction criticism has relied very heavily upon, the widely accepted solution to the synoptic problem (the numbering and describing of sources available to Matthew, Mark and Luke). The generally-held 'solution' has been termed, 'the two-document hypothesis', according to which both Matthew and Luke have independently used Mark's Gospel and a hypothetical source 'Q'. The results of literary-structural analysis which this book presents challenge this 'solution'. They suggest, as has been stated above, that Matthew used Mark's Gospel as his chief source and that in turn Luke used both Mark's and Matthew's Gospels.

In terms of literary-critical methodology the liveliest debate in recent years has centred on the validity and usefulness of structuralism. Analyses carried out along such lines have suffered, in the past, from incompleteness and from being highly subjective and interpretative in generalised and fluid fashion. Proponents have been viewed as having an anti-historical bias and as having a theological interest only in the texts. Opposers sometimes speak of their own predisposition to read texts that purport to be historical as sources of historical information and texts that give teaching as sources of teaching, rather than as skilful literary compositions that say something on a literary, aesthetic level. What is so easily overlooked is that literature itself, as in the six books of our study, is the means of communication of both history and teaching: understanding the forms and the purposes of this means of communication promises a clearer understanding of the contents of the books and, hence, a truer interpretation and application of the same. The examination of texts for their structures has this as its aim: it is a worthy pursuit.

The re-discovering, or un-covering, of numerical listings of parts, of simple parallelism, of chiastic parallelism, or of compounds of two or all three of these forms of literary-structural design has been no easy task. An objective, critical method of analysis has been wanting. In the succeeding chapters, are presented methodologies of literary-structural analysis which developed during the course of my work. It may be that they ought to be considered as existing in draft form only at this stage. It may be that these are worth further clarification by nomenclature in order that future work, on the Old Testament, or the New Testament Letters, might proceed with profit.

2 Mark's Gospel

What leading idea forms the basis of the composition of Mark's Gospel? This is clearly a key issue in understanding the book. We consider, but briefly, the very few possible answers to the question.

Flaccid, is how the many links between the pieces of the text have been described (notably, 'and', 'immediately', 'again', 'and it came to pass', 'and thence'): the result has been that no biographical or chronological interest has been established. Further, few direct, geographical conjunctions of the text are observable. Arguments have been put, therefore, for an essentially 'traditional' sequence of events. A theological scheme, repetitive of typological fulfilment of Old Testament texts, was entertained by Farrer. Carrington proposed that the sequence was the result of a liturgical intention for the Gospel (Goulder has developed this thesis). Beach identified what he thought were six stages of revelation of Jesus' messiahship. And Bowman claimed to have discovered parallels to the Jewish Passover Haggada. Nevertheless, 'Close examination of all these schemes', says Kummel (1), 'leads to no proof based on the text itself.'

Is it possible that the text on its own harboured the evidence we sought? The analysis of Mark's Gospel was approached with confidence: prior to it, the analyses of the Gospels of Luke and Matthew and the Acts of the Apostles had brought into the light the hidden evidence which defined the 'leading ideas' behind those compositions. The first step was to identify the material which appeared to give any hint at all of the presence of small and large scale constructions. Of the greatest significance, it seemed, was the 'seven days' of Mark's 'Holy Week'; this truly set the search for other 'series' of 'seven days'.

The analysis of the book, presented below, takes seriously the linkages between the Gospel pieces: they do appear, in fact, to assist in disclosing Mark's purpose of serialised continuity. For instance, the word, 'immediately', always deliberately brings into juxtaposition events in a 'day': only once does it begin a 'day's' telling and that is only in an act of qualification, 15. 1: 'And immediately early . . .' (lit.) meaning, 'Very early in the morning . . .', or 'Immediately in the morning . . .'. Another important linkage is the word which is translated 'again': we shall see in some cases how it is best represented by 'thereupon', or 'immediately-following', behaving like the word, 'immediately', in its general case.

The book, nevertheless, is still not true biography, nor is it fully the result of chronological interest. Rather, like what Beach proposes, it is a book which, for its leading idea, presents stages in the revelation of Jesus' life and mission: furthermore, they are stages which are so designed as to promote a clear understanding as well as a memorising of the book's contents.

Marcan infra-structure:

No apology is given for the use of the term, 'infra-structure': it is a perfectly good planning and architectural term which describes the basic structure, into which all the parts fit and to which all further sub-structures relate. It has its application here. The literary infra-structure to Mark's Gospel can be described as:

1. 1-20	Prologue (in four parts)	a
1. 21-5. 43	FIRST SERIES of Seven Days	b
6. 1-8. 26	SECOND SERIES of Seven Days	c
8. 27-10. 52	THIRD SERIES of Seven Days	c'
11. 1-16. 8	FOURTH SERIES of Seven Days	b'
16. 9-20	Epilogue (in four parts)	a'

where the major components correspond, a with a', b with b', and c with c', for sub-structure, themes and details. Though each of the four series is of 'seven days', the days are not all consecutive. Rather, they look more like the tellings of 'days' as if they were lifted from a diary: 'after some days', 'during those days', 'after six days', such phrases indicate there were many more days than those that are 'recorded' here. The Gospel does not present Jesus as a 'twenty-eight day wonder'.

THE PROLOGUE enjoys a title-verse, 1. 1: 'The beginning of the Gospel of Jesus Christ' (so witness the earliest manuscripts). 1. 2-8 describes, but briefly, the ministry of John the Baptist. 1. 9-13 is Mark's account of God's call of Jesus, and Jesus' immediate, yet forty-day, period of trial in the desert. 1. 14-20 describes the beginning of Jesus' ministry, in preaching the Gospel of God and in calling followers. Repentance and belief, immediacy of following, these are the only true responses. This basically four-part introduction describes adequately for Mark (and presumably, therefore, for his Church) the background and beginning to the days of Jesus' mission: 'the time is fulfilled', the waiting is over.

THE EPILOGUE is considered here. To include this as possibly 'original' is to risk the mockings of many scholars. We all know it to be a later addition! It is absent from the most reliable early manuscripts. It does not square with the preceeding passage, 16. 1-8. Its language is different from the rest of the text. We 'know' these things, yet . . .

The distinctive break in the text between 16. 8 and 16. 9 is justified, structurally and thematically: the Epilogue functions as 'follow-up' to the amazing resurrection-announcement; it moves through disbelief (a natural, reasonable first response) to commissioning, Jesus' ascension and an ending which speaks of a continuation of the story.

It is certainly not impossible that this (back page) Epilogue became separated from worn copy and lost in handling and re-transmission. It is not unlikely that it 'resurfaced' in later copy, or in the writing-down afresh of what had been committed already to memory.

THE PROLOGUE AND THE EPILOGUE serve similar functions: together they frame the Gospel. Like the Prologue, the Epilogue breaks down into four parts: 16.9-11, Jesus' first resurrection appearance, the telling of which is met with disbelief; 16. 12, 13, Jesus' second appearance to two 'walking in the country' (surely, this is what Luke was able to take and develop, in the concluding section of his Gospel); 16. 14-18, Jesus' third appearance to the Eleven, and their commissioning (surely, taken by Matthew and Luke, in turn); and 16. 19, 20, Jesus' ascension (rejected by Matthew, but developed by Luke) and the continuation of the story as it then focussed on the Eleven (the 'accompanying signs' give way in Matthew's account to an accompanying Jesus; Luke saves the theme for a whole book).

Some thematic and verbal details common to the Prologue and the Epilogue further suggest the Epilogue might be original. The ministry of the one coming before Jesus is spoken about in the Prologue: the ministries of those coming after Jesus are spoken about in the Epilogue. In the Prologue, disciples are called to follow and a promise is made regarding their future function: in the Epilogue, they are commisioned and given instructions of what to do. In the Prologue, the heavens open and the Spirit descends on Jesus: in the Epilogue, Jesus himself ascends into heaven. The little-used term in the Gospel, 'Lord', is applied to Jesus in both: see 1. 3 and 16. 19. The 'preaching of the Gospel' is a term common to both: in 1. 14, it is in reference to Jesus, in 16. 15, to the eleven. Galilee is the region of Jesus' first and last disclosures.

The relationships which exist between the Prologue and the present Epilogue are numerous. Is the Epilogue a later addition created by someone else to harmonise with the Prologue? Its priority over Matthaean and Lucan endings would appear to rule out this possibility. It is likely original!

THE FOURTH SERIES OF SEVEN DAYS is the most obvious of the four: we examine this first and the others in reverse order. It can be entitled: 'Jesus' Passion and Resurrection, the Jerusalem Days'. The series is as follows:

Day One	11. 1-11;
Day Two	11. 12-19;
Day Three	11. 20-13.37;
Day Four	14. 1-11;
Day Five	14. 12-72;
Day Six	15. 1-47;
Day Seven	16. 1-8.

The first six days are likely consecutive, Sunday through till Friday. The only reference to Holy Saturday in Mark's account (contrast Matthew's) is at 16. 1, but this is introductory to 16. 1-8, the telling of Day Seven, the Day of Resurection. We note the references, 'And when the sabbath was past . . . And very early on the first day of the week . . . as the sun rose . . .'

Day One begins (and begins the series) with the momentous words, 'And when they drew near to Jerusalem . . .': the day concludes, after Jesus' entry into Jerusalem and into the temple, 'but since it was already late in the day he went out to Bethany with the twelve.' Day Two's account begins, 'And on the morrow . . .': it ends with the words, 'And when it became late, they went out of the city.' The third consecutive day, Day Three begins, 'And passing along in the morning (early) . . .'. The common subject matter of Days Two and Three confirms the sequence. It may be judged that Day Four in the series is the very next day: Days Four, Five and Six are certainly consecutive. Day Four begins, 'Now the Passover and Unleavened Bread were after two days.' Properly under-stood it means the next day: consider the phrase, 'after three days' (8. 31, 9. 31 and 10. 34) which means 'the day after the following day'. Day Five begins, 'And on the first day of Unleavened Bread . . .' and Day Six begins, 'And immediately early . . .' or, 'As soon as it was morning . . .'. Again, as for Days Two and Three, the subject-matter of Days Five and Six demonstrates continuity.

Does Day Four follow Day Three? That is, if Day Four is the Wednesday (working back from the Sabbath, through Friday and Thursday) is Day Three the Tuesday? If it were, then Day One would be a Sunday. Church tradition certainly favours this conclusion.

Something very important was suggested by the analysing of this Series of Days. What appeared to be the case was that a 'day' in Mark's telling consistently assumed a period which was framed by 'sunrise' and 'just before sunrise' the next day. It includes the twelve hours of daylight (see, for reference, 15. 25, 33 and 34) and the four watches of the night (all known to Mark, see 13. 35). This series of days, the Gospel's Fourth Series, demonstrates this: investigation of the whole of the text of Mark's Gospel confirms this is so for all the series. Mark's 'day' is the 'civil day' as defined as a space of twenty-four hours, extending from 'sunrise' to 'sunrise'. Alternatively, the 'civil day' could be defined by the limits of 'sunsets': this we ordinarily associate with the Palestinian 'day' of this era. It would appear that Mark not only knows about but also recognises this

Jewish 'day' in his text, see 15. 42: but his Gospel certainly does not function in this way.

Justification of the title to this series needs no discussion here, it is plainly self-evident.

THE THIRD SERIES OF SEVEN DAYS can be given the title: 'The Days of Jesus' Journeying to the Cross and Glory'. The series is as follows:

Day One	8. 27-9. 1;
Day Two	9. 2-29;
Day Three	9. 30-50;
Day Four	10. 1-16;
Day Five	10. 17-31;
Day Six	10. 32-45;
Day Seven	10. 46-52.

The disclosures of 8. 27-9. 1 have long been recognised as particularly significant in Mark's scheme: readily, many will agree that a distinctively new series of revelations begins here in the text. Day One and this Series of Days begins with the words, 'And Jesus went out and his disciples to the villages of Caesarea Philippi: and on the way . . .'. In this series, 'the way' ('the journey') features strongly: also, the rhythm of new journey/new day is established. Day Two is partially exceptional: it begins, 'And after six days . . .'. Day Three begins with a report of a new journey: it continues in Capernaum where Jesus questions the disciples about what they were discussing 'on the way'. Day Three is not necessarily consecutive with Day Two, and neither is Day Four with Day Three. Day Four begins, literally, 'And from there, rising up . . .' (from sleep?). Day Four in the Second Series begins in a very similar way: see 7. 24. Day Five begins again with Jesus setting-out on his journeyings, 'And as he went out into the way . . .'. Day Six begins with words of great moment (note: for the first time in the Gospel and this series), 'And they were on the road going up to Jerusalem . . .'. And Day Seven begins, 'And they came to Jericho . . .'. Day Seven is not necessarily consecutive with Day Six. The last line of the Series is likely significant: once Bartimaeus, who had been begging 'by the way' (10. 46), is given his sight by Jesus, 'he followed him on the way'. The importance of 'following', we note, is established in this series in 8. 34, on Day One.

Justification for the title to this series of days is as follows. The journeying motif is maintained in Days One and Days Three to Seven. A journey up and down a mountain may qualify Day Two for inclusion too. Coupled with this, it is in this series that we find for the first time in the Gospel any explicit disclosure of Jesus' suffering messiahship. Five times, predictions are given: three sayings are similar, 8. 31, 9. 31 and 10. 33, 34; the two others are at 9. 12 and 10. 45. Their distribution is in Days One, Two, Three and Six. But it is not all gloom and doom: Jesus is to rise again after three days (three times we read this) and there is to be a glorious return (8. 38) and the saving of life (8. 35, compare also 10. 45). The central three days each record Jesus' teaching on life, eternal life and entering into the Kingdom. James and John perceive that Jesus' journeyings will end in glory (10. 37): it is where they too wish to be with him.

THE SECOND SERIES OF SEVEN DAYS can be entitled: 'Days of Increase in the Ministry of Jesus'. The days are:

Day One	6. 1-29;
Day Two	6. 30-52;
Day Three	6. 53-7. 23;
Day Four	7. 24-30;
Day Five	7. 31-37;
Day Six	8. 1-21;
Day Seven	8. 22-26.

Given any English translation only, Day One could look like several days. The significant feature of the Greek is that of an abundance of verbs in the imperfect tense, which are either inceptive or present-continuous. 6. 1, then, introduces the geographical context; 6. 2, 3, describes not only the temporal setting and the specific place but also the cause of the people's questioning; and 6. 4-6a describes Jesus' predicament, the solution to which he begins to put into effect in 6. 6b-13. The interlude, 6. 14-29, concerning Herod's questioning and the report of John the Baptist's execution is both repetitive of the people's questioning and an outcome (and hence a suitable place for such a report) of Jesus' effective solution.

Day Two begins after a passage of days: 6.35 describes what happens when it is late in the day (before sunset); 6. 47 describes what is happening at the onset of evening; and 6.48 (reference the fourth watch) indicates a night-crossing of the sea. Day Three begins with the crossing's completion. Days Two and Three are surely consecutive. Day Four is introduced in temporal and geographical terms, 'And from there, rising up, he went away into . . .' (compare 7. 24 and 10. 1). A passage of days is required before Day Five (the journey was a long one): the day begins, 'And again going out . . . he came through . . . to the sea . . .'. Day Six begins, 'In those days . . .': there is no geographical reference and the temporal reference is a general one. Nevertheless, 8. 2 suggests a passage of time of at least three days. 8. 10 describes a sea-journey but not a crossing: that comes at 8. 13. Day Seven begins with the completion of the likely night-crossing. Days Six and Seven are consecutive.

The title to this second series of seven days is suggested by the increase in the distances and geography of Jesus' journeyings (compare the first series), Jesus' sharing of his mission with his disciples, the extension of Jesus' ministry to include, amazingly, a Gentile woman and her daughter, an increase of food in his hands on two occasions, and a more generous than ever response to his healing work (7. 37).

THE FIRST SERIES OF SEVEN DAYS can be given the title: 'Jesus' First Days of Ministry, confined to Galilee and the Region of its Sea'. The series is as follows:

Day One	1. 21-38
Day Two	1. 39-45
Day Three	2. 1-22
Day Four	2. 23-3. 6
Day Five	3. 7-4. 41
Day Six	5. 1-20
Day Seven	5. 21-43.

For Day One, the following verses, timewise, are most significant: 1. 21, 'immediately on the Sabbath . . .'; 1. 32, 'When it became early evening, when the sun set . . .'; and 1.35, 'And very early in the night . . .' (literally). The day ends with revelation of Jesus' preaching itinerancy. Day Two begins simply with a general summary statement, expressive of a ministry which Jesus fulfils over a longish passage of time. 'And there came to him a leper . . .', is the phrase which as such begins the telling of this particular day's happenings. The record of Day Two ends with Jesus having now to stay in the countryside. Day Three geographically centres on Capernaum again (see Day One) and by the sea: thematically, the Day's account is much to do with 'sinners' and the first challenges to Jesus' authority. It can be seen in this series in particular how Mark introduces a new subject of teaching with each new day.

In 2. 13, is found an interesting feature of the Greek which is repeated in 3. 1 and 4. 1 (note, these are Days Three, Four and Five, the middle days of the series): the Greek word, *palin,* is usually translated 'again'. But, for illustration's sake, in 15. 13 we read, 'And they cried out again, "Crucify him." ' But, this is the first time, we are told, that the crowd so shouted! It is considered that all these usages of the word, *palin,* are the result of a poor translation of an Aramaic word, meaning 'thereupon'. In the above cases, with respect to Days Three, Four and Five, the meaning is closer to that of 'immediately-following' or 'thereupon' than 'again'.

Days Five, Six and Seven appear to be consecutive. Day Six records the event which follows the Gospel's first night-crossing of the sea (note 4. 35). Day Seven begins with the completion of the return-journey: here, *palin* ('again') enjoys its proper 'rursus' usage, marking a return over the same course in the reverse direction. The Day, and the Series, reaches its climax with the account of a raising of a dead child.

The title to this series is self explanatory.

THE FOUR SERIES IN PERSPECTIVE:

The First and Fourth Series of the Gospel bear comparison: we note how strikingly they both end with the only Gospel records of raisings from the dead. Both series relate Jesus' popularity, the crowds' astonishment at his teaching, conflicts over his authority, the wish of the Pharisees 'to destroy him', and Jesus teaching the crowds in parables and the disciples plainly. The betrayer is introduced in the former: in the latter, the betrayer acts. Many other details suggest that these Series do indeed lie parallel to each other in the Gospel. Comparisons of the Series, for their quantity of verses, supports such a conclusion too: the first is 172 verses, the second 119, the third 114 and the fourth 241. The First and Fourth Series are to be viewed as parallel, framing sections to the Gospel's main material.

The remaining two Series, the Second and the Third, have to be viewed, therefore, as the central sections to the Gospel. Equal in size, they are found to parallel each other in terms of content and arrangement. Days One in both Series cover similar material. Jesus' identity is questioned, and some of the details are the same and in the same order: compare 6. 3 and 6. 14-16 with 8. 27-29, noting especially: some said, 'John the Baptist . . .', others said, 'Elijah', and others said, '. . . one of the prophets . . .'. Days Seven in both Series cover similar material too: the only Gospel accounts of Jesus healing blind men are found in the telling of these days' activities (compare 8. 22-26 with 10. 46-52). Other thematic and detail parallels between these two Series could be listed.

Such an examination of the correspondences of the Series leads, therefore, to the following presentation of the Gospel's primary infra-structure: it can be described as:

$$I : (CI : CI') : I',$$

where I represents Series One, CI Series Two (C for central), CI' Series Three and I' Series Four. The Gospel's Series could be described, therefore, as being set in a four-part chiastic structure.

THE BOOK IN PERSPECTIVE:

We have seen how the weight of evidence favours the veiw that the framing pieces, the Prologue and the Epilogue, are parts also of the greater chiasm of the book. Diagrammatically, the complete infra-structure of the book can be represented by:

$$a : b : c : c' : b' : a'$$

as presented above at the beginning of these considerations, or by

$$p : I : (CI : CI') : I' : e.$$

Another further feature of Marcan structural-design requires atten-tion. Significant evidence exists for viewing the Series of Days themselves as chiasms, where Days One, Two, Three, Four, Five, Six and Seven might be represented by:

$$1 : 2 : 3 : C : 3' : 2' : 1'.$$

The major tell-tales are these. In Series One, we noted how in each of the middle three days the particularly interesting conjunction, *palin,* is similarly used. In Series Two, the Feedings of the Five and Four Thousands lie opposite each other, in Days Two and Six. In Series Three, Days One and Seven stress 'following'; Days Two and Six speak of 'glory' (then, in the first; future, in the second); Days Three, Four and Five record Jesus' teaching on life, eternity and entering the kingdom.

Another feature of the design, still more detailed, is that of the literary constructions of the 'days' themselves. At the centre of Series Four, Day Four of the Seven Days, is the anointing of Jesus in Bethany, 'beforehand for burying'. This day's central event is set clearly within the framework of plottings against Jesus: the structure of the passage is plainly, deliberately chiastic (consider, 14. 1, 2; 14. 3-9; 14. 10, 11). The fact is that chiasm and simple-parallelism are used in abundance, throughout the book.

So, are introduced what might be other, even more lengthy and involved, presentations of more detailed levels of structure. The purpose of this publication is necessarily limited. These details of structure are, however, accessible to those who would discover them for themselves.

Mark's role and purpose:
In the earliest testimony to Mark's Gospel that we possess (dated prior to 130AD), Papias, Bishop of Hierapolis, recalls the tradition:
i) that Mark was 'not a hearer or a follower of the Lord . . . but of Peter';
ii) that Mark 'became the interpreter of Peter';
iii) that 'he wrote down accurately but not in order as much as he remembered of the sayings and doings of Christ';
iv) that he 'adapted his teachings to the needs of the moment'; and
v) that he 'did not make an ordered collection of the sayings of the Lord' (like Matthew? like Luke? like John?).
This witness (2) to the Gospel of Mark and to Mark himself and indeed to his working-method is in no way contradicted by the discoveries of literary-order which are presented above. The internal evidence of the Gospel alone indicates that Mark was very much in control of his material and the methods of its presentation.

But, why did Mark choose to write as he did, in series of 'seven days'? And why did he choose 'four series'? It can be argued that he chose this aesthetic, not for its own sake, but for two reasons:
i) the structure is simple and memorable and it therefore assists the understanding and the memorising of the contents; and
ii) there would seem to be deep significance in the choice of the numbers as regards the Gospel revelations.
The number 'seven' enjoyed an eminent place among sacred numbers: it was associated with 'perfection', 'completion' and 'fulfilment'. The number 'four' in the scriptures, is also symbolic of 'completion' (Hebrew thought focussed on the square): it is also a prominent number in prophetic symbolism and apocalyptic literature. It is unlikely that Mark was unaware of these things. It is arguable, therefore,

that the structural-scheme itself was intended to reveal something of the dimensions of the GOOD NEWS which focusses on Jesus.

Why did Mark write in 'days'? Because it helps express 'immanence' and 'incarnation'? Or, did he entertain, at first, the possibility of writing a diary of events as they focussed on Jesus? Several possible answers could be entertained. It is suggested that Mark's work could attract one of two titles, either 'Days in the Life of Jesus' or 'The Day(s) of the Lord': the latter might be preferred for its apocalyptic appeal, and in the form, 'The Day of the Lord'. Mark's message may indeed focus on the historical day (age, period) of Jesus but it speaks clearly too of a future day.

Our task today:

Recovering the rhythms of this first-century book, born in content at least in the Middle East, allows us now, with our (more than Western) twentieth-century skills to present its message afresh in our age. Translators, Bible Editors and Publishers have their job to do. Theologians and Scholars, Teachers, Preachers, Evangelists and Commentators have theirs. It seems we ALL have a new opportunity to enjoy the book as it was enjoyed a long time ago, to learn from it, to apply it . . . and to memorise it? After what is undoubtedly a very long period of time, it seems now that Mark's intentions can be honoured again.

3 Matthew's Gospel

The study of the structure of Matthew's Gospel in modern times has been undertaken since at least 1930, the year that Bacon's (1) work was published. F. C. Grant (2) developed it: my summary outline of what he suggested is given below:

1.	1. 1-2. 23	The Infancy Narrative;
2.	3. 1-7. 29	Discipleship (including the first discourse);
3.	8. 1-10. 42	Apostleship (including the second discourse);
4.	11. 1-13. 52	The Hidden Revelation (including the third discourse);
5.	13. 53-18. 35	The Church (including the fourth discourse);
6.	19. 1-25. 46	The Judgement (including the fifth discourse);
7.	26. 1-27. 66	The Passion Narrative;
8.	28. 1-20	The Resurrection.

'It is evident', writes Grant, concerning the Gospel, 'that the work has been very carefully and artistically arranged. Like many ancient Jewish works, it is in five 'books' or main divisions.' He notes that these five divisions are similar in structure, that they each contain a narrative section followed by a didactic section.

Before him, Bacon had viewed Section 1 as the preamble and Sections 7 and 8 as the epilogue. Major stress is rightly placed on the recurring phrase, 'And when Jesus finished . . .' (7. 28, 11. 1, 13. 53, 19, 1 and 26. 1), but, as the table demonstrates, Grant is not consistent in his presentation of them. Further, he differed from Bacon in his placing of the phrase. Where should they be deemed to lie, at the beginning of a section, or at the end? My analysis suggests they are properly shown as links, independent of the sections themselves. But this is to discuss detail. Rightly in my view, R. G. Hamerton-Kelly (3) states that this structural breakdown 'has not stood the test of time'. That the infancy narratives and the passion and resurrection accounts lie outside of the main structure will not do for Hamerton-Kelly: he argues weakly that it 'is to overlook the fact that Matthew presents his Gospel as history, not as a law-code or a church-manual . . .'. This is an assumption which is unsupportable. Rather, the argument could be that the Gospel, by this breakdown, consists of a likely seven sections of equal status (sections 7 and 8 could be combined): it could then be claimed that the central five sections show similarities. But, this work has already been superceded.

It is worth noting here that a very different proposal has been entertained: Kingsbury (4) suggests that 4. 17 and 16. 21, 'From that time Jesus began . . .', mark points of new departure in the Gospel. His scheme which is based on this has attracted support from Hamerton-Kelly (for its advantages of including the birth narrative and the passion narrative within the main structure and of setting the account of Jesus within the framework of salvation history), but it has not attracted sizeable support.

It is to Bacon's kind of approach (and its development) that we return. Green (5), in 1936, and Fenton (6), more recently (by developing Green's scheme), have entertained the possibility that Matthew made use of chiasmus for his gospel-structure. In both cases, however, the arguments are under-developed. And Fenton (7) himself states that we cannot 'be certain that Matthew planned his work in this way'. He is certain of Matthew's skills of arrangement, however: but he is plainly unaware of other writers' similar abilities for he comments, 'Of all the Evangelists, Matthew has most obviously paid attention to arrangement' (8).

Arguing that the first teaching section (ch. 5-7) and the last (ch. 23-25) are similar (in length and subject matter: entry into the kingdom) and that the second (ch. 10) and the fourth (ch. 18) are of much the same length and comprise similar content (in the former, the sending-out of the apostles, and in the latter, the receiving of those who have responded), Fenton (9) discerns the possibility of the chiastic parallelism of these sections. He too sees the possibility that both the beginning and the end of the whole gospel match: he compares birth and resurrection, 'God with us' and 'I am with you always', baptism and death, temptations ('If you are the Son of God') and trials ('If you are the Son of God'). I would maintain he was on the right track! In my own case, I worked quite independently of Fenton: having established an eleven-section chiastic structure for the Gospel of Luke (and the Acts of the Apostles), I simply then examined Matthew's Gospel to see if it was composed in the same way. In general terms, omitting consideration of the linkages for the moment, the sections which I present agree with Fenton's in eight cases out of the eleven. I proceed now to the presentation of my work.

Matthaean infra-structure:

The basic framework to this Gospel, it would appear, is the same as that of the Gospel of Luke, and also of the Acts of the Apostles. Each side of a central section are five balancing sections. Numbered, these sections can be presented in the following way:

$$1, 2, 3, 4, 5, C, 5', 4', 3', 2'\ 1',$$

where themes and much detail content correspond, section for section, 1 and 1', 2 and 2', 3 and 3', and so on, around a central section, C. The particular uniqueness of Matthew's primary structure is that its sections enjoy independent linkages between them. In the chart below, they are presented as they behave: each one divides into parts one and two (suggestive of simple parallelism).

The Gospel appears to sub-divide as follows:

SECTION 1:	1. 1-4. 24	The Genealogy, Birth and Early Life of Jesus; John the Baptist; Jesus' Baptism, Temptations and Purpose; Old Testament fulfilment;
link A:	4. 25/5. 1, 2	
SECTION 2:	5. 3-7. 27	The Blessings; Jesus' Teaching on the Law, Prophets, Religion, the Coming Kingdom and Himself;
link B:	7. 28, 29/8. 1	
SECTION 3:	8. 2-9. 35	Jesus' Galilean Ministry; His Person and Purpose;
link C:	9. 36-38/10. 1-4	
SECTION 4:	10. 5-42	The mission of the Twelve; Jesus' Mission Instructions;
link D:	11. 1/2-6	
SECTION 5:	11. 7-12. 45	Disclosures of Jesus' Identity; the Response of Belief and Unbelief;
link E:	12. 46-50/13. 1, 2	
SECTION C:	13. 3-52	Parables of the Kingdom;
link F:	13. 53/54-58	
SECTION 5':	14. 1-16. 12	Disclosures of Jesus' Identity; the Response of Belief and Unbelief;
link G:	16. 13-17/18-20	
SECTION 4'	16. 21-18. 35	The Church and Jesus' Instructions to His Disciples;
link H:	19. 1/2	
SECTION 3'	19. 3-21. 13	Jesus' Judean Ministry; (Journeying to Jerusalem), His Person and Purpose;
link I:	21. 14-17/18-22	
SECTION 2'	21. 23-25. 46	The Woes; Jesus' Teaching on the Law, Prophets, Religion, the Coming Kingdom and Himself;
link J:	26. 1, 2/3-5	
SECTION 1':	26. 6-28. 20	The Betrayal, Arrest and Trials of Jesus; His Death and Resurrection; the Purpose of His Disciples.

It will be noted from the titles to the sections that those which are in bold, 2, 4, C, 4', 2', are collections of sayings of Jesus. Each of the linkages which follow these sections, significantly contains the words,

'And it came to pass, when Jesus finished . . .'. Found in the first part of each linkage, they confirm what both thematic and detail contents suggest is the basic structure. It is the discovery of Matthew's sub-structural methodology which provides further and more objective evidence: attention is paid, therefore, to the numbers of the component parts which each section comprises. Reference to what appear to be the Marcan pieces affords still more insight into Matthew's likely compositional endeavour.

SECTION C, 13. 3-52, is the first section that is examined. It is composed of twelve parts:

1.   13. 3-9   the Parable of the Sower;
2.   13. 10-17   the question about parables;
3.   13. 18-23   the explanation of the Parable of the Sower;
4.   13. 24-30   the Parable of the Weeds;
5.   13. 31, 32   the Parable of the Mustard Seed;
6.   13. 33   the Parable of the Leaven;
7.   13. 34, 35   the speaking in parables;
8.   13. 36-43   the explanation of the Parable of the Weeds;
9.   13. 44   the Parable of the Hidden Treasure;
10. 13. 45, 46   the Parable of the Pearl of Great Value;
11. 13. 47-50   the Parable of the Dragnet;
12. 13. 51, 52   the Parable of the Householder.

The title suitable to this section is most certainly, 'Parables of the Kingdom'. The parts which together make up this section are clearly defined in terms of subject-matter. It would appear that Matthew presents five Marcan pieces in order (1, 2, 3, 5 and 7), omitting Mk. 4. 21-29 and adding, in 2, from Mk 4. 25 and his own Isaianic reference. He supplies seven pieces himself from his own sources. At this the structural heart of his Gospel, Matthew chooses to present Jesus' teaching on the Kingdom, its beginnings, its growth, and its meaning.

SECTIONS 5 and 5′ are now examined. Section 5, 11. 7-12. 45, comprises the following twelve parts:

1.   11. 7-15   concerning John;
2.   11. 16-19   concerning this generation;
3.   11. 20-24   concerning cities;
4.   11. 25-27   concerning 'his own';
5.   11. 28-30   concerning 'all';
6.   12. 1-8   concerning himself and the sabbath;
7.   12. 9-14   concerning the sabbath and doing good;
8.   12. 15-21   concerning Isaiah's prophecy: Gentiles, Jesus, people and
                    healings;
9.   12. 22-32   concerning the Spirit of God;
10. 12. 33-37   concerning words;
11. 12. 38-42   concerning signs and this generation;
12. 12. 43-45   concerning unclean spirits.

Again, in terms of subject-matter the section seems quite simply to divide into twelve parts. The introductory linkage, 11. 2-6, supplied by Matthew, suggests the theme of this section might be that of Jesus' identity: he is 'Christ'. In 11. 14, he is the one who comes after 'Elijah'. Four times, in the section, we read 'Son of Man' sayings, 11. 19, 12. 8, 32 and 12. 40. He is the 'servant' of Isaianic prophecy, 12. 18, and the Son of David, 12. 23. He is the one on whom God's Spirit rests and the one through whom he works, 12. 18, 12. 28. His mighty works and healings are signs of the Kingdom. There are those who believe in him and those who do not: of the first consider 11. 5, 6, 15, 25, 27, 28, 12. 18, 21 and, from the conclusion-linkage, 12. 49 and 12. 50; of the second, consider 11. 16, 20-24, 25, 12. 2, 14, 24, 38, 39, 41, 42, 45 and, from the conclusion-linkage 12. 46. The title the section attracts seems properly to be, 'Disclosures of Jesus' identity: the response of belief and unbelief'. The section contains much teaching content, as does Section C, but it contrasts with that of Section C in that it is nearly all incident-attached. Further, and more decisively, Section 5 focusses plainly much more on Jesus and Section C on the Kingdom.

According to source considerations, it would appear Matthew is very much in control of his material. The introductory linkage, as stated above, is what Matthew supplies: he then provides his first five pieces and for the next five, adding further Isaianic material, he follows Mk. 2. 23-3. 30 for stories of conflict (omitting Mk. 3. 13-19, concerning the appointing of the twelve, which he uses in 10. 1-4). To conclude, he adds two more pieces from his own source. His conclusion linkage, 12. 46-50, is the next Marcan piece, Mk. 3. 31-35.

Section 5', 14. 1-16. 12, comprises the following twelve parts:

1.	14. 1-12	concerning John;
2.	14. 13, 14	concerning Jesus, crowds and healings;
3.	14. 15-21	the feeding of 5,000 men, also women and children;
4.	14. 22-33	walking on the sea, the Son of God;
5.	14. 34-36	concerning Jesus, men and healings;
6.	15. 1-9	concerning tradition and the commandment of God;
7.	15. 10-20	concerning words and actions;
8.	15. 21-28	concerning a Gentile and her daughter's healing;
9.	15. 29-31	concerning Jesus, crowds and healings;
10.	15. 32-39	the feeding of 4,000 men, also women and children
11.	16. 1-4	concerning signs and this generation;
12.	16. 5-12	concerning the leaven of the Pharisees and Sadducess.

Yet again, the section divides, by subject-matter, into twelve parts, Sections 4 and 4', 3 and 3', further so divide. Altogether, it seems the Gospel's middle seven sections divide in this way.

The introductory piece to Section 5' is 13. 54-58: the conclusion linkage is 16. 13-16. The conclusion to Section 5, 12. 6-50, and the introduction to Section 5', 13. 54-58, bear comparison: both query Jesus' indentity and do so in respect to Jesus' mother, brothers and sister(s). Likewise, the introductory piece to Section 5, 11. 2-6, and the conclusion linkage to Section 5', 16. 13-16, exhibit similarities concerning Jesus' identity: he is 'the Christ'.

The theme for this section, Section 5', seems set, therefore, to repeat that of Section 5. It does. As the first part of Section 5 concerns John, so also does the first part of Section 5': Herod is mistaken about Jesus' identity: it is John the Baptist, whom he killed, who is raised from the dead. The first part, like the introductory linkage, speaks of Jesus' mighty works, 13. 54, 58 and 14. 2. In the second part, the first of three, similar parts in this section, Matthew writes about Jesus, crowds and healings (parts 2, 5 and 9). The God of Israel is glorified in part 9. Isaianic prophecy is again fulfilled in Jesus. The 'feedings' of the massive crowds (parts 3 and 10) suggest something more about Jesus (and his identification with Elijah?). The episode of Jesus' walking on water and the wind being stilled as he got into the boat caused Jesus' disciples to worship him as 'the Son of God'. The only 'Son of man' saying in this section is found in 16. 13, the conclusion linkage. Jesus' mighty works and healings again can be likened to signs of the Kingdom.

Those who do not believe in Jesus seek signs, consider part 11. Herod is without belief as well as understanding. Pharisees and scribes, and also Sadducees, all contend with Jesus: they are denounced by Jesus, in parts 6, 11 and 12. Others believe in Jesus: they are those who are healed by him, the disciples and even a Gentile woman (see part 8, for two references to believing Gentiles).

In terms of sources, it is considered particularly noteworthy that Matthew follows Mark's Gospel, for content and order, in all the parts which make up this section. What is suggested by this is that this section was written prior to its parallel section, Section 5. As regards Section 5', Matthew demonstrates only a minor editorial role: of Mk. 6. 6b-8. 26, he omits only Mk. 6. 6b-13, the disciples' mission (which he incorportates in 9. 35, 10. 1, 10. 9-11, and 10. 14) and Mk. 8. 22-26, which he excludes from his Gospel altogether. We noted in our consideration of Section 5 how Matthew reserves use of Mk. 3. 13-19 for 10. 1-4. He had it in mind, it seems, as he composed these two sections, to write about these things in his Section 4.

It will be seen, from the presentations of Sections 5 and 5', why they are to be considered as parallel sections. Reference to the text itself highlights further reasons for comparison: for example, in Section 5, contention arises between Jesus and the Pharisees five times, (part 6, 7, 9, 10 and 11) and in Section 5', the same occurs three times (parts 6, 11 and 12).

SECTIONS 4 and 4' are now examined. Section 4, 10. 5-42, comprises the following twelve parts;

1.	10. 5-8	1st instruction: who to go to and what to do;
2.	10. 9-15	2nd instruction: take no money . . .;
3.	10. 16	3rd instruction: persecution, be wise and innocent;
4.	10. 17-20	4th instruction: persecution, the Spirit . . .;
5.	10. 21, 22	5th instruction: persecution and endurance;
6.	10. 23	6th instruction: persecution, the coming of the Son of man;
7.	10. 24, 25	7th instruction: persecution, disciple and teacher;
8.	10. 26-31	8th instruction: persecution, have no fear;
9.	10. 32, 33	9th instruction: acknowledging Jesus;
10.	10. 34-36	10th instruction: not peace, but a sword;
11.	10. 37-39	11th instruction: loving Jesus more than family . . .;
12.	10. 40-42	12th instruction: receiving and giving: reward.

It will be noticed, by comparison with the Nestle-Aland Greek text (10), that all the above sub-divisions are co-incidental with it. Other sections of the Gospel can be compared, more easily than this section, with a variety of translations and editions: it is surprising just how many times current presentations come close to agreement with what is presented in these pages.

The introductory linkage, 9. 36-38 (for the first part) and 10. 1-4 (for the balancing second part), well introduces the theme of this section, 'The Mission of the twelve: Jesus' mission instructions'. And source consideration would seem to suggest that Matthew is very much the collector and arranger of the pieces this section contains. From Marcan pieces, Mk. 6. 7-13, 34 and 3. 13-19, Matthew would appear to have begun his work of creating this compilation of instructions and warnings. It would seem probable that Matthew viewed his endeavour as that of taking Mark's record of a mission of the twelve and of adding from other sources of his own (including further Marcan pieces, Mk. 4. 22, 8. 34, 35, 38, 9. 37 and 9. 38-41) in order that he might establish a section on mission (and its hazards?) which would serve as instruction for the church.

Section 4', 16. 21-18. 35, comprises the following twelve parts:

1.	16. 21-23	Jesus' first prediction of his death and resurrection;
2.	16. 24-28	Instructions on discipleship;
3.	17. 1-13	Jesus' transfiguration: God's instruction;
4.	17. 14-21	A healing: Jesus' instruction;
5.	17. 22, 23	Jesus' second prediction of his death and resurrection;
6.	17. 24-27	The tax: Jesus' instruction;
7.	18. 1-4	'The greatest?': Jesus' instruction;
8.	18. 5, 6	Children and sins: Jesus' instruction;
9.	18. 7-9	Woe: Jesus' instruction on avoiding hell;
10.	18. 10-14	'Little ones': Jesus' instruction;
11.	18. 15-20	One at fault: Jesus' instruction;
12.	18. 21-35	Forgiveness: Jesus' instruction.

As Sections 5 and 5', so now Sections 4 and 4' compare well. Taking, in order, Marcan pieces from Mk. 8. 27-9. 48, omitting Mk. 9. 38-41 (which he uses in Section 4, 10. 42, and Section 5, 12. 30) and omitting 9. 49 and 9. 50 (which he uses in Section 2, 5. 13), Matthew has

created another series of twelve parts (basically, of instruction), by adding
parts 6, 10, 11 and 12 from his own sources. Worthy of particular mention
is the discovery of Mark's major sectional-division and piece (Mk. 8. 27ff)
performing similarly for Matthew: see 16. 13ff and 16. 21ff.

Again, the introductory linkage well presents the themes of this
section: the first part, 16. 13-17, completes the former section's
disclosures of Jesus' identity and, the balancing second part, 16. 18-20,
which is a Matthaean piece, introduces the theme itself, 'The Church and
Jesus' instructions to his disciples'. The content of these instructions, the
teaching, very much parallels that of Section 4: the major difference is
that the warnings of suffering which were given to the disciples and
applied to them, in Section 4, are now again given to the disciples but
applied, primarily, to Jesus. Further, Section 4 speaks of the mission of
the disciples to those 'outside' (the Kingdom?) and Section 4' speaks of
the disciples' role to those 'inside' (the Church?). Noted already above,
are the similarities of both conclusion linkages, particularly that is 11. 1
and 19. 1, 'And it came to pass, when Jesus finished . . .'.

One further observation is made: as Sections 5 and 5', where the
larger section is the one in which Matthew more faithfully follows Mark for
his material, so also here Section 4, 38 verses compares with Section 4',
70 verses. Could it be that Matthew unwittingly expresses hesitancy in
adding his own material?

SECTIONS 3 and 3' are now examined. Section 3, 8. 2-9. 35, comprises
the following twelve parts:

1.   8. 2-4   Healing of a leper: ref. Moses;
2.   8. 5-13   Centurion's son: faith;
3.   8. 14-17   Healing of Peter's mother-in-law and others: 'Isaiah'
                  is fulfilled;
4.   8. 18-27   Following Jesus: faith;
5.   8. 28-9. 1   Healing of two Gadarene demoniacs;
6.   9. 2-8   Healing of a paralytic;
7.   9. 9-13   Call of Matthew and call of sinners;
8.   9. 14-17   Fasting: bridegroom, cloth and wine;
9.   9. 18-26   Healing of woman and raising of a dead child;
10. 9. 27-31   Healing of two blind men;
11. 9. 32-34   Healing of a dumb man;
12. 9. 35   Teaching, preaching, healing.

It can be noted that Fenton (11) adopts the thirteen paragraphs set
out in the Revised Standard Version of the Bible for 8. 1-9. 34, but
topically 9. 9 (a paragraph in the RSV) belongs with 9. 10-13. The
number of parts reduces to twelve, therefore. However, I further include
9. 35 in the scheme: a Matthaean counterpart, 4. 23, 24 is also the final
part to Section 1. The number is again thirteen. But Schweizer (12) argues
that 8. 18-22 and 8. 23-27 (separate paragraphs in the RSV) belong
together. For him the miracle story of Mk. 4. 35-41 is given a new

function by Matthew who adds to the incident, concerning Jesus and his followers (his disciples), two 'would-be' followers. I am persuaded. Hence, twelve parts are again presented.

Three of the twelve parts are supplied by Matthew, in addition to the piece as discussed above: the remaining pieces come from Mark's Gospel. What is significant is that Matthew would appear to employ pieces freely from chapters 1, 2, 3, 4, 5 and 10 of Mark's Gospel. It would seem that he has created Section 3 to parallel his Section 3' in which he adds only one part of his own to what he takes in order from Mark's Gospel.

The content of this section is the first of its kind which we encounter in the Gospel. Only parts 8 and 9 fail to record healings or miracle-workings of Jesus. We read here in detail of what was stated only generally in 4. 23, 24. Further, what we read in detail here is reflected only generally in 11. 2 which prefaces a new series of healings. For the first time also in the Gospel we encounter a whole succession of specific details as regards Jesus' journeyings. Though it is nowhere clearly stated in this section, it is in 4. 23, it is a description of Jesus' Galilean ministry.

It will be observed that Section 3 differs in content from Sections 5 and 5' for it speaks more of Jesus' successes in provoking faith (belief) in himself. Matthew saves many of Mark's conflict stories for later use. The deeds as recorded serve to disclose details as to Jesus' person and purpose: he cleanses, he heals, he is to be followed, he exercises authority, he casts out demons, he forgives sins, he calls sinners, he is the 'bridegroom', he challenges traditions, he raises the dead and he heals the *blind* who (astonishingly) know him to be the Son of David. Matthew appears to be giving glimpses into Jesus' future work: his Isaianic reference is premature, 'He took our infirmities and bore our diseases' (8. 17), and the demons challenge Jesus (8. 29), 'Have you come here to torment us before the time?' (the time of his death?). Matthew appears only to have continued what Mark began: in Mk. 2. 20 we read, 'The bridegroom will be taken away'. The title the section attracts is 'Jesus' Galilean Ministry; his Person and Purpose'.

Section 3', 19. 3- 21. 13, comprises the following twelve parts:

1.	19. 3-9	Divorce: ref. Moses;
2.	19. 10-12	Marriage and the Kingdom of heaven;
3.	19. 13-15	Children and the Kingdom of heaven;
4.	19. 16-22	Eternal Life: commandments; treasure in heaven;
5.	19. 23-26	Riches and entry into the Kingdom of heaven;
6.	19. 27-30	Following: eternal life;
7.	20. 1-16	The Parable of the Labourers in the Vineyard;
8.	20. 17-19	To Jerusalem: prediction of death and resurrection;
9.	20. 20-28	Sitting at Jesus' side in the Kingdom: He came to serve and give His life;
10.	20. 29-34	Healing two blind men;
11.	21. 1-11	Entry into Jerusalem: Isaiah and Zechariah;
12.	21. 12, 13	Jesus' cleansing of the temple.

The division of this section into twelve parts raises only one real query. Fenton (13) and the RSV take 19. 23-30 as a whole. But, 19. 26 has a ring of finality about it. The editors of the Nestle-Aland Greek text recognise a break here. Further, the disciples' question has been answered: Peter asks another. We note too that Matthew is re-working Marcan material. The vocabulary of Mk. 10. 28 suggests a new paragraph: literally, it reads, 'And Peter began to say to him . . .'. Matthew has altered the verse: literally, 19. 27 reads, 'Then Peter answering said to him . . .'. Similarly, three other parts in my presentation begin with a use of the word, 'answering', they are 11. 25, 12. 38 and 22. 1, and the RSV itself agrees with these. Still further, we note a difference in the themes of the two parts.

Occasionally, it has to be added, 19. 3-12 is read as a whole. But, several commentators rightly agree, in my opinion, that 'this saying' (19. 11) cannot refer to what has preceded it, but only to what follows it (19. 12). Hence, 19. 10-12 represents a separate part. Lastly, the twelfth part, 21. 12, 13 is deemed to be complete: 21. 14-17 is complete in itself and forms the first of the two balancing parts to the conclusion linkage, 21. 14-22.

In the discussion of sources to Section 3, we noted that this section, Section 3', comprises basically Marcan pieces in order. Matthew follows Mk. 10. 1-11. 11 and adds only part 7, 20. 1-16. Mk. 11. 12-25 provides the material for the conclusion linkage. We see evidence of Matthew's editing of the Marcan pieces. Again, he introduces another ancient scripture, we observe his predilection for such: in fact it is a blending of Isaiah 62. 11 and Zechariah 9. 9, see 21. 5.

For content, this section and its following linkage, therefore, basically matches that of Days 4 to 7 of Series 3 and Days 1, 2, and part of 3 of Series Four in Mark's Gospel (see the preceding chapter). This section, it follows, is no simple 'Journey to Jerusalem' or 'Journeying to the Cross and Glory'. It would appear to be an account of Jesus' Judean ministry. And as such, throughout the section, Matthew presents details about Jesus' person and purpose: he receives children and blesses them; one who seeks eternal life approaches him; in the 'new world' the Son of man will sit on his glorious throne (with the disciples sitting on their thrones judging Israel); he is worth following, he 'pays the wages' (consider the parable, 20. 1-16); in Jerusalem, the Son of man will die and be raised; he will sit in his Kingdom after 'drinking the cup'; he came to serve and to give his life as a ransom for many; he is the 'Son of David', say two blind men; and at his entry into Jerusalem, he is 'the Lord', Zion's King, the cleanser of the temple and the one who heals there. The title which seems best to express these contents is, 'Jesus' Judean Ministry (journeying to Jerusalem): his Person and Purpose'.

Sections 3 and 3' compare for their themes and details; we note the decisive difference in their geography. Discussion of these correspondences could be lengthy: I refer to two details only. In parts 1 of both sections, significantly, we read of references to Moses' commands. In parts 10 of both sections, we discover what appears to be Matthaean developments of the same Marcan piece, Mk. 10. 46-52! Comparison of the tables presented and, of course, the texts themselves will reward enquiry.

SECTIONS 2 and 2' are now examined. For the first time in this presentation of the results of the Gospel's literary analysis, different sectional structures are encountered. Section 2 comprises the following parts:

1.	5. 3	Blessed: poor . . . Kingdom of heaven;
2.	5. 4	Blessed: mourn . . . comfort;
3.	5. 5	Blessed: meek . . . inherit;
4.	5. 6	Blessed: hunger . . . satisfied;
5.	5. 7	Blessed: merciful . . . mercy;
6.	5. 8	Blessed: pure . . . see God;
7.	5. 9	Blessed: peacemakers . . . sons of God;
8.	5. 10	Blessed: persecuted . . . Kingdom of heaven;
9.	5. 11, 12	Blessed: reviled . . . reward in heaven;
10.	5. 13	You are salt (. . . thrown out);
11.	5. 14-16	You are the light (. . . glory);
12.	5. 17-20	Law and Prophets (entry into the Kingdom; doing/teaching);

1.	5. 21-26	I say to you . . . killing;
2.	5. 27-32	I say to you . . . adultery;
3.	5. 33-37	I say to you . . . swearing;
4.	5. 38-42	I say to you . . . revenge;
5.	5. 43-48	I say to you . . . love, hate;
6.	6. 1	Please God, not men . . . reward;
7.	6. 2-4	Give alms . . . reward; hypocrites;
8.	6. 5, 6	Praying . . . reward; hypocrites;
9.	6. 7-15	In praying . . . forgiveness;
10.	6. 16-18	Fasting . . . reward; hypocrites;

1.	6. 19-21	Treasure, in heaven;
2.	6. 22, 23	Eye, light and darkness;
3.	6. 24	Serving two masters;
4.	6. 25-34	Do not be anxious;
5.	7. 1-5	Do not judge;
6.	7.6	Do not give to dogs . . .;
7.	7. 7-11	Ask . . ., good things; heavenly father;
8.	7. 12	Whatever you wish . . ., law and prophets;
9.	7. 13, 14	Enter by the narrow gate . . .;
10.	7. 15-20	Beware . . . false prophets (. . . cut down, thrown);
11.	7. 21-23	'Lord, Lord . . . heavenly father';
12.	7. 24-27	Hearing and doing, parable of the house-builder.

Framed by the linkages, 4. 25-5. 2 and 7. 28-8. 1, the second part of the former, 5. 1, 2 introduces what is presented as the Sermon on the Mount, and the first part of the latter, 7. 28, 29, concludes it. What the section contains suggests the title: 'The Blessings: Jesus' teaching on the

Law, the Prophets, Religion, the Coming Kingdom and Himself'. The arrangement of this material appears to be that of a twelve-ten-twelve part chiasm, where the central content, five sayings on the Law and five sayings on Religion, is bordered by two balancing series of twelve parts, which both end with sayings on doing what is taught.

Section 2, in terms of sources, is almost entirely non-Marcan: it is assembled by Matthew from his own sources basically. It seems that Matthew has make use of Mk. 9. 50, 4. 21, 9. 43-48, 10. 11, 12, 11. 25, 26, 4. 24 and 1. 22 alone and in the order presented. It is a very small percentage of the whole of the contents. In contrast to this, is the Marcan content to the Gospel's balancing section, Section 2'. Structured in the same way as Section 2, to a twelve-ten-twelve part chiasm as we will see below, the first series is built on material from Mk. 11. 27 to 12. 37a. Providing parts 2, 3 , 7 and 8 himself, Matthew closes it with Mk. 12. 34b. For the balancing series, the last of the three series, he follows Mk. 13. 1-32, using only one verse from Mk. 13. 33-37, and adds his own material in parts 5 and 8 to 12. The central series of ten parts is built on Mk. 12. 37b-40, but mainly with Matthew's own material. Again, as in the above parallels of sections, it is the Section which is found in the latter half of the Gospel, based on Mark's Gospel, which would appear to have been written first. The same is also true of Sections 1 and 1'. Consideration of Matthew's likely sources, coupled with an examination of the Gospel's structures, would seem to allow us the luxury of describing his working method.

Section 2', 21. 23-25. 46, comprises the following parts:

1.	21. 23-27	Jesus' authority is questioned;
2.	21. 28-31a	A question about two sons;
3.	21. 31b, 32	Tax collectors and harlots enter the Kingdom;
4.	21. 33-41	The Parable of the vineyard tenants;
5.	21. 42-44	The rejected stone: Kingdom given to others;
6.	21. 45, 46	Response to parables: attempt at arrest;
7.	22. 1-10	The Parable of the marriage feast;
8.	22. 11-14	The Parable of the wedding garment;
9.	22. 15-22	Taxes to Caesar: hypocrites;
10.	22. 23-33	A question about marriage and the resurrection;
11.	22. 34-40	The greatest commandment; the law and the prophets;
12.	22. 41-46	The Christ, David's Son and Lord;

1.	23. 1-12	Doing deeds, seen by men;
2.	23. 13	Woe: hypocrites: shut the Kingdom, do not enter;
3.	23. 14	Woe: hypocrites: devour houses, long prayers;
4.	23. 15	Woe: hypocrites: child of hell;
5.	23. 16-22	Woe to you blind guides;
6.	23. 23, 24	Woe: hypocrites: law, justice and mercy;
7.	23. 25, 26	Woe: hypocrites: outside of cup;
8.	23. 27, 28	Woe: hypocrites: whitewashed tombs;
9.	23. 29-36	Woe: hypocrites: tombs of prophets, hell;
10.	23. 37-39	O, Jerusalem: house forsaken and desolate;

1.	24. 1, 2	The temple will be destroyed;
2.	24. 3-8	Last things: the beginnings, leading astray;
3.	24. 9-14	Persecution, falling away, endurance;
4.	24. 15-22	The desolating sacrifice;
5.	24. 23-28	Here is the Christ, false christs;
6.	24. 29-31	After the tribulation, the coming of the Son of man;
7.	24. 32-35	The fig tree: heaven and earth will pass away;
8.	24. 36-44	The Day: the parable of the householder;
9.	24. 45-51	The faithful and wise servant: hypocrites out;
10.	25. 1-13	Kingdom of heaven: parable of ten maidens;
11.	25. 14-30	Kingdom of heaven: parable of the talents;
12.	25. 31-46	King and judgement: sheep and goats.

Again, a cryptic presentation will have to suffice. Further descriptions of the form of this section can be discussed. The first series of twelve parts represents Jesus' teaching in the context of the temple, about himself, the Kingdom, about giving to God, the resurrection, the Law and the Christ. Luke, we will see, creates a whole section for his Gospel on the subject of Jesus' teaching in the temple. Matthew's first sub-section begins with Jesus entering the temple, 21. 23. The balancing sub-section, the third series, begins with Jesus leaving the temple, see 24. 1. For content, it begins also with Jesus' teaching about the destruction of the temple. It continues with teaching on the 'last days' and the coming of the Son of man and the Kingdom. It compares with the first series, but, most noticeably, whereas, in the first, it is Jesus who is to be rejected, to suffer and to die and be raised, in the second, it is his followers who will face these things. The central series of ten parts could be entitled, 'the Woes'. Here, Jesus denounces the scribes and the Parisees by reference to the Law, the Prophets, their hypocritical religious practices and the coming Kingdom. Overall, the content of the section seems best represented by the title, 'The Woes: Jesus' teaching on the Law, the Prophets, Religion, the Coming Kingdom and Himself'.

On Sections 2 and 2' (my designation), Fenton (14) wrote, 'Certainly the first teaching section (5-7) and the last (23-25) are similar both in length and subject matter (entry into the Kingdom)'. Comparison of the lengths of the sections which are presented above does not lead to such a conclusion, however: Section 2 is 107 verses and Section 2' is 206 verses. But the internal structures and the subject-matter do correspond remarkably. And, we note again the similarities of the conclusion-linkages, their first parts, 7. 28, 29 and 26. 1, 2.

The 'Blessings' of the earlier section seem to be balanced by the 'Woes' of the later one, though I am not suggesting they balance either for number or for detail. We note too that they occupy different positions in the structures. It is fascinating to find that Luke brings both 'blessing' and 'woe' into juxtaposition in his 'Sermon on the Plain', his counterpart to the 'Sermon on the Mount'. Furthermore, he brings them into exact balance, for number and for detail.

SECTIONS 1 and 1' are now examined. For only the second time in the presentation of the analysis is a new sectional structure encountered. It can be described as a pair of seven parts. It is interesting to note at the outset that, in his opening piece to the Gospel, Matthew demonstrates a predilection for the number fourteen, which he establishes by sacrificing historical details (omitting three names: Ahaziah, Joash and Amaziah) and by counting the name of Jechoniah twice.

Section 1, 1. 1-4. 24, comprises the following parts:

1. 1. 1-17   The Book of the Genealogy of Jesus;
2. 1. 18-25   The Birth of Jesus;
3. 2. 1-6   Visitors from the East seek the King of the Jews;
4. 2. 7-12   The visitors find Jesus; they worship him;
5. 2. 13-15   Jesus is taken to Egypt;
6. 2. 16-18   Herod's killing of young, male children;
7. 2. 19-23   Herod dies: Jesus is taken to Nazareth;

1. 3. 1-3   John the Baptist, preaching in Judea;
2. 3. 4-12   John's ministry in Judea;
3. 3. 13-17   Jesus' baptism by John;
4. 4. 1-11   Jesus' three trials in the wilderness;
5. 4. 12-17   Jesus, preaching in Galilee;
6. 4. 18-22   Jesus calls men to follow him;
7. 4. 23, 24   Jesus' ministry in Galilee.

The Genealogy begins the first series of seven parts and it is plainly a whole part: it is presented as a 'book'. The six other parts, for their sub-divisions, agree with the presentation in the RSV. In subject-matter, this first series is clearly distinguishable from the second, though we note their balance, for their references to Old Testament scriptures, and for their Galilean conclusions. The second series begins with an Isaianic introduction to John (Matthew has corrected Mark's, by omitting Mk. 1. 2b): part 5, in introducing Jesus in a similar way, reflects part 1. Part 2 is judged to be a whole: the RSV reads four paragraphs. The remaining parts are likewise deemed to be complete units. For a comparison of final parts, consider 4. 23, 24 and 9. 35, the final parts, that is, of Section 1 and Section 3. The linkage which follows, 4. 25-5. 2, well concludes this first section of the Gospel and plainly introduces the contents of the next. It comprises two balancing parts, 4. 25 and 5. 1, 2.

Many of the pieces which make up Section 1 are Matthaean. The first series is entirely his. The second series follows Mk. 1. 1-20 for both order and content. Some of the pieces are developed by Matthew from his own source. Omitting Mk. 1. 21-34, for use in 7. 28, 29, 8. 14-17, and omitting Mk. 1. 35-38 altogether, Matthew builds the last part to the Section on Mk. 1. 39.

The specific contribution this Section makes to the Gospel as a whole can now be assessed. A brief statement will have to suffice. Matthew is clearly presenting material which demonstrates that the truths that centre on Jesus can be fully grasped, only, against the background of

Old Covenant literature. On the basis of subject-matter, the Section maybe fully described by, 'The Genealogy, Birth and Early Years of Jesus; the Purpose of John the Baptist; the Baptism, Temptations and Purpose of Jesus: all as viewed against the background of the Old Covenant scriptures'.

Section 1', 26. 6-28. 20, comprises the following parts:

1. 26. 6-13   Jesus' anointing for death;
2. 26. 14-16   Judas' plot against Jesus;
3. 26. 17-30   The Last Supper: its preparation, the meal-time;
4. 26. 31-35   Jesus' prediction of Peter's denial;
5. 26. 36-56   Jesus' three 'trials' and arrest in Gethsemane;
6. 26. 57-75   Jesus before the council: Peter observes and denies;
7. 27. 1-10   Jesus is condemned: Judas repents;

1. 27. 11-26   Jesus before Pilate and delivered for crucifixion as 'King of
                  the Jews';
2. 27. 27-56   Jesus is mocked, crucified and dies;
3. 27. 57-61   Jesus is buried;
4. 27. 62-66   The guard at the tomb;
5. 28. 1-10   Jesus is risen: women see him;
6. 28. 11-15   The guard's report;
7. 28. 16-20   The Great Commission.

The first series describes the events, step by step, which lead up to the final scenes of Jesus' earthly-life, the second series. The connecting linkage, 26. 1-5, concludes the previous section and adequately, but briefly, introduces this final section. The parts which make up this (two series) presentation are judged to be complete wholes in themselves. The Greek, more than the English, in its conjuctions and participles, lends weight to the argument.

Throughout the Section, Matthew has followed in order all Mark's pieces from Mk. 14.1 to 16.8. The following passages are from Matthew's own sources: 27. 3-10 (the death of Judas), 27. 62-66 (the posting of the guard) and 28. 11-15 (the guard's report). If it is correct that the larger ending to Mark's Gospel is original, then the Great Commission of 28. 16-20 is primarily Marcan. Throughout the Section, Matthew's editorial activity is displayed: most noteworthy is the change in the post-resurrection response of the women (compare 28. 8-10 with Mk. 16. 8).

The title to this Section is suggested in the introductory linkage which can be amplified: 'the Delivering up of Jesus to be Crucified, his Death and Resurrection: his Commissioning of his Disciples'. Inclusion of other words might be in order too, for example, Jesus' arrest and trials, and his disciples' purposes.

We turn to a comparison of these sections, Sections 1 and 1'. Fenton (15) has observed how 'the beginning of the whole Gospel matches the end of it: the birth of Jesus (ch. 1) and his resurrection, or rebirth (ch. 28); the first quotation from the Old Testament, 'God with us' and the last words of Jesus, 'I am with you always'; his baptism (ch. 3) and his death, which he speaks of as his baptism in Mk. 10. 38 (ch. 27); the temptations, with the twice-repeated, 'If you are the Son of God' (ch. 4) and his trials before Caiaphas and Pilate, and temptation to come down from the cross, 'If you are the Son of God' (ch. 27).

To these parallels, we can add others. Both sections speak of 'purpose': in the first it is of John the Baptist and Jesus; in the second it is of Jesus and, at its conclusion, the disciples. We identify also the significance of the phrase, 'King of the Jews': in the Gospel it is found only within these sections, see 2. 2 and 27. 11, 29, and 37 (see also 27. 42, for 'King of Israel'). In thematic terms, we might consider that a parallel can be established between Jesus' three temptations in the wilderness (a Matthaean piece) and his three prayers in Gethsemane. By direct reference and allusion, both sections demonstrate scripture fulfilment. Both sections speak of making disciples: in Section 1, it is Jesus calling the two pairs of brothers (to the first pair, he commands, 'Follow me and I will make you fishers of men.'); in Section 1', it is Jesus' command also, 'Make disciples of all nations'.

The 'wise men', on seeing Jesus, 'fell down and worshipped him' (2. 11, see also 2. 2 and 2. 8): the women, similarly, 'took hold of his feet and worshipped him' (28. 9) and his disciples too, when they saw him, 'worshipped him' (28. 17). Injunctions 'not to fear' are given to Joseph (1. 20) and to the women (28. 5), in both cases by 'angels of the Lord' (a phrase which is found only in 1. 20, 24, 2. 13 and 28. 2). We note, in 2. 13, Jesus' life is sought by Herod: it is under Pilate that he is crucified. In 1. 21, Jesus' work is announced by the angel of the Lord, 'he will save his people from their sins': his death and resurrection is the salvation-event (this parallel Luke sharpens in his record of Jesus' commissioning of his disciples, see Lk. 24. 47).

Structure, themes and details, all appear to confirm Matthew's endeavours: for his opening and closing sections to his Gospel, as for all his other, paired sections (around the central one), he intended balance.

Matthew's compositional approach:

Such a compositional approach to western, twentieth-century minds, seems at first surprising, to say the least! But when we consider that this Middle-Eastern, first-century Gospel was written to be read by the few in the hearing of the many, we can, maybe, judge the structure and the sub-structures to be appropriate to the task. Systematic presentation of this kind could be judged to be of the very greatest assistance, in the assembly and at a time given over to instruction and exposition, for both understanding and memorising Gospel truths (note, eternal, rather than purely historical, truths). The proposition that this Gospel was 'designed for learning' is quite clearly before us. It seems our definition of what a Gospel really is (consider also the presentations in chapters 2, 4 and 5 of this book) will have to take account of the uncovering, the qualities and the purposes of such literary-structures.

Questions arise concerning the overall scheme, 1-5, C, 5'-1'. Is the number of eleven sections meaningful? The Gospel ends with eleven witnesses. Is it significant that the 'teaching'-blocks number five, like the number of books in the Law and the number of books in the Psalms? Or, is it significant that the sections, each side of the central one, number five? Does the sectional-form suggest that the Gospel was written as a lectionary scheme? Does the evidence square with the theory that Matthew developed Mark's Gospel?

And questions too arise concerning Matthew's use of sevens, or fourteens, twelves and tens. We can compare Mark's use of fours and sevens. As for Mark, so also for Matthew, they would appear to be helpful in terms of promoting both the understanding and the memorising of the Gospel's contents. We have already noted above Matthew's interest, in his opening Gospel-piece, in symbolic numbering. It is reckoned that 'fourteen', in terms of gematry (favoured in first-century religious circles), is the numerical value of the Hebrew letters which spell the name 'David' (D.V.D.). Symbolically, the genealogy may well point, three times over, to Jesus being a second David. It may be, as Richards (16) states, that the list of names is also meant to convey six sevens: if that is so, 'Jesus would mark the beginning of the seventh seven, or the fullness of time'. 'Seven' indeed implied 'perfection', 'completion' or 'fulfilment'. It seems likely that Matthew knew this, to use the number as he has done. 'Twelve' was traditionally viewed as indicative of God's elective purposes. 'Ten' may have been reflective of the decalogue (the ten commandments). We surely come close to the thinking of Matthew.

Our task today:
Plainly, the structural-scheme demands our attention. What is presented above can be fully sifted. And, further, there is much more detail, in terms of argument and evidence, that waits to be shared. It may be that some preachers and teachers will feel confident enough already to tackle the work of communicating this Gospel as it seems Matthew intended. The above disclosures seem to beg editorial revisions to the laying-out of the book and the sub-titling of its sections. A new means of comparing the material and composition of the synoptic gospels of Matthew, Mark and Luke is very clearly before us. It seems there is much, for many, to do!

4 The Gospel of Luke and the Acts of the Apostles

The prologues to the two books:
In his Prologue to the Gospel, Lk. 1. 1-4, Luke promises 'order'. He does so by direct statement and by his very structuring of his opening paragraph. Literally, it might read:

1. 'Inasmuch as many have undertaken to draw up a narrative
2. concerning the matters accomplished among us
3. as the eye-witnesses and attendants of the word from the beginning delivered to us,
1. it seemed good to me also having investigated all things from their source
2. to write to you carefully in order most excellent Theophilus
3. that you might have the certainty of the things in which you were instructed disclosed to you.'

It can be described as 'a threefold protasis balanced by a threefold apodosis' (see Talbert [1]) or as 'one long periodic sentence, each of whose two parts contain three matching phrases' (see Marshall [2]).

The emphasis, to Goulder (3), falls on the word, *kathexes,* meaning 'in order'. 'Carefully in order', is proposed. Most commentators and translators take the word, *akribos,* meaning 'carefully' (or 'accurately', or 'exactly') to qualify Luke's investigation of 'all things from their source'. But, the two words, *akribos* and *kathexes,* are in juxtaposition in the text and they can be read together. The discovery of Luke's consistent application of structural-principles would seem to warrant this. It is argued below that the 'order' to which Luke writes is neither chronological, nor geographical, nor primarily theological, nor primarily liturgical (for lectionary purposes): each of these ideas has been entertained already but without lasting support. Rather, the 'order' to which Luke writes, the evidence seems to suggest, is primarily that of 'literary order'.

But, why should Luke seek to impose new order upon an already existing narrative (or narrative collection, see Lk. 1. 1), especially when he seems to infer no disparagement of such earlier work (see Lk. 1. 2)? The answer would appear to lie in the last line of the prologue. But, here

49

another translation difficulty is encountered, in establishing the force of Luke's meaning: *epignos* is variously translated in the Gospel and Acts by 'recognise' (majority-usage), 'learn' (next, in order), 'perceive', 'know', 'see', 'ascertain', 'find out', 'identify', 'grasp' and 'understand'. The common denominator and principle of all these translations is that of 'disclosure'. We us the verb with the indirect object in this way, 'it is disclosed to me': hence, my translation above. It would seem, therefore, that Luke's reason for re-structuring the 'good news' is to make clear its truths.

When we speak of 'order', we speak of the absence of 'chaos'. Clarity, we say, aids understanding and appreciation: it aids disclosure. Further, Luke contrasts his purpose with what he understands to have been the purpose of earlier writers: in the Prologue, we read that their work was to 'draw up a narrative', his work was to write 'carefully in order' to disclose the truths. It would seem that Luke's intention was not to correct earlier stories about Jesus, but was to disclose, by his careful application of order, the theological, or Christological, depths of the truths. It is in the penultimate clause of the Prologue that the (likely) patron of the work is first addressed, and it is in the final clause that the purpose, in respect to him, appears to be fully and clearly described. In this way the sense of the Gospel's prologue would seem to be established.

What is raised by this line of approach, is a questioning of the narratives available to Luke. Most scholars would agree, for a variety of reasons, that Luke knew Mark's Gospel, but was he aware of Mark's structure? Few scholars would agree that Luke knew Matthew's Gospel, but the presentation below suggests that he did. It would seem highly likely that he knew Matthew's basic structure of an eleven-section chiasm and copied it himself in his own writings: but was he aware of its numerical listings of sectional parts? Luke's own distinction between his own work purpose and that of his predecessors would seem to suggest the possibility that all but the major sectional divisions of these two books had dissolved into copy prior to his possessing them? It may be though that the differentiation to be made between 'narrative' and 'careful ordering' is in danger of being exaggerated.

One further detail, incorporated within the concluding piece of the Prologue, is also worthy of discussion: Theophilus has already been 'informed' about the 'good news'. The Greek word is *katecheo,* which can also mean 'report' or 'inform'; it is the word from which is derived the English word, 'catechism'. In its technical sense of formal instruction in the church, Maddox (4) argues that it does not make its appearance until the second century (2 Clements 17. 1) but that it is foreshadowed in Paul's usage (Gal. 6. 6, 1Cor. 14. 19 and Rom. 2. 18) and in one of four usages in Luke-Acts (Acts 18. 25). Given Luke's likely Pauline-discipleship and his likely literary-purpose, we might consider too that his whole work (of two books) foreshadows the church's use of catechism.

The Prologue to the Gospel would seem to promise carefully-ordered instruction, to disclose the depths of the truths about the things that have been happening: the book itself would appear to fulfil this purpose.

The Prologue to the Acts of the Apostles, 1. 1-5, expresses continuity in Luke's purposes. There is to be a change of emphasis, however, Jesus is now to be represented by his apostles. It is they who are to take centre stage, though it is Jesus who is still to command the attention. The two prologues demand comparison. The two books are written for the same reader and the two prologues attempt to state clearly the purposes attached to the books, but the first is clearly differentiated from the rest of the text whereas the second appears integral with it. The first is short and well-balanced: the second is clearly longer and less obviously balanced. It may be, however, that it breaks down, structurally, in the following (and, therefore, similar) fashion:

1. 'The first account I make concerning all things, O Theophilus,
2. which Jesus began both to do and to teach
3. until the day on which, having given commands to the apostles whom he chose through the Holy Spirit, he was taken up;
1. to whom also he presented himself living after he suffered
2. by many sure proofs through forty days being seen by them and speaking the things concerning the Kingdom of God;
3. and meeting with them he charged them, "Do not depart from Jerusalem but wait for the promise of the Father which you heard from me: for John indeed baptised in water but you will be baptised in Holy Spirit after not many days.'''

Notably, the Nestle-Greek Text (5) presents one continuous sentence. The Nestle-Aland (6) text, however, does not: the first and the second three pieces are separate sentences. As with the Gospel's Prologue so also here the final piece discloses the greater force of emphasis. There are not a few of us who would like to re-title the book it introduces, 'the Acts of the Holy Spirit'.

Order in Luke-Acts: A summary of earlier studies:
Talbert (7) is one who has had work published on the structures of Luke-Acts as a whole. He recognises 'remarkable correspondences both in content and sequence between the events and persons' found in both books. He presents many lists of so-called correspondences. He demonstrates usages of both chiastic and simple parallelism, but he is unable to present them in any meaningful summary-form. He discerns many parallels which are in sequence, but many which are not. I cannot do full justice to his work here: I can only refer the reader to his work. What he correctly draws attention to is the Tubingen School's attack on the historicity of Luke's second book (8): correspondences were deemed to be found between chapters 1 to 12 and chapters 13 to 28. But, again it is noted, these correspondences disclose only a very loose parallelism of content and sequence.

One very recent publication requires mention. David Gooding (9) has produced a 'new exposition on the Third Gospel' and in it he displays evidence of a keen investigation into the organisation of Luke's writing, its themes, its details and its 'flow'. In short, Gooding proposes that the book is in two parts: 'the coming of the Son of God from glory' and 'his return to glory'. The pivotal point of his scheme is 9. 51, 'When the days drew near for him to be received up . . .'. Each 'part', according to Gooding, has five 'stages' and each stage has 'movements': these vary in number (2, 4 and 8) and in design (simple parallelism and chiasm). What Gooding's work amply illustrates, however, is the trap prepared for any would-be literary-structural analyst. To button your waistcoat to your jacket is the easiest thing to do. Many times over, Gooding has done just this by paralleling passages which do not parallel and not paralleling those that do: for example, in the first case, consider 7. 36-50 and 8. 43-48, and in the second, consider 10. 25, 26 and 18. 18, 19.

The force of the episode describing Jesus' anointing by a 'woman of the city' (7. 36-50) is not the same as that of his healing of the woman with the issue of blood (8. 43-48). It is in fact the same as that of his healing of the paralysed man lowered down to him on a stretcher (5. 17-26). It is: Jesus has authority to forgive sins. Gooding does not want to recognise the story as told by Mark and Matthew (and placed elsewhere in their Gospels) as the same one retold by Luke with a new emphasis. One of Gooding's prejudices, it seems, is to maintain the historicity of every Lucan account, at whatever cost to understanding Luke's methods of approach and his own commentary on the actual text. Luke does in fact retell the story differently to establish the parallelism he needs, to shape a section of his Gospel to his literary-scheme. Luke has reworked much Marcan and Matthaean material to create his literary-artistic designs. He has reworked both Marcan and Matthaean passages to create the great pillars of his central sub-section to the Gospel. In 10. 25, 26 and 18. 18, 19, containing the phrase, 'What must I do to inherit eternal life . . .?', we discover a common usage of no less than twelve Greek words. The constructions are so similar too. Gooding misses seeing the significance of these, and many other parallel pieces. His work suffers, sadly, from a lack of completion in the analysis.

It is in regard to the central section of Luke's Gospel that the more reliable and more significant work has been done so far. Nevertheless, this work also begs completion. In one of the latest commentaries on Luke's Gospel (10), structural interests are mentioned, but no new developments are presented. So, what is the work which has been done? Goulder (11), Bailey (12) and Talbert (13) have offered evidence in support of chiasm within the central section. Goulder has put forward a fifteen-part chiasm with limits of 10. 25 and 18. 30; Bailey's scheme is of a nineteen-part chiasm with limits of 9. 51 and 19. 48; and Talbert has advanced a twenty-one part chiasm with limits of 10. 21 and 18. 17 (including 18. 18-30 repositioned within his scheme). Commentators and scholars vary in their responses to these schemes. No doubt, as a result of these differences, Marshall (14) says, 'They are not possible without doing some violence to the text'. All these schemes do indeed displace pieces.

The riddle of the composition of the central section is brought closer to a solution, however. Marshall, in rejecting any or all of these possible solutions, has to admit that he fails to define its general theme or to establish 'any kind of thread running through it'. Goulder (15), who thought he had solved the problem, stated, 'Criticism has despaired of it and indeed much critical theory, like the Q hypothesis, has been born from this despair.' Unfortunately for Goulder, because other schemes differ markedly to his, the weakness of his argument is exposed: 'It is possible to trace the mind of the evangelist from sentence to sentence and from word to word', he writes (16). Bailey, too, exhibits over-confidence: he says, 'the schematic correspondences between the units are very strong and need no comment' (17). These statements must be excused, though: the process of unravelling the strands to this section of the Gospel was well begun by them.

In a more recent paper on the central section, Blomberg states that Luke 'did not create any new chiasmus' but utilised and preserved an already-existing, chiastically-constructed parable source. He speaks of 'Luke's apparent disinterest in chiasmus elsewhere' (18). But, the three sub-sections of the central section are set in chiastic arrangement and they are also, themselves, chiastically-organised and likewise are their central parts. Indeed, all the Sections of the Book would appear to be set in chiasm, and in all of them chiasm would appear to be much in evidence! Talbert, who demonstrates a concern to attribute this method of presentation to the editor rather than to the sources Luke possessed, would seem to be entirely vindicated.

Miesner, working from Bailey's thesis, it seems, and adopting Dibelius' view that Acts 13. 1-21. 16 is the central part of the message of the Acts of the Apostles, seeks to demonstrate that Luke utilised a similar structure to that of the central part in his Gospel to serve corresponding thematic purposes (19). Miesner also cites support for his thesis in the works of Cadbury and Harnach, on the importance of journey-motif in Luke-Acts, and in the work of Selby, who sees the corresponding sections as literary parallels. That there is a structural principle of relationship between the two books is what is demonstrated in what I present: but the sectionalising to which I have come, by way of my methods of analysis, is very different.

Notes on presentation and analysis-methodology:
At the outset, it has to be clearly stated that what is presented here is a summary of 130 pages of text and 23 A1-size charts: space allows for an introduction only, to detailed considerations. For instance, my analysis exposes eleven levels of order. The first level of order is that of the sections which both books comprise, Section 1, Section 2, etc. (eleven

sections in each). The second level of order is that of the Sub-sections which each Section contains. The third level of order is that of the sub-divisions of the second; the fourth level of order is that of the sub-divisions of the third, and so on. It is these lower levels, more detailed levels, of order which both demonstrate and confirm the patterns and balance of content at the higher orders. For the most part, the presentation below is of the first three or four levels of order.

In considering Luke's Gospel for the possible sources behind it, of Mark of Matthew and Luke's own, the notes have had to be kept to a minimum. It is the argument, based on sources, which, as for Matthew's Gospel with respect to Mark and Matthew's own source, at times can confirm sub-divisions in the text, and throughout can point to the reasonable nature of the writer's compositional method. Other commentators on Luke's Gospel would have chosen to consider Q source, instead of Matthew, but Farrer (20), rightly in my judgement wrote, 'To be rid of it we have no need of a contrary hypotheses, we merely have to make St Luke's use of St Matthew intelligible.' The discovery of Luke's compositional purpose and method is sufficient, I would maintain, to answer this challenge.

Further, a whole variety of texts have had to be consulted: they include that of Bodmer Papyrus P75 (21), dated variously between 175 and 225 AD, which is the most significant, Codex Alexandrinus, and the Nestle-Kilpatrick and Nestle-Aland Greek New Testaments. Space does not allow for a fuller discussion of the texts than is presented. That they have been influential in the sub-dividing of the books and in the determining of the parallels of themes and details needs to be recognised. Plainly, it is reference to the more literal translations which will enable the reader to weigh the force of the arguments that are presented below.

During the course of the analysis, a methodology developed. It basically adds up to a series of questions that needed to be addressed:

1. What is the distinctive contribution of this piece of the whole work? That is, what are its main themes? Are these in terms of story-line or in terms of the meaning(s) of the story-line?
2. What is the quantitiy and quality of detail which confirms the fixing on the theme, or themes?
3. Do the opening and closing sub-sections, or paragraphs, or verses, frame, introduce, conclude or climax the presentation of the theme or themes?
4. In what sense, or in what ways, can this piece of the whole work be considered to parallel another, or others? Are these parallels sufficiently distinctive: are they in any way exclusive, so as to suggest a real significance of relationship?
5. What other factors (source, structural or textual) support the limits of the pieces and their relationships with others?

In such a way, the search has been made of Luke's writings for his employment of structural-principles of literary-order. The results of this investigation would seem to suggest that the two-book work we are handling is literature of a most beautifully, and most consistently, organised kind. In every way, the discovery of such order is fully concomitant with the view that Luke is a great literary-artist. He, whom legend declared also to be a painter, the Church appointed as Patron, not only of Doctors but also of Artists. Maybe Luke will yet be appointed to the role of Patron of Writers.

Lucan infra-structure:

The Gospel of Luke and the Acts of the Apostles would appear to be structured in the very same way:

$$1, 2, 3, 4, 5, C, 5', 4', 3', 2' 1',$$

where, because of thematic and detailed content, Section 1 can be said to correspond with Section 1', Section 2 with Section 2', and so on around a central Section, C. Further, the two books seem to display correspondences in themes and details, on a section to section basis, that is, Sections 1 in both books, Sections 2 in both books, etc. Additionally, sections of the two books could be said to correspond chiastically: that is Section 1 of Luke with Section 1' of Acts, Section 2 of Luke with Section 2' of Acts, and so on. But, these are, in the general case, the least apparent. Luke Section 1' and Acts Section 1, the last section of the Gospel and the first section of the Acts, do display, however, many common features.

The basic structural-scheme of the two books, it is noted, is equivalent to what is presented above in Matthew's Gospel, but comparisons of the sectional-contents of Luke's two books with Matthew's suggest no intention on the part of the writers to establish further, meaningful correspondences. The proposition is that the two books comprise the following sections:

The Gospel of Luke				*The Acts of the Apostles*		
P	1. 1-4	4 verses				*verses*
1	1. 5-80	76		1	1. 1-26	26
2	2. 1-52	52		2	2. 1-42	42
3	3. 1-4. 44	82		3	2. 43-5. 42	110
4	5. 1-8. 21	159		4	6. 1-9. 31	146
5	8. 22-9. 43a	77½		5	9. 32-11. 26	86
C	9.43b-19.46	434½		C	11.27-15.35	144
5'	19. 47-21. 38	87		5'	15. 36-18. 23	103
4'	22. 1-53	51		4'	18. 24-22. 29	153
3'	22. 54-23. 25	42		3'	22. 30-26. 33	122
2'	23. 26-53	28		2'	27. 1-28. 15	59
1'	23. 54-24. 53	55		1'	28. 16-31	15
		1,148				1,006

The numbers of verses are, to some degree, provisional: future textual studies may affect them by one, or two, or so. They are given so that comparisons can be made easily in regard to the sizes of the sections.

Immediately observable is the more controlled nature of the sizes of the sections of the Acts: they vary widely but, section for section (1 and 1', 2 and 2', etc.), they give greater evidence of correspondence that do those of the Gospel. This feature is perhaps not surprising: the distinct likelihood is that the writer was much more in charge of his material in ordering a book on the Church than he was in re-ordering and re-working Gospel-material on Jesus. Also, immediately observable is the size of the Gospel's Central Section. It accounts for over a third of the Gospel. Perhaps, Luke's work began with a composing of such a chiastically-organised collection of the teachings of Jesus. Maybe, he then tackled a re-presentation of the whole of the Gospel, along similar structural-lines, incorporating the section he had already done by adding travel details. Certainly, few scholars would argue that the Central Section represents true travel narrative. It may now be properly titled, 'Jesus' Journey to Jerusalem', but the travel details themselves are few and most-times detached: further, many of the same characters keep on popping-up in the account where one would not expect.

The Sections themselves are now presented. A beginning is made with Sections C, firstly, that of the Gospel, and secondly that of Acts. The reasons are twofold. The Central Section of the Gospel is the one which has received the most attention already: its true construction needs to be demonstrated at the outset. Also, the principal feature of chiasm is that its central part enjoys a place of importance.

Luke's Gospel, Section C, 9. 43b-19. 46:

The section attracts the title, 'Jesus' Journey to Jerusalem'. It consists of three basic parts:

> I: 9. 43b-10. 24   'Setting out for Jerusalem';
>   C: 10. 25-18. 30   'Jesus' teaching, on the way';
> I':   18. 31-19. 46   'Arriving in Jerusalem'.

They are in chiastic arrangement, hence they are described by:

$$I : C : I'$$

The outer sub-sections are structured in the same way and the contents of each are similar, consider I:

1:	9. 43b-50	Jesus' fate, disciples (know,concealed),
2:	9. 51-56	Messengers are sent ahead, Son of man came to save,
C:	9.57-62	'Would-be disciples' and the Kingdom of God,
2':	10.1-20	Seventy are sent ahead,
1'	10. 21-24	Blessedness of disciples (hidden, know);

and I'

1:	18. 31-34	Jesus' fate, disciples do not understand,
2:	18. 35-19. 10	Son of David, Son of man came to seek, to save,
C:	19. 11-28	Parable on discipleship, the Kingdom of God,
2':	19. 29-40	Davidic blessing; entry into Jerusalem,
1':	19. 41-46	Jerusalem's fate (do not know, hidden).

Most scholars seem to agree that 9. 51 begins the section. Rather, it does seem that the unlikely half-verse, 9. 43b, properly begins the section, with the very generalised statement, 'While they were all marvelling at everything he did . . .'. It is followed by Jesus' prediction of his being 'delivered into the hands of men', a saying which Jesus' disciples

        1)   did not understand
    for 2)   it was concealed from them
  and 3)   they were afraid to ask him about it.

The parallel to this is clearly found in 18. 31-34, the first part of the opposite sub-section. Here, Jesus again makes a prediction about himself: he is to be 'delivered to the Gentiles' as a fulfilment of scripture. It is a more extended saying than the former, but it evokes a very similar response from the disciples who

        1)   understood none of these things
    for 2)   this saying was hid from them
  and 3)   they did not grasp what was said.

With these passages then, it is reasoned that the peripheral parts of the Central Section begin.

They conclude in the latter case with Jesus' lamentation over Jerusalem (and its fate which is hidden from its occupants) and the fulfilling of scripture in Jesus' judgement on the temple, and in the former case with Jesus' exultation over his disciples, who are blessed indeed for having had revealed to them things hidden to many. The parallels are clearly evident.

A brief discussion of sub-section I is completed here. The content of 9. 51-56 is clearly paralleled in the more extended account, 10. 1-20: both speak of a sending ahead of messengers, reception and rejection, and judgements (?) of a village and of cities. The Gentile mission is often said to be pre-figured in the latter. 'Rejection' and 'cities' feature in the opposite sub-section, 18. 31-19. 46, in which it is Jesus who 'goes ahead', 19. 28. At the heart of this first sub-section, 9. 57-62, is a chiastically-organised threesome of 'would-be' followers: 9. 57, 58; 59, 60 and 61, 62. To two Matthaean pieces, Mt. 8. 19-22, Luke adds a third. It is argued in this fashion: no reference to 'Q' is required. The material from 9. 51 to 18. 14 is sometimes referred to as the 'large insertion': what is likely demonstrated by the literary analysis is that Luke freely composes the major part of his Central Section from Matthaean pieces and form his own sources. Only very occasionally do we encounter possible Marcan material. Also, what is noticed, in both peripheral sub-sections, is how Luke has grafted his own composition onto the pieces of Marcan material which he selects for use.

A brief discussion of sub-section 1' can be completed now. For content and structure, 18. 35-19. 10 and 19. 29-40 correspond. They each sub-divide in similar geographical ways:

> i   18. 35   . . . as he drew near to Jericho;
> ii 19. 10   . . . he passed through Jericho;
> i   19. 29   . . . toward the Mount called Olives;
> ii 19. 37   . . . the descent of the Mount of Olives.

For content similarities, consider Jesus' necessities, Son of David and the Davidic greeting, rebukings, shoutings, and praise to God. It can be noted that all the parts which are arranged around the centres of these opening and closing sub-sections divide into two. At the heart of this sub-section, as in the former one, is another chiastically-organised piece, 19. 11-28, the Parable of the Minas. The framing, and therefore, corresponding pieces are 19. 11-15 and 19. 24-28: consider references to Jerusalem, 'minas' and those who did not want the nobleman 'to be king' over them. At the heart of the passage, 19. 16-23, we encouter another threesome (compare 9. 57-62), of 'servants' and the responses their actions attract.

Structure, detail of content, source-considerations, the reasonableness of compositional-method, all these things together disclose and confirm Luke's design strategy. His systematic approach to composing the first and last sub-sections of his Central Section, 9. 43b-10. 24 and 18. 31-19. 46, can be summed up in the following way: they are both designed to the pattern:

$$1, 2, C, 2', 1';$$

where 1, 2, 2' and 1' divide into i:i' (simple parallelism), and where C divides into i:c:i' (chiastic parallelism).

The central sub-section, C, 10. 25-18. 30, follows the same systematic approach, only it is extended: it is designed as follows:

$$1, 2, 3, 4, 5, C, 5', 4', 3', 2', 1';$$

which is the same as that of the book's structure, and where 1, 2, 3, 4, 5, 5', 4', 3', 2' and 1' divide into i:i (simple parallelism), and where C divides into i:c:i' (chiastic parallelism).

Bailey, Goulder, Talbert and myself agree on seven of the eleven sub-divisions: they are 10. 25, 11. 1, 11. 14, 13. 10, 16. 1, 17. 11 and 18. 18. Bailey, Talbert and myself agree on a further sub-divsion, 18. 1. We enjoy a measure of agreement on aspects of correspondence. But, the scheme to which I have come is as follows:

1:	10. 25-42 (18vs)	The Inheriting of Eternal Life: Law and Love;
2:	11. 1-13 (13vs)	Prayer: the Holy Spirit is given to those who ask; persistence;
3:	11. 14-12. 12 (53vs)	The Kingdom of God: what is internal, not external, is of importance;
4:	12. 13-48 (36vs)	Earthly and Heavenly Riches: the coming of the Son of man;
5:	12. 49-13. 9 (20vs)	Divisions: warning and prudence; repentance of sinners;
C:	13. 10-14. 24 (50vs)	Sabbath Law: Kingdom of God and Entry; Jerusalem, Jesus is to be killed there;
5':	14. 25-15. 32 (43vs)	Divisions: warning and prudence; repentance of sinners;
4':	16. 1-17. 10 (41vs)	Earthly and Heavenly Riches: judgement, reward and punishment;
3':	17. 11-37 (27vs)	The Kingdom of God is within; it is not coming with signs; judgement;
2':	18. 1-17 (17vs)	Prayer: receiving the Kingdom; persistence;
1':	18. 18-30 (13vs)	The Inheriting of Eternal Life: Law and Love.

The title already given above, to this sub-section, is that of 'Jesus' Teaching, on the way (to Jerusalem)'. The number of verses are again given so that comparisons, for size, can be made readily. The parts are discussed below in their pairs, 1 and 1', 2 and 2', and so on; the central part is presented last.

Parts 1 and 1' (10. 25-42, 18. 18-30) begin in very similar fashion: no less than twelve Greek words are common to both, and the constructions are the same. Luke's source for 18. 18, 19 is likely Mk. 10. 17ff: he tailors it to suit his requirements. His sources for 10. 25f are Mk. 12. 28-31 and Mt. 22. 34-40. His purpose it seems is clear: he is creating parallels, with deliberate intention. Parts 1 and 1' begin, therefore, with the same question, 'What must I do to inherit eternal life?' Nowhere-else in the Gospel is this language used. In the first, the Shema (Dt. 6. 5) is presented and, in the second, the Decalogue (Dt. 5. 16) is. Love of neighbour is taught in both: in the first, it is the Parable of the Good Samaritan and, in the second, it is the dominical command, 'Sell all that you have and distribute to the poor'. The primacy of love for the Lord is the closing teaching in both.

Parts 2 and 2' (11. 1-13, 18. 1-17) begin by introducing the subject of 'prayer'. In the whole of the Gospel, these are the only two places we find direct teaching on prayer. In the first, following Mt. 6. 9-13 and his own source, Luke opens by presenting the Lord's Prayer as a right way to pray. He uses Mk. 10. 13-16 and his own source in the second. The teaching of the parables in both parts is similar: consider the friend's boldness, and the teaching of 11. 9, 10, in comparison with the widow's persistence. Right praying is illustrated in the second part in the parable of the Pharisee and the tax-gatherer. Both parts speak about children.

'Entry', in the second, and 'Knock, and it will be opened for you', in the first, appear to parallel. It would seem, therefore, that Luke is paralleling the receiving of the Spirit and entry into the Kingdom.

Parts 3 and 3' (11. 14-12. 12, 17. 11-37) both begin with examples of Jesus' exercise of power and authority. Both give details of Jesus' difference of opinion with Pharisees. Both speak to the same theme: what is internal (in the heart) is what really matters. We can compare 11. 20, 'the Kingdom of God has come upon you', with 17. 21, 'the Kingdom of God is among/within you'. We note, further, a trio of characters in both: in the first, Jonah, Sheba (un-named) and Soloman and, in the second, Noah, Lot and his wife (un-named).

Parts 4 and 4' (12. 13-48, 16. 1-17. 10) are about earthly and heavenly riches, judgement (reward and punishment). 12. 13-15 introduces the subject in the first part: a parable on 'a rich man' follows. In the second part, two parables on rich men are found. Both parts speak on servanthood, the first in relation to the coming of the Son of man: the eschatological image of 'sitting at table' is presented in both.

Parts 5 and 5' (12. 49-13. 9, 14. 25-15. 32) begin with what appears to be material from Mt. 10. 34-39: half is found in the first and half is found in the second. This is a most significant discovery, in matters of determining compositional-method. Hence, both parts begin with the theme of 'division'. Warnings, prudence and repentance of sinners are the themes which follow. A structural similarity is observed, too: each comprises two closely-related teachings connected by 'or', followed by a longer parable. Details like 'tower' and 'dung' are common to both parts and appear significant! They are not found elsewhere in the whole of the Gospel.

Part C (13. 10-14. 24) sub-divides into chiasm:

i.   13. 10-30   Sabbath healing (ox and ass, watered); parables of the Kingdom; humble exalted; entering the kingdom (we ate and drank . . .);
c.   13. 31-35   Jerusalem: Jesus is to be killed there; he laments for it;
i'. 14. 1-24   Sabbath healing (ass and ox, well); parables of the Kingdom; humble exalted; repayment and resurrection; invited into/ being in the Kingdom; banquetting.

The bordering pieces, i and i', further incorporate language which is highly expressive: consider 'strive to enter' 13. 24, 'thrust out' 13. 28, and 'compel people to come in' 14. 23. Sayings on reversal and rejection are common to both, likewise parables (of the kingdom) and other significant details, such as 'streets'.

The central piece, c, represents the centre-point of Part C, also of Section C and, naturally, also of the Gospel. Verses 31-35 of chapter 13 hold prime place. The motif of the Journey to Jerusalem, the theme of the Central Section, is presented here. Clearly, Jesus is going to be killed there, but nothing will deflect him from this. It seems that at the very heart of the Gospel, we encounter that which is at the heart of evangelical faith. It is a masterful piece of Lucan organisation. It serves as further evidence of Luke's intent, in so structuring his Gospel, to disclose the deep truths of the 'Good News'.

The passage sub-divides chiastically again: the centre, .c, breaks down into two parallel pieces, .ci and .ci':

.i   v31   Herod wants to kill Jesus;
    .ci   v32   'Behold, I cast out demons and perform cures today and
                       tomorrow, and on the third day I finish my course.'
    .ci'   v33   'Nevertheless I must go on my way today and tomorrow and
                       the day following; for it cannot be that a prophet should
                       perish away from Jerusalem.'
.i'   v34, 35   Jerusalem kills prophets; Jesus is going there.

With this, we move to a close in our considerations of the Gospel's Central Section. Space has not allowed for a detailed presentation of all the evidence of correspondences, nor has it allowed for a detailed presentation of all the structures, in their lower levels of order. What has been presented is what is deemed the basic material. It demonstrates that the 'bone-structure' of the section is the main theme of 'Jesus' Journey to Jerusalem': the arrangement of the sub-sections discloses this; the first is the 'setting-out to Jerusalem', the middle one is 'on the way to Jerusalem', and the last is the 'arrival in Jerusalem'. The 'flesh' of the Section is the teaching. Salvation, eternal life, entry into the Kingdom, repentance of sinners, the matter of riches, warnings, judgement, reward and punishment, prayer, law, love, the Holy Spirit, reversals, what is within the heart, divisions, prudent action . . . these are the issues. Simply, Luke has organised them. He has also set the teachings against the background of the incidents and encounters of Jesus' daily-life. If we are to distinguish between the 'flesh' and the 'blood' of the section, then the 'blood' is surely that of the teaching on discipleship, the following of Jesus, his example and his teaching, in obedient response to his commands. The opening and closing sub-sections, the framing sub-sections to the central sub-section, adequately present this theme. The 'heart' of the section is, truly, Jesus and the course which he is taking to his death.

The Acts of the Apostles, Section C, 11. 27-15. 36:

The section attracts the title, 'Three Journeys of Saul and Barnabas'. It consists of three basic parts:

I: 11. 27-12. 25   'From Antioch to Jerusalem, and back';
   C: 13. 1-14. 28   'From Antioch on a Mission, and back';
I':   15. 1-35   'From Antioch to Jerusalem, and back'.

Just like the Central Section of the Gospel, the three sub-sections are in chiastic arrangement: the journey-motifs obviously warrant such a conclusion. Correspondence with the Gospel's Central Section is clearly suggested, by the way Jerusalem features and dominates in both pairs of framing sections. But, note, Paul's journey to Jerusalem, to his arrest and trials, does not come until Section 4': it is this later journey in which many of the things that happened to Jesus happen to him, but, I stress, these things are those which are found in the Gospel's Section 4'.

Another similarity between the central sections of both books is that the sub-sections are constructed in the same way, though the central one here is not extended: all three are the same. And, again, it is the framing sub-sections which are very much smaller in size than the central sub-section. The sub-sections are constructed as follows: consider I:

```
1:    11. 27-30   Saul and Barnabas are sent to Jerusalem to take relief,
   2:    12. 1-4      Peter is imprisoned by Herod who has killed James,
      C:    12. 5-17    Peter is miraculously released,
   2':   12. 18-23   Herod kills sentries, he himself dies,
1':   12. 24, 25   Barnabas and Saul return to Antioch.
```

and C:

```
1:    13. 1-3      Barnabas and Saul are sent on a mission,
   2:    13. 4-13    A Jew and a Gentile,
      C:    13. 14-52   In Antioch of Pisidia; 'We turn to the Gentiles',
   2':   14. 1-22    Gentiles and Jews,
1':   14. 23-28   Paul and Barnabas return to Antioch to report.
```

and I'

```
1:    15. 1-6      Paul and Barnabas are sent to Jerusalem,
   2:    15. 7-11    Peter speaks, concerning Gentiles,
      C:    15. 12      Barnabas and Paul speak, concerning Gentiles,
   2':   15. 13-21   James speaks, concerning Gentiles,
1':   15. 22-35   Paul and Barnabas return to Antioch and stay there.
```

In the Central Section of the Gospel, all the non-central parts of the sub-sections divide into i:i' (simple parallelism), and all the central parts divide into i:c:i' (chiastic parallelism). In the Central Section of Acts, all the parts which comprise the flanking sub-sections divide into i:i', that is, 1, 2, C, 2' and 1' of I and I'. Symmetry is maintained in the central sub-section, C, but in the following way:

```
          1:        i:i      (13. 1: v2, 3)
          2:        i:c:i'   (v4, 5: v6-12: v13)
          C:        i:i'     (v14-43: v44-52)
          2':       i:c:i'   (14. 1-7: v8-18: v19-22)
          1':       i:i'     (v23-26: v27, 28)
```

This structural detail is presented in order to demonstrate Luke's consistency of craftsmanship. For size, the central part is the largest: it also demonstrates unequal sizes of pieces. We examine this feature, but briefly.

The two opening verses, 13. 14 and 13. 44, introduce sabbath-happenings. It is pointed out that, in the central part of the Gospel's

Central Section, we found the same: see Lk. 13. 10 and 14. 1 for the verses which begin the bordering pieces. In this case in Acts, however, we find that they appear to introduce further chiasms: consider:

i:	(i)	(13. 14, 15)	and i':	(i)	(v44, 45)	
	(ci)	(v16-25)		(ci)	(v46, 47)	
	(ci')	(v26-41)		(ci')	(v48, 49)	
	(i')	(v42, 43)		(i')	(v50-52)	

What takes up the space in the presentation is Paul's speech! See i: (ci) and (ci'). Luke preferred not to shorten it, for the sake of a quantitative balance, it seems. His structural harmony sufficed.

The above serves as an introduction to the discussion which must follow now on the detail of the contents of the Section and how it compares with that of the parallel Central Section in the Gospel. Given that the correspondences in journey-motifs and in structural-terms seem to be sufficiently established, we turn to other things.

It is for the purpose of taking famine-relief that Barnabas and Saul first go to Jerusalem, but Luke takes the opportunity of telling about another anxiety the church there was facing, Herod's violent attack on it. It is for the purpose of seeking a decision on circumcision and the law, as it affects Gentiles, that Paul and Barnabas go the second time. Gatherings are held in both cases: the different anxieties are addressed. Peter is prominent in both episodes. Further, the name of 'James' is common to both. Mention of the people of Tyre and Sidon in the first part could be significant: in the first part of the Central Section of the Gospel mention is also made. Coupled with this mention is their 'asking for peace': this is something we also encounter in the Gospel's Central Section, see Lk. 14. 31-33.

The central content of the section is presented in the context of a missionary journey, sub-section C, which contrasts responses of Jews and Gentiles. It is in the central part of the central sub-section, which reports the happenings in Antioch of Pisidia, where we come across the most significant details. It is here that Paul announces to the Jews, 'you judge yourselves unworthy of eternal life, behold, we turn to the Gentiles.' Paul, has already taught them, before then, that by Jesus, 'everyone that believes is freed from everything from which you could not be freed by the law of Moses.' Both 'eternal life' and 'the law' are issues common to the two books' Central Sections, issues which are so addressed nowhere else in the books: see Lk. 10. 25, 18. 18, v30 and Acts 13. 46, v48. Further, as Paul and Barnabas left Antioch of Pisidia, 'they shook off the dust from their feet against' the Jews there: it is another phrase which is nowhere else repeated in Acts. A parallel to this is found in the Gospel's Central Section: see Lk. 10. 11, but see also Lk. 9. 5 for a further use of the phrase (in Section 5). That the mission succeeds more in regard to Gentiles than to Jews, and that Paul 'turns to the Gentiles', suggests a parallel to the pre-figuring of a Gentile mission in the Gospel's Central

Section: see Lk. 10. 1-20. Sabbath occasions, common to both Central Sections, have been mentioned already above: a word which means 'following', as in 'On the following sabbath', Acts 13. 44, or 'next', is rendered by a little-used Greek word, *erchomeno,* which is also encountered in the central part of the Gospel's Central Section, see Lk. 13. 33. It is a strange parallel, but it is one that Papyrus P75 supports. Only one further usage might be found in the two books, in Acts 20. 15: uncial D supports its use, but against all the other, available papyri.

A further parallel, between the Central Sections of the two books would appear to be that of the use of the phrase, 'entry into the Kingdom of God': they are found in Acts 14. 22 and Lk. 18. 17, v24, v25 alone and they occupy almost the very same positions in the two structures.

To discuss the Central Sections in more detail would be to protract this presentation beyond what is required here, but without a doubt there is much more that could be argued on the issues of mission, the old law, the new law, Moses and Jesus. What we view in these sections does indeed give us more than a glimpse into the resultant tensions as they focussed on Jesus, also in the church, and through their common mission. The case for my presentation of the literary structures of the Central Sections of the two books, and the ways in which they relate, must rest here. We turn now to a study of Sections 5 and 5'.

Sections 5 and 5' of Luke's Gospel and the Acts of the Apostles:

Luke's Gospel, Section 5, 8. 22-9. 43a, and Section 5', 19. 47-21. 38

They both comprise the same, compound chiastic-structures and, according to the method of presentation used above, they can be described by:

$$I (1 : 1') : C (1 : 1') : I' (1 : 1').$$

Section 5:

I: 8. 22-56   A lake-crossing, and return, with incidents   (8. 22-39: v40-56);
   C: 9. 1-27   The disciples are sent out; they return: 'Who is this . . ./
                  Who . . .?; 'The Christ'; he is to suffer, die, be raised and
                  come in glory;   (9. 1-9: v10-27);
I':   9. 28-43a   A mountain ascent, and descent, with incidents
                                                              (9. 28-36: v37-43a).

Section 5':

I: 19. 47-20. 26   Teaching daily in the Temple; Jesus' authority; a parable
                      on his death and judgement; an attempt to trap him;
                                                         (19. 47-20. 8: 20. 9-26);
   C: 20. 27-21. 4   Resurrection is questioned (ref. a widow); 'The Christ';
                      condemnation (ref. a widow);   (20. 27-38: v39-21. 4);
I': 21. 5-38   The destruction of the Temple and the last things; he will
                      come in glory; his words have authority; he teaches daily in
                      the Temple;   (21. 5-28: v29-38).

The Gospel's Section 5 is clearly structured: in the first sub-section, I, 8. 22ff speaks of a lake-crossing, 8. 40ff records what happened on the return; in the central sub-section, C, 9. 1ff tells of the disciples being sent out, 9. 10ff tells of their return and what follows; and in the last sub-section, I', 9. 28ff tells of a mountain ascent and 9. 37ff speaks of what happens after the descent. The rhythm, when once observed, is so obvious. Likewise, Luke's handling of the details of the contents, to create this structure, becomes clear.

A feature of this section, when compared with Mark's Gospel, is that of Luke's 'great omission' of Mk. 6. 45-8. 26. Many reasons have been suggested for this: the one which is most obviously before us now is that Luke saw the chiastic potential of bringing into juxtaposition Mk. 6. 14-16, Herod's wondering about Jesus, and Mk. 8. 27-33, Jesus' questioning of his disciples. Mark has already used these himself as parallel pieces. It seems Luke is fully aware of this! Concomitant with this, it would seem Luke identified the further paralleling potential of Mk. 5. 1-20 and Mk. 9. 2-8, two miraculous events which Peter, John and James witness (Lk. 8. 49-56 and Lk. 9. 28-36), and also Mk. 5. 1-20 and Mk. 9. 14-29, two events of Jesus casting out evil spirits (Lk. 8. 26-39. and Lk. 9. 37-43a). From the beginning to the end of Section 5, Luke follows Mk. 4. 35 through to 9. 29: all his editorial activity is to create the compound chiasm as presented above.

Section 5', like Section 5, requires no major addition by Luke: again he follows Marcan material, editing it, in order to create the same structure as he has used, or will use, in Section 5. His purpose is to present Jesus within the Temple for the whole of the section: contrast Mk. 13. 1 with Lk. 21. 5, and consider the opening and closing pieces, Lk. 19. 47 and 21. 37, 38. It would seem that Luke saw the potential for this compound chiasm in Mark's material. As this section does much less violence to Mark's writings than its parallel section, and as it is by no means as obvious, it might be considered that it was Section 5' that was written first. We examine its construction and its contents.

The common denominator of the two pieces which comprise the central sub-section, 20. 27-38 and 20. 39-21. 4, is that of 'widows': it would seem that Luke spied the possibility of their juxtaposition in Mk. 12. 18-44. He achieves this by omitting Mk. 12. 28-34a which he adapts, or has already adapted, for use in his Central Section, Lk. 10. 25-28. Significantly, the material on 'the Christ', Mk. 12. 35-37/Lk. 20. 41-44, parallels that in the centre of Section 5. In all the $434\frac{1}{2}$ verses of the Central Section the word, 'Christ', is not mentioned once. Similarly, no mention of the word, 'Christ', is found in Sections 4 and 4'. Also, we note that 'resurrection' which is an issue at the centre of Section 5' gets a double-mention at the centre of Section 5.

In each of the sub-sections of Section 5', we observe, Jesus is being questioned. In sub-section I, and its first part, 19. 47-20. 8, questioned and challenged about his authority, Jesus proceeds to tell a parable about his coming death and the judgement the questioners will suffer as a result. That they are already seeking to destroy him is presented in 19. 47. In the second, balancing, part, 20. 9-26, reckoning that Jesus told the parable against them, they attempt to capture Jesus, and when they realise that this is not possible, they seek to trap him in order to deliver him to the authority of the governor.

In sub-section I', its first part (21. 5-28), Jesus provokes the questioning of his disciples: speaking of the 'last things', Jesus gives warnings of suffering and death for the disciples, coupled with a coming judgement, but they will live. The balancing part, 21. 29-38, which contains the only wholly Lucan piece of the section, 21. 34-36, and an ending, 21, 37, 38 (which Luke has very much built himself, on Mk. 11. 19 and Mt. 21. 17?), is deliberately created to conclude the presentation of Jesus' teaching in the Temple and, at the same time, reinforce his warnings. Of the ten verses, five are Marcan (Mk. 13. 28-31).

To conclude this examination, further parallels between Sections 5 and 5' can be considered. In both, the disciples are prepared by Jesus for mission and testimony: compare 9. 1-6 and 9. 23-26 with 21. 8-36. The Son of man's coming in clouds and glory is expressed in these passages, as is also the disciples' losing of their lives and their gaining them. It seems that the matter of Jesus' authority is deliberately presented in both: compare the miraculous stilling of the storm, the exorcisms and the healings, (note, the raising of a child from death), and Jesus giving his authority to his disciples, in Section 5, with the questioning and challenging of his authority 'to do all these things' ('What things?' we might, otherwise, ask), in Section 5'. Beyond any doubt is the paralleling of the Transfiguration command of God to the three disciples 'to listen to him' (Jesus), in Section 5, with the people's listening to Jesus in the Temple, in the opening and closing pieces to Section 5'.

The Acts of the Apostles, Section 5, 9. 32-11. 26, and Section 5', 15. 36-18. 23:

As sections 5 and 5' of the Gospel, so also Sections 5 and 5' of Acts are composed to the compound chiastic-structure:

$$I (1 : 1') : C (1 : 1') : I' (1 : 1').$$

Section 5:

I: 9. 32-43   Peter's mission leads to people 'turning to the Lord' and 'believing in the Lord';   (9. 32-35: v36-43);

C: 10. 1-11. 18   The conversion of Gentiles, Cornelius and his household believe and are baptised; Peter's report; the role of vision and the Spirit; Jesus is 'judge';   (10. 1-48: 11. 1-18);

I':   11. 19-26   The mission of others leads to Greeks 'turning to the Lord' and others being 'added to the Lord'; in Antioch, the term 'Christians' is first used;   (11. 19-21: v22-26).

Section 5':

I: 15. 36-16. 10   Paul (and companions) set out, strengthening the
                         churches: the role of vision and the Spirit;
                                                        (15. 36-16. 5: v6-10);

   C: 16. 11-18. 8   Believers and households are baptised; an exorcism
                         and a prison miracle; Jesus is 'judge';
                                                        (16. 11-40: 17. 1-18. 8);

I':   18. 9-23   Paul (and companions) according to vision and God's
                         guidance, stay and travel; disciples are strengthened;
                                                        (18. 9-17: v18-23).

In Section 5, Peter is prominent: in Section 5', Paul dominates the episodes. It may be that Luke intends to confirm Paul's status as an apostle in this way: what is certain is that the book's attention from Section 5' to the end focusses on Paul.

Examination of the texts will show that by means of simple-parallelism throughout the chiastically-arranged sub-sections, most noticeably of a more complex variety in the central sub-section, Luke presents his material again in a most orderly fashion. Key themes, phrases and words suggest the structures presented, they include: increase in numbers in the churches (compare 9. 42 with 16.5); the roles of vision, the Spirit and God's guidance in missionary activities; the believing and baptising of households; the teachings that Jesus is 'judge' (in both Sections, in the central sub-sections); the teachings about his death and resurrection, and continuing ministry through the apostles (see 9. 34, 10. 36-43), that the Christ should suffer and is Jesus (17. 2, 3, 18. 5); the ministries to Jews and Gentiles/Greeks, with the emphasis on the latter throughout; the recapitulating of events in the central sub-section of Section 5; the repetitions of similar material in the central sub-section of Section 5'; the only use of the phrase in the book, 'they turned to the Lord', 9. 35 and 11. 21; the correspondences of interest in Paul's travelling companions, in Section 5'; journey-details in both sections (most clearly, suggesting the limits of Section 5', compare Syria, 15. 41 and 18. 18, also Phrygia and Galatia, 16. 6 and the last verse of the section, 18. 23); the telling of events which are city-related; the whereabouts of Silas and Timothy (in 17. 1-15, they stay in Beroea, in 18. 1-8, they rejoin Paul: these fall opposite each other in the more minor structures of 17. 1-18. 8); and others.

It is the consideration of these things which leads to a determining of the structures to the two parts, in simple parallelism, which the central sub-sections comprise. Their chiastic structures are briefly presented here:

Section 5, sub-section C, 10. 1-11. 18:

                C1, 10. 1-48:   i: 10. 1-16
                                     c: v17-23a
                                     i':   v23b-48;

                C1', 11. 1-18:   i: 11. 1-3
                                     c: v4-17
                                     i':   v18;

Section 5', sub-section C, 16. 11-18. 8:

C1, 16. 11-40:	i:	16. 11-24
	c:	v25-28
	i':	v29-40;
C1', 17. 1-18. 8:	i:	17. 1-15
	c:	v16-34
	i':	18. 1-8

It is this kind of structural-detailing which confirms what is presented on the more basic levels of order. These structures, themselves, further break down in simple parallelism.

Luke-Acts, Sections 5 and Sections 5':

We have seen above how they correspond in basic structural terms. How do they compare for contents? In the introduction to Lucan infra-structure, it is claimed that Sections 5 of both books correspond and that Sections 5' of both books correspond.

In Sections 5 of both books, we notice what might be a possible primacy of Peter. In the Gospel's section, he is the one who speaks with Jesus, Lk. 8. 45 (Mark says it was 'his disciples', Mk. 5. 31), he is the one who answers Jesus' question, 'Who do you say that I am?', he is present (with James and John) at the raising of the dead-girl and also at the Transfiguration, he is the one who asks to build three booths. No other disciple individually contributes anything in this section. Compare, therefore, Section 5 of Acts.

We further notice comparable raisings of the dead in both Sections 5: Jesus raises a dead girl, Peter raises a dead woman. Parallels in details are observed: weeping attends both occasions; Jesus permits no one to enter . . . Peter puts them all outside; they each command 'arise' (though the Greek is different); Jesus holds her hand, Peter gives his hand; she rose up, he raised her up. We do find other raisings of the dead in the two books, but none of the other stories compare, detail for detail, as these do.

It may be that we should see the parallels in terms of 'missions': both mission accounts speak of preaching and healing. Maybe, mention of John the Baptist in both is significant (Lk. 9. 9, v19 and Acts 10. 37)? The teaching that Jesus is 'ordained judge of the living and the dead' (Acts 10. 42) and that Jesus will judge, at his parousia (Lk. 9. 26, 27) is surely significant.

The future role of Jesus, as judge, perhaps, is even more strongly put in Sections 5': compare Lk. 21. 5-36 with Acts 17. 30, 31. Examination of Sections 5' suggests other possible correspondences. Jesus is teaching in the Temple, Paul is speaking in synagogues and, in Athens, in the Areopagus (where Ares, the Greek God of war, is worshipped). The subject of the 'resurrection' is ridiculed, in these places: compare Lk. 20. 27-40 and Acts 17. 18, 32. Teaching his disciples in the Temple, Jesus warns them that they will be 'delivered up to synagogues and to prisons'

(Lk. 21. 12), Paul certainly suffers at the hands of the Jews and also at the hands of the authorities, in prison. Teaching on 'the Christ' is common to both: compare Lk. 20. 41-44 and Acts 17. 3, 18. 5.

Similar studies into possible correspondences between the books, section for section (that is, Luke 4 with Acts 4, Luke 3 with Acts 3, and so on), will show that the relationships of Sections 5 and of Sections 5' are the weakest of all. We turn now to Sections 4 and 4'.

Sections 4 and 4' of Luke's Gospel and the Acts of the Apostles: Luke's Gospel, Section 4, 5. 1-8. 21, and Section 4', 22. 1-53:

They both comprise the same, compound chiastic-structures:

$$I(1:1'): C(1:C:1'):I'(1:1')$$

Luke's chief source would again seem to be that of Mark: as before, for Sections 5 and 5', his creation of chiasm gives the explanation for his rehandling of his source. Two further points can be made. The first is that we discover for the first time that Marcan material is also re-worked for the purpose of correspondence between the Sections. For Section 4', Luke begins by following Mk. 14. 1, 2: omitting 14. 3-9 (the anointing at Bethany) he, therefore, brings Mk. 14. 10, 11 into simple parallelism with Mk. 14. 1, 2. What he has omitted, he remodels for use in Section 4. The second is that we encounter what appears to be, Luke's clear rehandling of Matthaean material, to help him complete Section 4 and shape its central sub-section. Luke provides a number of his own pieces in both sections, again it seems, for his structural and thematic purposes of correspondence. The results of his work on these sections can be presented in the following way:

Section 4:

I: 5. 1-6. 19   Jesus' ministry to 'sinners'; questions of law and custom;
                                                        (5.1-26: 5. 27-6. 19);
   C: 6. 20-49   Jesus' sermon on 'discipleship': sinners and disciples are
                       compared;   (6. 20-26: v27-38: v39-49);
I':   7.1-8. 21   Jesus ministry to 'sinners'; questions of prophethood;
                                                        (7. 1-35; 7. 36-8. 21).

Section 4'

I: 22. 1-13   Plot to betray Jesus; preparation of the Passover:
                                                        (22. 1-6: v7-13);
   C: 22. 14-30   Jesus and disciples at table; the betrayer is present; at table
                       in the Kingdom;
                                                        (22. 14-20: v21-23: v24-30);
I':   22. 31-53   Preparations for disciples and Jesus; Jesus' betrayal and
                       arrest;   (22. 31-38: v39-53).

In both cases, the structures appear to be confirmed by what appears at the centres. It is easier to describe in Section 4': at the heart of the meal-time presentation the subject of 'betrayal', the subject of sub-sections I and I', finds sole use of this place. Other details further support the thematic presentation: one not alluded to above is that of 'Satan', 22. 3 and v31 (these mentions lie opposite each other).

The central sub-section to Section 4 needs to be given more attention. At the heart of the Sermon on Discipleship, the 'Sermon on the Plain', are three sayings which contrast the life of 'sinners' and 'disciples'. These sayings follow the summary commandment, 6. 31, which in Mt. 7. 12 is 'the law and the prophets'. Together, these pieces comprise the central part and it more than adequately focusses special attention on the issues presented in turn each side of the central sub-section. The full structure of the Sermon is worthy of a brief discussion: it can be described as:

i: 6. 20-26   Four blessings and woes;   (v20, v21a, v21b, v22, 23:
                                                                          compare v24, v25a, v25b, v26);
    c(i):   6. 27-30   Eight commands;
      c(c):   6. 31-34   Four statements; summary command and three
                             statements;   (v31, v32, v33, v34);
    c(i'):   6. 35-38   Eight commands with reasons attached;
i':   6. 39-49   Four parables on blessing and woe;
                                                             (v39, 40, v41, 42, v43-45, v46-49).

It will be observed that, in c(i, c and i'), the commands and summary command's supporting statements all begin with, firstly, 'love' and, secondly, 'do good'. Further, the blessings and the woes correspond, the first with the first, the second with the second, and so on. The sermon, it seems, is deliberately constructed for memorising: it would seem that Luke has re-organised Matthew's Sermon on the Mount and added his own pieces to complete his Sermon on the Plain. Luke's purpose as described in the Prologue is furthered by such presentation. He promised a carefully-ordered account: he fulfils his promise.

The sermon's theme is that of 'discipleship'. This theme is in fact introduced in the opening part of the first sub-section, see 5. 1-11. Luke's source is Mk. 1. 16-20. We note that he has already used, or saves for use, Mk. 1. 21-39: it is found in Section 3 in a chiastic-form. What seems certain, therefore, is that Luke swaps these pieces to achieve his thematic purposes. In adapting this Marcan piece, and by adding to it, he not only introduces his 'discipleship' theme but also his concurrent theme of 'sinners'. Jesus' miracle catch of fish serves, to Luke, possibly a triple-purpose. It evokes the thematically-significant response from Peter, 'Depart from me, for I am a *sinful* man, O Lord.' It also suggests reason for Peter's eventual following. It further suggests something of the proportions of the future catch of men (sinful men?). Reference to any concordance will show that, in this Section 4, compared with the rest of the Gospel, there is an abundance of use of the words, 'sin', 'sinner' and 'sinful'. The themes of 'discipleship' and 'sinners' seems well set. Confirmation of this could be said to be provided by the opening part of the second half of the first sub-section, 5. 27-32, which is that of another call to discipleship (deliberately brought into parallel, by Luke, from

Mark). Jesus is provoked to declare, 'I have not come to call the righteous, but sinners to repentance.'

The title which Section 4 begs is surely, 'From Sinners to Disciples'. Space, unfortunately, does not allow further consideration of this section, save to comment: what we handle here is a most skilfully-produced and most purposefully-contrived piece of revelation.

A title for Section 4' might now be considered: 'From Disciples to Sinners' is proposed. Satan enters Judas and has designs on Peter. The first betrays Jesus, the second will three-times deny Jesus. The disciples squabble over who is the greatest. They are all to be identified as law-breakers: to fulfil scripture, they take up two swords. Indeed, one of them cuts off the right ear of the high priest's slave. The word, 'sinner' is nowhere found in this section: there is, nevertheless, something compelling about this title.

We observe how Section 4 tells of the calling and choosing of disciples: it reports the coming together of Jesus and the twelve. Section 4' speaks of their being separated. Reference to Judas, the betrayer, is not found outside Sections 4 and 4'. References to meals, eating and drinking, outside of the Central Section, are found only in Sections 4 and 4'. The 'new wine', 5. 37, 38, and 'the bread of the Presence', 6. 4, in successive passages, appear to parallel the elements of the supper, 22. 17-20. In 5. 33-35, Jesus is challenged about his disciples not fasting: he responds, 'Can you make wedding guests fast while the bridegroom is with them? The day will come when the bridegroom is taken away from them . . .'. The day comes, in the opposite section. We note that, after a sabbath healing, 6. 6-10, the Pharisees and scribes were 'filled with fury and discussed with one another what they might do to Jesus.' This is the first threat we read of: with the last, the opposite section begins. The only Gospel references to 'kissing' are found in these parallel sections, see 7. 38, v45 and 22. 48: the only other reference in the two-book work is in Acts 20. 37, notably in Acts, Section 4'. We now turn to an examination of Acts, Sections 4 and 4'.

The Acts of the Apostles, Section 4, 6.1-9. 31, Section 4', 18. 24-22. 29:

The structures of these sections are the same. Comparison with the opposite Gospel Sections 4 and 4' will show, however, that, for the first time, we encounter a difference in the basic schemes. This is the case also with Sections 3 and 3' and 1 and 1', when compared in the two books. What we do find is that Acts Sections 3, 4, 4' and 3' all follow the same broad patterns. These can be described as:

$$I (1 : C : 1') : I' (1 : C : 1').$$

In contrast to Section 3 and 3', in which the sub-sections break down further into simple parallelisms, in Sections 4 and 4' they each constitute chiasms: hence, I (1[i:c:i'] : C[i:c:i'], and so on. Section 4 is as follows:

I: 6. 1-8. 3   The church in Jerusalem, the events leading up to its
                     persecution:
1:    6. 1-7   Hellenists and Hebrews; the calling/choosing of the 'seven';
                     the church in Jerusalem grows;   (6. 1: v2-6: v7);
  C: 6. 8-8. 1a   Stephen's ministry and martyrdom; his speech on the Law
                     and the Prophets;   (6. **8-15**: 7. 1-53: v54-8. 1a);
1':   8. 1b-3   The church in Jerusalem is persecuted and is scattered;
                                                                       (8. 1b: v2: v3);
I':   8. 4-9. 31   The scattered church: the events which follow its persecution:
1:    8. 4-40   The ministry of Philip and of the apostles (from Jerusalem);
                                                            (8. 4-13: v14-25: v26-40);
  C: 9. 1-22   Saul's call and purpose: the persecutor becomes the
                     proclaimer of Jesus;   (9. 1,2: v3-19a: v19b-22);
1':   9. 23-31   Paul and the apostles (in Jerusalem); Jews and Hellenists; the
                     church, in peace, grows;   (9. 23-25: v26, 27: v28-31).

An examination of the text will show that the chiasms (their verses are
given in brackets) break down further into simple parallelisms. 7. 1-53,
Stephen's speech, is worthy of special attention as it is the largest. Simply,
we have a question, 7. 1, and an answer, 7. 2-53. The answer appears to
follow the structure:

    (i) 7. 2-40   Regarding the writings of 'the Law':
    .i 7. 2-34   the history;
    .i' 7. 35-40   Stephen's judgements, based on this history;
    (i') 7. 41-53   Regarding the writings of 'the Prophets':
    .i 7. 41-50   the history;
    .i' 7. 51-53   Stephen's judgements, based on this history.

The above presentations summarise, adequately for our present purposes, the results of the analysis which takes into consideration themes and
details, and matter of structural harmony. We turn to Section 4'.
Section 4';

I: 18. 24-20. 16   In Ephesus, Paul's ministry and troubles: he resolves to go
                       to Jerusalem (and later, Rome); he hurries to get there:
1:    18. 24-19. 22   Apollos, then Paul, ministering in Ephesus; Paul is to go to
                       Jerusalem;   (18. 24-19. 7: v8-17: v18-22);
  C: 19. 23-41   Paul's causes an uproar in Ephesus;
                                                          (19. 23-27: v28-34: v35-41);
1':   20. 1-16   Paul's continuing ministry, travelling; and then, making for
                       Jerusalem;   (20. 1-6: v7-12: v13-16);
I'   20. 17-22. 29   Paul says his 'Farewells'; he is going to Jerusalem, to
                       imprisonment and troubles; he arrives and, after a few days
                       is arrested:
1:    20. 17-38   Paul's farewell speech to Ephesian elders;
                                                          (20. 17, 18a: v18b-35: v36-38);
  C: 21. 1-30   Paul is warned; he arrives in Jerusalem, causes an
                       uproar and is set upon;   (21. 1-14: v15-17: v18-30);
1':   21. 31-22. 29   Paul's speech in Jerusalem; 'Away with him', his
                       citizenship is questioned; `   (21. 31-40: 22. 1-21: v22-29).

The detailed structures are too numerous to present: all the chiasms break down further, mainly into simple parallelisms. The exceptions are worthy of note: they are 19. 28-34 (a three-part chiasm: v28, 29: v30, 31: v32-34); 20. 18b-35 (a four-part chiasm: v18b-21: v22-24; v25-31: v32-35); and 22. 1-21 (a four-part chiasm: v1-5: v6-11: v12-16: v17-21). Details of content are arranged with the same kind of Lucan dexterity that we have evidenced in the previous sections.

Sections 4 and 4' of Acts correspond in many ways. The accounts of Paul's ministry in Ephesus and Philip's in Samaria display a host of similarities: additional to the receiving of the word and Holy Spirit (in similar circumstances), are the working of miracles, baptisms, believing-responses, ministries to those who practised magic, healings and casting out of evil spirits. Nowhere-else in the Acts are these many, similar features so compactly presented. We note also the dominance of Saul/Paul in both sections, further, the telling of his persecution of the church, conversion, call and purpose. In the audience of Agrippa, in Section 3', Paul relates his experience as he did in Jerusalem, but the fuller, more detailed account is found in Section 4'. Stephen's death, Paul's approval of it, his keeping the garments of those who killed Stephen, these are found in Section 4'.

Further, significant correspondences include the charges against Stephen, in Acts 4, and the charges against Paul, in Acts 4': they concern the law of Moses and the Temple. Philip finds mention in only Sections 4 and 4' of the book: likewise, 'the seven' are mentioned only in these sections. Paul speaks of 'the law of our fathers' in his Jerusalem speech, and 'prophets' feature in Caesarea (21. 9, 10): is any parallel intended to Stephen's Jerusalem speech? Maybe also, the early Jewish plots against Saul, and the message to Ananias about Saul's future 'suffering' (9. 16) find their parallels in these later incidents. The uproar which Paul causes in both Ephesus and Jerusalem (structurally opposite in Section 4', and told in similar words and phrases) might be interpreted as persecution against the church and hence as paralleling Saul's own earlier work of persecution. He sought those belonging to 'the way', 9. 2: the same is found in 22. 4. Further references to 'the way' in Section 4' suggests the use of the term is significant: see 18. 25, v26, 19. 9, v23 (two other references only are found in the book, they are 24. 14 and v22, in Section 3').

Luke-Acts, Sections 4 and Sections 4':

The sections of the two books do not correspond for their designs of basic structure, but they do for their themes and details. Comparing Sections 4, we note the two principal features of 'the Law' and 'the Prophets'. The nature of the challenges which Jesus faced, over the law, the church also faced. We find the choosing of the twelve, in the Gospel, has its counterpart in the Acts, the choosing of the seven. The calling of disciples, we might add, is similar in both.

Sections 4' exhibit correspondences. Both speak of the arrests of the principal characters, in Jerusalem. Many of the details which precede these arrests are similar: consider 'the days of Unleavened Bread' (Lk. 22. 1, v7, and Acts 20. 6, note one other mention, Acts 12. 3); the passover meal of Jesus and his disciples, and Paul breaking bread in Troas; the ways in which their arrests are foretold; the finalities of Jesus' meal with his disciples and Paul's farewells; Peter's readiness 'to go to prison and to death' and Paul's similar readiness, 'to be imprisoned or even to die in Jerusalem'; Jesus' prayer, 'not my will, but thine, be done', and Paul's friends, failing to persuade him otherwise, saying, 'The will of the Lord be done'; Jesus' kneeling down and praying (Lk. 22. 41, the only such reference in the Gospel) and Paul's kneeling down and praying (Acts 20. 36, 21. 5), compare Stephen kneeling (Acts 7. 60) and Peter (Acts 9. 40); and lastly, the 'kissing' at Jesus' betrayal and at Paul's departing from the Ephesian elders.

Sections 4 and 4' of the two books are clearly designed with each other in mind.

Sections 3 and 3' of Luke's Gospel and the Acts of the Apostles:
Luke's Gospel, Section 3, 3. 1-4. 44, and Section 3', 22. 54-23-25:
The Sections both comprise the same, compound chiastic structures:

$$I(1:C:1'):C(1:C:1'):I'(1:C:1')$$

Section 3:

I: 3. 1-20   A dating; John's Ministry; he is not 'the Christ'; his imprison-
                    ment;   (3. 1-9: v10-14: v15-20);

 C: 3. 21-4. 30   Jesus is the Son of God: his baptism; son of Joseph, son of
                   God; his three trials; Joseph's Son (?), rejected prophet;
                                           (3. 21-38: 4. 1-15: 4. 16-30);

I': 4. 31- 44   Jesus' Ministry; three rebukings; he is 'the Holy One of God',
                   'the Son of God', 'the Christ';   (4. 31-37: v38, 39: v40-44).

It is observed that the first three sections of the Gospel begin with 'datings'. All the sub-sections break down into simple parallelisms, with the exceptions of 3. 10-14 which is a three-part chiasm (see: 'What shall we do . . .?'); 4. 1-15, which is a Lucan re-arrangement of Matthew's three temptations of Jesus' in the wilderness, to a three-part chiasm: v1-4 ('If you are the Son of God . . .'): v5-8: v9-15 ('If your are the Son of God . . .'); and, likely also, Luke's genealogy of Jesus. 3. 23e-38 would seem to be an eleven-part chiasm, with each part containing seven names:

1: **of Joseph** .... **of Joseph;**
 2: **of Mattathias** .... **of Mattathias;**
  3: of Semein .... of Salathiel;
   4: of Neri .... **of Jesus;**
    5: of Eliezer .... **of Joseph;**
     C: of Jonam .... **of David;**
    5': of Jesse .... of Admin;
   4': of Arni .... **of Abraham;**
  3': of Terah .... of Shela;
 2': of Cainan .... of Enoch;
1': of Jared .... **of God;**

The bold names are the ones considered to be of thematic and structural importance. We note that this scheme accentuates the issue of 'Jesus' sonship, that of Joseph and of God. It well fits its context: firstly, sub-section C could be entitled, 'The Son of God', secondly, the balancing part, 4. 16-30, raises again the question of Jesus' sonship (of Joseph?). Luke's scheme demonstrates, it seems, that with Jesus the twelfth era of 'sevens' begins. Matthew's genealogical-scheme, of three periods of fourteen generations, bears comparison. It would seem that Luke has developed a Matthaean idea: only now, the scheme suggests that with Jesus the perfect age of election has arrived ('seven' signifies perfection, 'twelve' signifies the election of God). It is to be noted that this chiasm reflects that of the Gospel as a whole, as does that of the central sub-section to the Central Section. Further comparison with Matthew's genealogy shows that there may be significance in Luke's descent of Jesus through Nathan, the son of David: was he here identifying the prophetic figure and, therefore a prophetic line for Jesus? If so, Luke's genealogy would even more perfectly balance its opposing part, 14. 16-30.

Section 3' might be given the title, 'The Rejections and the Three Trials of the Prophet, the Christ, the Son of God, the King of the Jews': the correspondences with Section 3 are plain. Luke's thematic and structural scheme is perfectly balanced:

Section 3':

I: 22. 54-62   Peter's three denials/rejections of Jesus;

(v54-57: v58: v59-62);

C: 22. 63-23. 12 Jesus is mocked as a prophet; his three trials; he is mocked again;

(22. 63-65: v66-71: 23. 1-5: v6-10: v11, 12);

I': 23. 13-25   The crowd's three rejections of Jesus;

(v13-19: v20, 21: v22-25).

At the centre of the five-part chiasm of sub-section C, we identify another equally well-balanced chiastic structure, 23. 1, 2: v3: v4, 5. All the other parts of the sub-sections divide into simple parallelisms.

Comparisons of the details of the three 'trials' (temptations) in the wilderness, at the centre of Section 3, with the three 'trials' (interrogations?), at the centre of Section 3', disclose a similarity of order: the question of Jesus' sonship; the consideration of his kingship; and a request for a sign.

Source considerations of both Mark and Matthew give indication of Luke's working-method: again such a study exposes what he includes from his own sources. The distinct likelihood is that he creates some of the details himself to further his tightly-spun design. The possibility has arisen before, but nowhere is it more clearly evident than here, in Section 3 and 3'. We turn to the parallel sections in the Acts.

The Acts of the Apostles, Section 3, 2. 43-5. 42 and Section 3', 22. 30-26. 32:

Because few translations show any emphasis of division at 2. 43, reason for the opening verse to Section 3 may be presented straightaway. The structural scheme of the two sections is as follows:

I (1 : C : 1') : I' (1 : C : 1')

What is found, in Section 3, to introduce sub-section I(1), is found also to introduce sub-section I'(1). The content of 2. 43-47 parallels that of 4. 32-37: each speaks of believers sharing their possessions. An example of what 2. 43 actually speaks about, 'wonders and signs done through the apostles', follows in 3. 1ff. These sub-sections, I and I' therefore, begin in similar fashion: they also continue in similar ways. They both tell of incidents which lead, in turn, to arrests of apostles, to trials and to judgements against them.

Section 3:

I: 2. 43-4. 31	The developing church in Jerusalem; arrests, trials and judgements against two apostles:	
1: 2. 43-3. 26	Wonders and signs, the church; a healing leads to preaching in Solomon's Portico;	(2. 43-47: 3. 1-26);
C: 4. 1-4	Peter and John are arrested for preaching about Jesus and the resurrection; the church grows;	(4. 1-3: v4);
1': 4. 5-31	Tried by the council, they are charged not to preach; on release, they report (signs and wonders);	(4. 5-22: v23-31);
I': 4. 32-5. 42	The developing church in Jerusalem; arrests, trials and judgements against all the apostles:	
1: 4. 32- 5. 16	The church; two deaths, signs and wonders, and together in Solomon's Portico;	(4. 32-37: 5. 1-16);
C: 5. 17-21a	The church grows: their arrest, because of jealousies; their freeing;	(5. 17, 18: v19-21a);
1': 5. 21b-42	Freed, they teach in the temple; tried by the council, they are charged with teaching in the name of Jesus; beaten, they are released;	(5. 21b-32: v33-42).

The two sub-sections clearly balance for their systematically similar presentations and contents. The detailed sub-divisions (shown in parenthesis), and others too, disclose familiar rhythms. We consider Section 3'. Again, its basic structure is the same. For contents, the theme of 'trials' continues. Similarities are observed between those of the Apostles and those of Paul: they are tried, before the high priest and members of the council, for preaching Jesus and the resurrection; Jerusalem is 'filled' with the apostles' teaching (5. 28), Paul is credited as an agitator among all the Jews throughout the world (24. 5). The Temple features in both accounts. The two Acts references to 'Satan' (3. 19 and 26. 18) appear significant: one is in Section 3, the other is in Section 3'. The phrase, 'repent therefore and turn again' (3. 19) finds a parallel, 'repent and turn to god' (26. 20), likewise, the references to Moses and the prophets that Christ should suffer (3. 18, v22 and v24: 26. 22, v23). The theme of Apostolic-trials provides the main point of contact between the two sections, the structures and some details would appear to confirm Luke's sectional-paralleling. Section 3' is presented below.

Section 3':

I:	22. 30-24. 27	Paul before the tribune and the council in Jerusalem; his transfer to Caesarea; Paul before the governor, Felix:
1:	22. 30-23. 22	Paul, before the tribune and the council in Jerusalem; a Jewish plot is discovered and reported; (22.30-23. 11: 23. 12-22);
C:	23. 23-35	Paul's transfer to Caesarea; (23. 23-30: v31-35);
1':	24. 1-27	Paul, before the governor, Felix, who delays decision and leaves Paul in prison for two years; (24. 1-21: v22-27);
I':	25. 1-26. 32	Before the governor, Festus, Paul 'appeals to Caesar'; Festus arranges with King Agrippa for him to hear Paul; Paul before Agrippa:
1:	25. 1-21	Festus is informed about Paul, Jews plot again, Paul 'appeals to Caesar'; Festus informs Agrippa: (25. 1-12: v13-21);
C:	25. 22	Festus arranges a hearing, for Agrippa; (v22a: b);
1':	25. 23-26. 32	Paul, before Agrippa: he could have been freed if he had not appealed to Caesar; (25. 23-26. 23: 26. 24-32).

The case for 25. 22 needs to be put. It is the shortest of all central sections in both books, indeed there could hardly be one shorter! The one that comes nearest to it, for size, is in the opposing section 3, in the first sub-section. This may indeed be significant. Comparisons of the centres of the sub-sections of these two Sections with others in the two-book work, which are consistently longer, suggest that this is a proper feature of the construction. Thematically, 25. 22 compares with its opposite centre, 23. 23-35: they both speak of a 'transference'. Further, grammatically, 25. 22 appears to be unique and, therefore, forceful: the Greek reads, 'And Agrippa to Festus . . .'; no verb is given. The verse itself comprises two balancing sentences. Also, it appears to stand as separate from what precedes it: what is given as a report by Festus to Agrippa, 25. 13-21, is a thorough recapitulation of the events and details of 25. 1-12.

Luke-Acts, Sections 3 and Sections 3':

As Sections 4 and 4', so also Sections 3 and 3', when viewed in the two books, do not correspond for their designs of basic structure. Sectional-parallelism is suggested alone by the contents, in particular, the theme of 'trials' and, further, the many significant details.

Sections 3 present comparable details: the trials of Jesus at the hands of the devil and the trials of Ananias and Sapphira who succomb to Satan; the ethical teaching of John appears to be given expression in the Church, in the selling of possessions, in the sharing of the proceeds and in the distribution to the poor among them; the 'gathering together' against Jesus (Acts 4. 27) and the rejection of Jesus in Nazareth; Jesus being 'full of the Holy Spirit' (Lk. 4. 1), also the apostles and their friends (Acts 4.

31); references to 'the Holy One and Righteous One' (Acts 3. 14) and 'the Holy One of God' (Lk. 4. 34); and John the Baptist's experience of prison, likewise of Peter and John and, in turn, all the apostles. Another possible common feature might be that of the use of the number 'forty': Jesus was forty days in the wilderness; the lame man who was healed was forty years old. Forty Jews plot to ambush Paul: see the opposing Acts section.

Sections 3′ appear to parallel the trials of Jesus with the trials of Paul. The Jews reject Paul as they did Jesus. Each of them appears before the council, the governor and the king (Paul, before two governors, with two years in prison between). We note that before Jesus is brought to the council he is 'struck': in the council-hearing, Paul is 'struck on the mouth'. Before Felix, Paul is charged as being 'a pestilent fellow, an agitator among all the Jews, a ringleader of the Nazarene sect' (Acts 24. 5). Jesus, before Pilate, is accused of perverting the nation, forbidding tribute to Caesar, and stirring up the people (Lk. 23. 1, v2 and v5). It is leading Jews, in both case, who make the accusations. We note that Pilate declares, of Jesus, 'I find no crime in this man' and, 'Behold, nothing deserving death has been done by him' (see Lk. 23. 4, v15). Festus recognises Paul's innocence: 'I found that he had done nothing deserving death', he says to Agrippa (Acts 25. 25, see also 26. 31).

The correspondences, again, would seem to be established.

Sections 2 and 2′ of Luke's Gospel and the Acts of the Apostles: Luke's Gospel, Section 2, 2. 1-52, and Section 2′, 23. 26-53:

Like Sections 4 and 4′, Sections 2 and 2′ are designed to a compound chiastic-structure described by:

$$I(1:1'):C(1:C:1'):I'(1:1')$$

Section 2:

I: 2. 1-20   A dating; Mary and Joseph go to Bethlehem where Jesus is born; angels announce the news of Jesus' birth to shepherds, who go to find Jesus;   (2. 1-7: v8-20);

C: 2. 21-40   Mary and Joseph go to Jerusalem to fulfil the requirements of the Law; at Jesus' presentation, Simeon and Anna bear witness;   (2. 21-24: v25-38: v39, 40);

I′: 2. 41-52   Mary and Joseph take the twelve-year old Jesus to Jerusalem, at the Passover; he separates from them but is found in the Temple, after three days;   (2. 41-45: v46-52).

Section 2′:

I: 23. 26-31 Jesus is led away to his death, Simon of Cyrene carries his cross; many follow, Jesus laments for the women;   (23. 26, 27: v28-31);

C: 23. 32-46 Jesus is crucified; he is mocked on his cross but one of the criminals sympathises; Jesus dies; (23. 32-34: v35-43: v44-46);

I′: 23. 47-53 The people change thier minds about Jesus; he is taken down from the cross and buried in the tomb of Joseph of Arimathea;   (23. 47-49: v50-53).

All the parts, which are described by the verses in the brackets, can be said to break down into simple parallelisms. They serve to maintain the rhythms of revelation. One part, however, gives cause for hesitation: it is that of 2. 25-38. Based on attention to the prominent characters alone, it could be argued that here is another simple parallelism: 2. 25-35 tells about Simeon and his witness, 2. 36-38 tells about Anna and her witness. What is not balanced, however, is the number of lines, and the reason for this is that one of the characters is quoted and the other is not. The following, possible detailed break-down, therefore, has to be considered:

i) 2. 25-28   Simeon, 'looking for the consolation of Israel', came into the
                Temple, and took Jesus in his arms;
ii) 2. 29-32   The first quotation;
c) 2. 33, 34a Joseph and Mary marvel;
ii') 2. 34bc, 35 The second quotation;
i') 2. 36-38   Anna, regularly in the Temple, came up at that moment, and
                spoke of Jesus to 'all who were looking for the redemption of
                Jerusalem'.

The rhythm of these pieces seems well described in this way. The Lucan tendency, however, is to give complete parts: he shows elsewhere no pre-disposition to fudge his parts. The first breakdown of the central part is favoured, therefore. The bordering parts to the above, 2. 21-24 and 2. 39, 40, well balance: they introduce and conclude this episode.

The central sub-section of Section 2', 23. 32-46, is also worthy of special attention, but for different reasons. Here the balance of parts particularly exposes Luke's thinking:

1: 23. 32-34 Jesus is crucified; 'Father forgive . . .'; his garments are divided;
C, i): 23. 35-38 (a) rulers scoff: 'save . . . Christ . . .';
                  (b) soldiers mock: 'King . . . save . . .';
C, i'):23. 39-43 (a) criminal rails: 'Christ . . . save . . .';
                  (b) the other: 'remember me . . . kingdom . . .';
1': 23. 44-46 Darkness came; the Temple curtain is torn; 'Father, into your
              hands . . .'; Jesus dies.

Luke cannot have been unaware of the usefulness of this 'order' for the preacher or expositor. This shaping of Section 2' was achieved only by a substantial editing of Mk. 15. 21-47, on Luke's part, and the additions of Jesus' address to the women of Jerusalem, Jesus' two prayers, Jesus' discussion with the criminal, and the first criminal's railing. Simultaneously, Luke presents both a historical event and its deep significance.

Section 2 and Section 1 are normally thought to be dependent of Lucan sources alone. Luke, clearly, includes much material of his own, but Drury (22) has shown persuasively how many Matthaean pieces are represented and developed. His arguments are supported now by the results of literary-structural analysis and by what appear to be Luke's motives in so writing.

In structural terms, Sections 2 and 2' correspond. They do so also for their themes and many details. Section 2 tells of the birth of Jesus: Section 2' tells of his death. His death under Roman law (but in fulfilment of the Law, of the Jews, and the Prophets) may find correspondence with Jesus' being born in Bethlehem (in fulfilment of scripture), due to the Roman decree regarding the census. Luke tells us in Section 2 that Jesus' parents did everything in accordance with the Jewish Law: note Jesus' circumcission, their purification, his presentation as a baby and his Passover attendance at the Temple at the age of twelve. In Section 2', it may well be that Luke intends that the meaning of Jesus' death be understood in respect to the law. Luke clearly demonstrates its meaning as regards salvation, in both sections: compare their central teachings and note the announcements of the angels to the shepherds. In both sections, named characters are 'looking for' 'the consolation of Israel' (2. 25), 'the redemption of Jerusalem' (2. 38) and 'the Kingdom of God' (23. 51). Compare also Anna and the 'daughters of Jerusalem'. The 'wrappings' of the body of Jesus and the 'placing' of him may be significant: compare 2. 6, v7 and v23 with 23. 53. Sectional mentions of Jerusalem, the Temple, references to 'country' and 'fields' (2. 8 and 23. 47), the glorifying of God (2. 14, v20 and 23. 47), and the witnessing to Jesus (of Simeon, Anna and the Centurion) may all be considered to be significant for establishing correspondence.

The Acts of the Apostles, Section 2, 2. 1-42, and Section 2', 27. 1-28. 15:

The structures of Sections 2 and 2' follow the same pattern as above:

I (1 : 1') : C (1 : C : 1') : I' (1 : 1')

Section 2: The birth of the Church's mission:

I: 2. 1-13   The Holy Spirit is given; Jews are amazed and perplexed;
                                                                    (2. 1-4: v5-13);
C: 2. 14-36   Peter's Speech: Joel's prophecy is fulfilled; Jesus whom they
               killed is raised; Jesus and David are contrasted/the promise
               is fulfilled;   (2. 14-21: v22-28: v29-36);
I': 2. 37-42   Those who were previously amazed ask what they should do:
               Peter tells them; the response is great;   (2. 37-39: v40-42).

Section 2': Paul's Journey to Italy and Rome:

I: 27. 1-12   Setting out; centurion is kind; Paul's warning of disaster is
               unheeded;   (27. 1-8: v9-12);
C: 27. 13-44   Storms and shipwreck: Paul's warning is acted upon; they are
               all saved;   (27. 13-26: 27-32: 33-44);
I': 28. 1-15   Stay on Malta; the natives show kindness and are amazed Paul
               does not die; arrival in Rome;   (28. 1-10: v11-15).

Section 2 is arranged around Peter's Pentecost, three-part (three point?) sermon: the first and last parts are primarily about the pouring out of the Spirit; the central part is about Jesus. The first part speaks of prophecy, regarding the Spirit, as fulfilled: the last part speaks of the Spirit as the proof of Jesus' exaltation (his promise is fulfilled). Each side of the sermon, the crowds are provoked to question: in the first, they ask, 'What does this mean?, in the last, 'What shall we do?'

Section 2' is arranged around the action-packed, three-part telling of the storm at sea and the shipwreck. In each part, Paul is taking the lead: in the balancing first and last parts Paul gives encouragement, and in the central part he contributes to the saving of everyone. The opening sub-section gives details of the setting-out for Italy and the negative responses Paul attracts: the closing sub-section details the positive responses Paul attracts and the completion of the journey.

In Section 2, Peter is the central character, in Section 2' Paul is. Already established, in the examination of other sections, is Luke's interest in setting Peter and Paul as equal, in apostolic status. In both sections, as we have noted, their influence causes a change in the attitudes and responses of the people around them. Some details suggest further correspondence: there is common mention of Rome, Asia, Crete (also Egypt/Alexandria?) there is an emphasis of salvific language (2. 21, v40 and 27. 20, v31, v35, v43, v44, 28. 1, v4); there are common references to breaking of bread; to 'a number' of souls; to 'fire'; to 'wind' (in the Greek, 2. 2 and 27. 40, the only uses in the book); and to a violent wind, in 2. 2, and a tempestuous wind, in 27. 14. What we surprisingly do not find is any common reference to the 'Spirit'!

Luke-Acts, Sections 2 and 2':

The basic structural similarities have been noted. Possible thematic and detailed corresondences are now examined.

Luke Section 2 tells of scripture-fulfilment and the fulfilment of angelic promise in relation to Jesus' birth: Acts Section 2 tells of scripture-fulfilment and the fulfilment of the risen Jesus' promise in relation to the birth of the Church's mission. Heavenly-happenings introduce the events: amazement, bewilderment, marvelling and fear are the common responses (see Lk. 2. 9, v18, v47 and Acts 2. 6, v7, v12). The Holy Spirit causes the principal characters to bear witness: compare Simeon and Peter (and all the others, Acts 2. 4). And Jerusalem features in both sections, at the times of major Jewish festivals.

Luke Section 2' tells of Jesus' death as a saving act. Acts Section 2' tells how Paul comes near to death (by drowning, at the hands of the soldiers and by snake-poisoning): it tells of his role in saving everyone in the ship. Like Jesus, Paul is in the company of other prisoners. Soldiers feature in both episodes. We note favourable attitudes to the principal characters from centurions (Lk. 23. 47, Acts 27. 3, v43); the changing of people's opinions (Lk. 23. 47, 'he was righteous', Acts 28. 6, 'he is a god', also Lk. 23. 48 and Acts 27. 11, compare 27. 31, 32, also 27. 33-36); and similar details of sky-conditions (Lk. 23. 44, Acts 27. 20).

Sections 1 and 1′ of Luke's Gospel and the Acts of the Apostles: Luke's Gospel, Section 1, 1. 5-80, and Section 1′, 23. 54-24. 53:

For the first time in our examination of Luke's Gospel, we encounter two sections which are designed to a non-chiastic scheme: we find instead a simple-parallelism of two pairs of chiasms:

$$I\,(1:1') : I'\,(1:1').$$

Section 1:

I: 1. 5-38   An angel's announcements of births: Zechariah's disbelief and Mary's belief:

1: 1. 5-25   John: Elizabeth is old and barren; they are blameless before the law; (chiasm: v5-12: v13-20: v21-25);

1′: 1. 26-38   Jesus: Mary is a young virgin; she is favoured; (chiasm: v26-29: v30-37: v38);

I′: 1. 39-80   The exultations and announcements of Elizabeth, Mary and Zechariah; before and after John's birth:

1: 1. 39-56   Jesus is witnessed to by John (in utero); Elizabeth and Mary exult; (chiasm: v39, 40: v41-55: v56);

1′: 1. 57-80   John is born, people rejoice; John is named, Zechariah exults; (chiasm: v57, 58: v59-79: v80).

Just like the Gospel Sections 2 and 3, Section 1 begins with a dating (1. 5: compare 2. 1, 2 and 3. 1, 2). Unmistakeably, these four episodes of Section 1 are both clearly defined and easily related. The disposition of all the pieces, to demonstrate the similarities of these two pairs of stories and their real, and theological, points of difference, invites a major discussion. Luke's presentation begs pages of exposition. Space allows for neither of these things: the above resumé will have to suffice. The cryptic presentation of the contents is intended to give guidance to those who would examine these things for themselves. Additional notes are kept to a minimum.

It will be seen that at the hearts of the first two episodes there are similar questions (posed to the angel): Zechariah asks, 'According to what shall I know this?' (1. 18, literally) and Mary asks, 'How will this be . . .?' (1. 34). Central to both episodes, these questions arise, as a result of what has already been said, and as a lead into what is then said by the angel. We discovered something very similar to this in Section 2, 2. 21-40. The centres of I, 1 and 1′, therefore, express the differences of response of Zechariah and Mary, and attract our comparison of the two episodes regarding matters of disbelief and belief. This is further confirmed by what the angel had to say to Zechariah (1. 20) and the sign that was given, of his dumbness, and later, in sub-section I′, in the fulfilment of the sign (1. 64) and in what Elizabeth had to say to Mary (1. 45). Just as the first pair of episodes contain the angel's announcements about the different purposes of God, in John and Jesus, so also the second pair, in the exultations of Mary and Zechariah, contain announcements of God's purposes and the different roles of Jesus and John. We observe that, in 1. 32, Jesus is 'the

Son of the Most High' and, in 1. 76, John is 'the prophet of the Most High'. Luke, with his customary adroitness, has woven together, for our understanding, several strands of gospel truth: profoundly, they are the status and roles of John and Jesus, matters of law and grace (favour), and the issue of belief and disbelief. Such are the themes, with which he introduces his Gospel. Fascinatingly, these are the very same themes that John presents in the first section of his Gospel.

Section 1':

I: 23. 54-24. 11 Angels announce to the women that Jesus has risen: their report to the men is not believed:

1: 23. 54-56   The women see how the body of Jesus is laid; they return from the tomb;   (23. 54: v55, 56a: v56b);

1' 24. 1-11   The women find the tomb empty; angels announce that Jesus is risen; returning, they report; they are not believed;
                                                       (24. 1-3: v4-8: v9-11);

I': 24. 13-53   Jesus' appearances result in belief; he instructs them in the scriptures and in what they are to do; a new promise is made:

1: 24. 13-32   Jesus appears to two disciples; he instructs them in the scriptures; disbelief turns to belief, Jesus vanishes;
                                                       (24. 13-16: v17-27: v28-32);

1': 24. 33-53   Jesus appears to them all, in Jerusalem; he instructs them in the scriptures, describes their purpose and makes a new promise; he parts from them;   (24. 33-43: v44-49: v50-53).

Anouncements of angels, and of Jesus, issues of belief and disbelief (the woman believe, the men at first do not: compare with Mary and Zechariah), the prospect of a new promise being fulfilled, descriptions of the roles of the disciples, these are matters which suggest that it is not only the structures of Sections 1 and 1' that are similar. Examination of the details of both sections confirm the correspondence: note, for example, Mary is to be overshadowed with 'the power of the Most High' and the disciples are to be 'clothed with power from on High'; also, John will preach 'forgiveness of sins', likewise the disciples will. It might be properly argued that the Sections both present matters of scripture-fulfilment, though, in Section 1, it is more by allusion: compare, nevertheless, the announcements and exultations of the angel, Mary and Zechariah, with Jesus' instructions on the scriptures. The Gospel clearly closes as it began, in expectation.

We observe, in Section 1', that two pairs of chiasms are again Luke's choice (compare Section 1): further, all the pieces break down, as in Section 1, into simple parallelisms. Sub-section I, because of textual difficulties and because of differences of punctuation in the popular Greek New Testament texts, has been most difficult to analyse. What is presented is the result of an examination of the verbal details of available textual synopses and an assessment of their value. Plainly, the details of 23. 54-56 are a part of this section, with 24. 1-11 containing the same details (women, Galilee, tomb, body, preparation, spices and returned). The first chiasm of the section sets up the material that will contrast with that of the second. In such a way, Luke cleverly emphasisis what is the startlingly incredible, yet true, revelation of Jesus' resurrection. As with Section 1, so it is with Section 1': it is the fine balancing of detail and the creative juxtaposing of contrasting story-lines that inform. Luke's creative genius is surely well-demonstrated in these sections. Helpful too, is the clear differentiation of episodes which these sections comprise. In each, they number four.

The Acts of the Apostles, Section 1, 1. 1-26, and Section 1', 28. 16-31:

The structures of these sections are as those immediately above:

I (1 : 1') : I' (1 : 1').

Section 1:

I: 1. 1-11:   Prologue: proofs of Jesus' resurrection; 'stay in Jerusalem' . . . the promise of the Spirit; witnesses; Jesus' ascension and angels' announcements:

1: 1. 1-5   Integral prologue: the story up to Jesus' ascension, proofs of Jesus' resurrection; his speaking of the kingdom; his command: 'stay in Jerusalem; John's baptism, the promise of the Spirit;
(v1, 2: v3-5);

1': 1. 6-11   The promise of the Spirit . . . witnesses in Jerusalem, Judea . . .; Jesus' ascension and angels' announcements;
(v6-8: v9-11);

I': 1. 12-26:   In Jerusalem, the eleven and others at prayer and choosing a resurrection witness replacement for Judas:

1: 1. 12-14   Returning to Jerusalem, the eleven and others assemble; with the women, including Jesus' mother Mary, they pray;
(v12, 13a: v13b, 14);

1': 1. 15-26:   Under Peter's guidance and by lot a replacement for Judas is appointed; it is one who accompanied them from John's baptism to Jesus' ascension, a witness to Jesus' resurrection;
(v15-22: v23-26).

Section 1'

I: 28. 16-22   In Rome, Paul stays by himself: leading Jews hear him:

1: 28. 16   In Rome, Paul stays by himself, with a soldier guarding him; (a:b);

1': 28. 17-22   He seeks to be heard by leading Jews and explains his situation, because of the hope of Israel;   (v17-20: v21, 22);

I': 28. 23-31   Jews, in larger numbers come to where Paul is staying:

1: 28. 23-28:   They come to Paul in large numbers; he instructs them in the scriptures; some were convinced, others disbelieved; '. . . the Gentiles will listen';   (v23: v24-28);

1': 28. 30, 31   Paul lives there two years, preaching the Kingdom of God and teaching about Jesus;   (v30: 31).

this chapter: the content of verses 6-11 reflects it and takes up the story. From the chart on the two books, in the section on 'Lucan Infra-structure', it is clearly shown that Acts Sections 1 and 1' are the shortest of Luke's work. They, nevertheless, contribute much. The settings are different: the first is Jerusalem, the second is Rome. The book takes us, significantly, from the principal city of the Jews to the principal city of the Gentiles. Christian witness first went out from Jerusalem, to Jews: it now proceeds, at the last, from Rome, to Gentiles. Acts 1. 8, 'you shall be my witnesses . . . to the end of the earth' finds now more certain fulfilment. The central placing of Antioch, in Luke's second book-scheme, likewise, is clearly significant: Antioch provided the mission-base for a ministry among both Jews and Gentiles.

Details, which might confirm correspondence between Sections 1 and 1', might include: apostles and friends (leading members of the Church) and 'leaders of the Jews' in gatherings (1. 6, v12-14, 28. 17); references to the Kingdom (1. 3, v6, 28. 23, v31): the references in the book are possibly, deliberately chiastically-distributed, see Sections 1, 4, C, 4', 1'); scripture-fulfilment regarding Judas (1. 16, v20), and the Jews (28. 25-27); and the fact that Judas deserved to die (1. 18), but Paul did not (28. 18).

Luke-Acts, Sections 1 and 1':

The Prologues have already been discussed. Sections 1 may be said to correspond for the following reasons. We note the common importance of Jerusalem. We note the common features of angelic appearances and announcements: we can compare the announcement of Jesus' birth with that of Jesus' return. Promises expressed in both can be compared, of births, in the Gospel, and of the Holy Spirit, in Acts. Fulfilment of scriptures is found in both. They speak of prayer and answers to prayer (Lk. 1. 13, Acts 1. 14, v24), also, of 'lots' (Lk. 1. 9, Acts 1. 26). They both quote Psalm 69: v31 in Lk. 1. 46; v25 in Acts 1. 20. The Holy Spirit is coupled with 'power' in Lk. 1. 35 and Acts 1.8. But, the strongest comparisons to be made, perhaps, lie with the roles of the principal characters as witnesses to Jesus. It may be that Luke makes his appeal to the continuing church, to do the same. It may be that, from the beginnings of his books, he is simply giving evidence for the reliability of their contents. John, Elizabeth, Mary and Zechariah all qualify as witnesses, likewise also, all the apostles and the others (including Mary, Jesus' mother), who have been with Jesus from the beginning (his baptism, not his birth) till his ascension.

Sections 1', concluding the books, present the issue of belief and disbelief. It may be that Luke, in this way, makes his appeal to 'would-be' followers, who might be listening to the reading of his works. It may be that, in the Gospel, he simply seeks to show reasonable disbelief giving way to reasonable belief and, in the Acts, unreasonable disbelief giving over to condemnation. The matters of 'seeing' and 'the heart' are presented in both (Lk. 24. 16, v25, v31, v32, v38; Acts 28. 26, v27). Scripture-fulfilment is more clearly a parallel here (compare with the above): references to the law of Moses and the prophets, as they concern Jesus, are found in Lk. 24. 25-27, v44 (where they are in parallel) and Acts 28. 23. Witnessing, too, is perhaps (compare with the above) more plainly featured: compare Lk. 24. 48 and Acts 28. 22, v30, 31. We note also the reference, 'after three days' (Acts 28. 17) and 'on the third day' (Lk. 24. 7, v21, v46).

Because Sections 1 and Sections 1' clearly correspond, and because Sections 1 and 1', within each book, correspond, the possibility arises that Section 1 in one book might be found to correspond also with Section 1' of the other. This issue has been introduced already in the opening to the presentation of Lucan infra-structure. Only in Sections 1 and 1' is it a matter of importance (other sections show little such correspondence). For example, examining Gospel Section 1 for para- llelism with Acts Section 1', we might consider that Isaiah 6, quoted in Acts 28. 26, 27, is alluded to in Lk. 1. 8-23. After much investigation, however, I conclude that the Gospel's final section and the Acts first section are the only ones which correspond significantly. Any examina- tion of the two will reward enquiry. And the explanation for this, I would proffer, is that Luke began his second work ('the Acts of the Holy Spirit') by thoroughly fixing it, at its beginning, to that which concluded the Gospel, in order to establish it, beyond question, as a continuance of the same story. I would further suggest that, as he continued in writing his second work, he had to hand his own first work, deliberately repeating themes, details, issues and forms of structural presentation, to his literary and theological ends. The simplest way of putting the latter is that, to Luke, the life of Jesus is lived again in the life of the Church, a life and a mission which the Spirit brings to birth and sustains.

Our task today:
Clearly, we are to enjoy this discovery and learn afresh from the contents of these two books. There is much to assimilate. Additional details, over and above those mentioned here, are there to be examined: consider the Gospel's Sections 3 and 4, for their structural use, in turn, of 'threes' and 'fours'. Plainly, new presentations are demanded, printed and spoken. Textual and translational issues can be tackled in new ways. A clearer and more accurated understanding of Luke's theological approach can be grasped. Issues which have oppressed successions of readers can be laid aside. No longer do we need Q source to help us: the synoptic problem is not. A more unified approach to the study of the Gospels of Mark, Matthew and Luke and to the study of the Acts of the Apostles is promised: though, I doubt not that this will come about only at some cost. What will not be lost will be the honest endeavour of these book- evangelists, who call us to faith in Him who is at the centre of all history and eternity. This is their faith, it can be ours too.

5 John's Gospel

Griesbach (1), in the late eighteenth century, separated the first three Gospels from the fourth and presented them in parallel columns under the title, 'A Synopsis of the Gospels of Matthew, Mark and Luke'. Since then, it has been common practice to consider John's Gospel in isolation. It cannot be the case when we are discussing literary-structures. John's Gospel can be examined now, with the benefit of having completed the study of the others.

'Simple in outline, complicated in detail', is how Barrett (2) describes the Gospel's structure which he presents:

1. 1-18	Prologue;
1. 19-12. 50	Narratives, Conversations and Discourses;
13. 1-17. 26	Jesus alone with his disciples;
18. 1-20. 31	The Passion and Resurrection;
21. 1-25	An Appendix.

But, he also presents Miss Guilding's alternative:

1. 1-18	Prologue;
1. 19-4. 54	The manifestation of Messiah to the World;
6, 5, 7-12	The manifestation of the Messiah to the Jews;
13-20	The manifestation of the Messiah to the Church;
21	Epilogue;

and C. H. Dodd's:

1	the Proem;
2-12	The Book of Signs;
13-20	The Book of the Passion.
(21)	

Whilst they demonstrate some measure of agreement and similar simplicities of outline, their differences suggest that schemes of this kind cannot be totally convincing. Other variant schemes would appear to differ little from these given above. Plainly, they require discussion, but what is presented below has little in common with them and is not based on them. They, therefore, without a presentation of their merits or demerits, simply describe the limited progress which until now has been made. Of all the investigations of the Gospels for their literary-structures, those of John's, it would seem, have led, thus far, to the least success.

Some general agreement, however, is enjoyed concerning the discovered dislocations, or displacements of the present text: for example, 3. 22-30 is considered better placed after 2. 12, and 3. 31 after 3. 21. Eight possibilities of displacements are often addressed. The old theory, that these are the result of accidental re-arrangement, has given way to the new theory, that they are the result of an intent on the part of an editor. But, what lay behind the intent? And, did this accord with the wishes of the original author? Until now, we have been some distance from finding any satisfying answers. But, it would seem that the discovery of the structure of the current version of the Gospel, as presented below, when considered in tandem with the proposed displacements, leads to a plausible theory which takes account also of material like that of chapter 21 which is by many scholars considered to be a later addition.

The current version of John's Gospel would appear to be the result of a re-shaping and an enlarging of an earlier, quite differently-structured version. Clearly two stages in this presentation are required. The first is to describe the structure of the current version of the Gospel and the way in which it was discovered and confirmed. The second is to examine the evidence for that of the possible, earlier version.

Johannine infra-structure, Part I:

John's Gospel as we presently know it would seem to be arranged in the following chiasm of seven sections (of twelve parts each), where 1 and 1', 2 and 2', 3 and 3' denote sections which correspond in themes and details around a central section C:

$$1, 2, 3, C, 3', 2', 1'.$$

A search was made, first of all, for possible 'signifiers' of structural divisions. Comparison with the synoptic gospels focussed attention on the three particular, recurring emphases of John's Gospel. They are (i) 'the signs' that are recorded in detail and which, in most cases, attach to illuminations of a spiritual kind, (ii) the reasonably regular references to 'feasts' and (iii) the unique 'I am' sayings of the longer variety (with predicates). In turn, these were listed and assumed, for the sake of making a start, to warrant different sections, that is, each of their kind. Judgements were made, at the same time, regarding possible introductions and conclusions to the sections.

The 'signs' (of the kind mentioned above) were identified and arranged in sections, as follows:

1) 1. 1-2. 12   'water' into 'wine' (2. 1-11);
2) 2. 13-4. 54   'the healing of an official's son' (4. 46-54);
3) 5. 1-47   'the healing of a paralysed man' (5. 1-9);
4) 6. 1-71   'the feeding of the five thousand' (6. 5-14);
5) 7. 1-9. 41   'the healing of a blind beggar' (9. 1-12);
6) 10. 1-11. 54   'the raising of Lazarus' (11. 1-44); and
7) 11. 55-21. 25 'Jesus' death and resurrection' (19. 1-21. 25).

Explanation is given for the division between 9. 41 and 10. 1: it may appear to be an abrupt entry, but the content of 10. 1-21, concerning 'sheep', seemed to demand it belonged with 10. 22ff.

The references to 'feasts seemed to warrant no change to this scheme:

1)	2. 1 (v8, v9)	'the marriage feast';
2)	2. 13	'the Passover of the Jews';
3)	5. 1	'a feast of the Jews';
4)	6. 4	'the Passover, the feast of the Jews';
5)	7. 2 (v8, v10, v11, v14, v37)	'the feast of the Jews, Tabernacles';
6)	10. 22	'the (feast of) Dedication';
7)	11. 55 (12. 1, v12, v20, 13. 1, v29)	'the Passover of the Jews'.

The present ordering of the feasts is a reasonable one: the last four succeed each other on the annual calendar.

The 'I am' sayings, of the kind described above, were then identified, plotted against the proposed sectional scheme and taken to suggest further sub-divisions:

1) 1. 1-2. 12
2) 2. 13-4. 54
3) 5. 1-47
4) 6. 1-71   'I am the bread of life' (6. 20, v48);
5) 7. 1-9. 41 'I am the light of the world' (8. 12, 9. 5);
6) 10. 1-42   'I am the door of the sheep' (10. 7);
               'I am the good shepherd' (10. 10);
7) 11. 1-54   'I am the resurrection and the life' (11. 25);
8) 11. 55-14. 31 'I am the way, the truth and the life' (14. 6);
9) 15. 1-21. 25 'I am the true vine' (15. 1, v5).

The close proximity of the sayings in section 6 demanded they both occupy the same section. It was noticed that the first five sections were unaltered: sections 6 and 7, therefore, begged closer scrutiny.

Some features of these two sections strongly suggested that they needed to be seen as balancing each other. In section 6, we read: 'if anyone enters by me, he will be saved' (10. 9); 'I came that they may have life and have it abundantly' (10. 10b); 'The good shepherd lays down his life for the sheep' (10. 11b); and of 'other sheep . . . not of this fold; I must bring them also' (10. 16). In section 7, we read that Jesus is 'the resurrection and the life' (11. 25) and in the conclusion (11. 45-54) we find a passage that looks very much as if it was included to satisfy balance. It is highly significant that, without 11. 49-52, the conclusion would still make good sense. It is within these verses that we read Caiaphas' counsel that 'it is expedient . . . that one man should die for the people, and that the whole nation should not perish . . . and not for the nation only, but to gather into one the children of God who are scattered abroad.' (It is noted how the second series of statements appears to explain the first.) It did seem that the two previous, possible 'signifiers' had suggested that sections 6 and 7 should be viewed as a whole.

The possibility, therefore, clearly arose that sections 6 and 7 were two balancing parts of a central section. Further, because the sections preceding it numbered five, the possibility that this gospel was arranged like that of Matthew and Luke was too obvious to ignore. What then became likely, straightaway, was that the first and the last 'I am' sayings were sectionally parallel, the first being that of the 'bread' and the last being that of the 'true vine'. The 'I am' sayings would then occupy the central five sections of the book.

Reference to the earliest Church manual (3) that we possess, for the liturgy of the eucharist, appears to confirm this balance. Thanks to God were expressed firstly over the chalice, 'for the holy Vine of thy servant David', and then over the particles of bread, for 'the life and knowledge thou hast make known to us through thy servant Jesus.' The order, it is recognised, is reversed in the Gospel, but the sentiments expressed, as regards the different elements, are so plainly similar.

A close examination of 11. 55-21. 25 followed. It did seem that the likely sections 5' to 1' were being given over to the greatest of all the signs, the seventh, Jesus' death and resurrection. An assumption was made (for later testing) that the resurrection narratives might occupy Secton 1' as in Luke's Gospel. Further breaks in the text were deemed to be likely between 14. 31 and 15. 1, 16. 33 and 17. 1, and 18. 27 and v28. The reason for the first of these is simply that of the content of 14. 31: 'But I do as the Father has commanded me so that the world may know that I love the Father. Rise let us go hence.' The reason for the second of these is that Jesus' prayer, chapter 17, is called traditionally, 'the High Priestly Prayer', and that chapter 18 contains no fewer than nine references to the then 'high priest'. It seemed likely that Jesus and the High Priest were being compared and contrasted here. As all use of the term, 'high priest', ceases abruptly at 18. 26, 18. 27 seemed a likely last verse to the section. 18. 28 clearly begins a new episode: 'Then they led Jesus from the house of Caiaphas to the praetorium . . .'. The passages, 18. 28-19. 42, on the trial of Jesus before Pilate, Jesus being handed over for crucifixion, his death and his burial, did seem that they very much held together for their twelve references to Jesus being 'King (of the Jews)'.

The likelihood, therefore, was that the Gospel was designed to the following chiasm:

```
      1   1. 1-2. 12
        2   2. 13-4. 54
          3   5. 1-47
            4   6. 1-71
              5   7. 1-9. 41
                C   10. 1-11. 54
              5'   11. 55-14. 31
            4'   15. 1-16. 33
          3'   17. 1-18. 27
        2'   18. 28-19. 42
      1'   20. 1-21. 25.
```

It was judged worthy of a detailed structural examination. Would the Gospel's sections be found to consist of numerical listings of pieces, like Matthew's? Or, would they be found to be a blend of chiasm and simple-parallelism, as in Luke's two books? It soon appeared that a hybrid of the two was possibly the case. What is presented is a brief summary only of much analysis.

Sections 1 and 1' were examined first.

	Section 1:				Section 1'	
I	1	1. 1-18		I	1	20. 1-18
	2	1. 19-28			2	20. 19-29
	3	1. 29-34			3	20. 30, 31
I'	1	1. 35-42		I'	1	21. 1-14
	2	1. 43-51			2	21. 15-23
	3	2. 1-12			3	21. 24, 25.

Comparison with the structure of Luke's Prologues seemed not unreasonable, though, of course, these are much larger. Section 1, I, in its three parts, is devised to demonstrate the contrast to be made between John the Baptist and Jesus. It is very much John's testimony to Jesus, in all its parts. Section 1, I', in its three parts, which are the first three days of Jesus' ministry, connects by way of a repetition of John's testimony and proceeds to present Jesus' own witness to himself.

Section 1', for its episodes, would seem to be correctly sub-divided: they further divide into 20. 1-9: v10-18; 20. 19-25: v26-29; 20. 30: v31; 21. 1-3: v4-14; 21. 15-19: v20-23; and 21. 24: v25. Witness is given to Jesus' resurrection: at the conclusion of series I, he is most clearly his own witness, but at the conclusion of series I', it is John the Apostle who is his witness.

The book, in its present form, would seem to present Jesus as witnessed to by John the Baptist at the beginning and John the Apostle at the end. The mention of 'the third day' (2. 1) is not without its significance. Nathanael, 'of Cana in Galilee' (21. 2) is mentioned in both Sections. Simon Peter is called, in the first, and commissioned, in the last.

Section C, as it suggested itself to be a two-part, simple parallelism, attracted attention next. It did seem that it constituted the following:

		Section C:				
I	1	10. 1-6		I	1	11. 1-5
	2	10. 7-18			2	11. 6-16
	3	10. 19-21			3	11. 17-37
I'	1	10. 22-30		I'	1	11. 38-44
	2	10. 31-39			2	11. 45-53
	3	10. 40-42			3	11. 54.

Changes in setting and subject matter suggest these divisions. For example, compare 10. 21 with 11. 37 (reference: the opening of the eyes

of the blind). Similarities between 10. 40-42 and 20. 30, 31 (Section 1')
for brevity, and 'sign' and 'belief', are discerned. Similarities with Section
1, for 'beyond the Jordan', 'John' and 'baptised' are also apparent. It has
been noted, in the examination of Luke's Gospel, how the chiastically-
central pieces reflect, to some degree, those of the beginning and the end
of the total structure. We observe, it seems, the very same feature again.
Details like 'lamb' (1. 29, v36), 'little lamb' (21. 15) and 'sheep' (10.2, v3,
v4, v7, v8, v11, v12, v13, v15, v16, v26, v27 and 21 v16, v17) suggest
interdependency too: nowhere-else in the Gospel are such references
found. For further discussions on this section, see above.

Sections 2 and 2' appeared to be arranged in the same way. A
common elemental pattern of sectional structure seemed to be emerging:

		Section 2:				Section 2'
I	1	2. 13-22		I	1	18. 28-40
	2	2. 23-3. 21			2	19. 1-12
	3	3. 22-36			3	19. 13-16a
I'	1	4. 1-26		I'	1	19. 16b-22
	2	4. 27-42			2	19. 23-30
	3	4. 43-54			3	19. 31-42.

Temporal and geographical references seem to suggest these
divisions: changes in themes and repetitions of detail seem to suggest the
arrangements.

The first succession of parts in Section 2 is: Jesus' Passover visit to
Jerusalem; Jesus' conversations with a night visitor; and Jesus' in Judea.
4. 1, 2 clearly links the following material with what has preceded it, but
equally clearly introduces the return-journey. The three parts are: Jesus'
conversation with a Samaritan woman; what follows from it; and what
happens on his return. 4. 54, 'This was the second sign . . .' echoing 2.
11, is clearly an appropriate sectional ending.

Section 2' comprises three rejections of Jesus by the Jews, in its first
half, and as a consequence of these rejections, Jesus' crucifixion, death
and burial, in the second half. The balance of these two sets of three parts
is, therefore, thematically-justified. The linkage of the themes, between
the two series, is further strengthened by the repeated reference, by
question and challenge, to Jesus 'kingship'.

Sections 2 and 2' would seem to correspond for reasons of both
themes and details. In Section 2, Jesus condemns the old sacrificial way
and points to a new one, 'Destroy this temple . . .' (2. 19ff). In the
teachings, in the remainder of the section, Jesus' role in the salvation of
the world and the transition from sacrificial to spiritual worship are clearly
presented. We note the movement also is from a nationalistic to a
universal religion. The context lends support to these teachings: from
Jerusalem, Jesus journeys into Judea and then into Samaria on his way
back to Galilee, where he heals a Gentile's (centurion's) son. The scheme

seems to echo that of Acts 1. 8. Section 2' presents Jesus' death which is already interpreted (see 10. 9; v11b, 11. 49-52, 18. 14): we say, 'it is a once and for all sacrifice'. Consider also John 3. 16. One detail comparison between the two sections is the mention of Nicodemus (3. 1, v4, v9 and 19. 39): he who went to Jesus with his questions now brings myrrh and aloes, in great quantities. Further, both sections have their location in Jerusalem at the time of the Passover.

Sections 3 and 3' were found to break down again in the very same way:

Section 3:		Section 3'	
I 1	5. 1-9a	I 1	17. 1-5
2	5. 9b-13	2	17. 6-19
3	5. 14-18	3	17. 20-26
I' 1	5. 19-30	I' 1	18. 1-11
2	5. 31-40	2	18. 12-18
3	5. 41-47	3	18. 19-27

Section 3 of the Gospel, in the first part of its first series, opens with a reference to a 'feast' and a report of a healing-miracle. Part two takes up the story, it was a sabbath . . .. Part three tells of the worsening charge against Jesus. It introduces the teaching themes of the second series: Jesus 'can do nothing of his own accord . . .'. The three parts of this series speak in turn about matters of 'judgement and life'; about matters of 'testimony' (of John, of the Father's works and of the scriptures); and about the issue of 'glory' (praise) and its coming from man or from God.

The first series to Section 3' is taken up entirely with Jesus' 'high-priestly prayer': it divides into three parts which appear to sub-divide further: 17. 1, 2: v3-5; v6-11a: v11b-19; v20-23: v24-26. The basic divisions would seem not to be set by any usage of the term 'Father', or by anything other than the themes of the prayer (firstly, Jesus himself; secondly, the apostles: and thirdly, all believers). The second series is suggested by the following alternation of the leading characters:

18. 1-9	Jesus	a
18. 10, 11	Peter	b
18. 12-14	Jesus	c
18. 15-18	Peter	d
18. 19-24	Jesus	e
18. 25-27	Peter	f

Not a few commentators and scholars would like to rewrite this chapter: but once this identification of rhythm is made, and once it is seen in relation to the previous chapter, an acceptance of it is secured. Written that we might compare (and contrast?) the true high priest (of chapter 17) with the then high priest (of chapter 18), both series maintian closely interwoven presentations of Jesus and his disciple(s) which beg further considerations of comparison. Hence, a and b, c and d, and e and f are linked.

We observe that Sections 3 and 3' frame the central five sections which contain the longer 'I am' sayings. They would appear, therefore, to introduce and conclude a series of teachings in the Gospel, which, in a characteristically different way, focus upon the divine-relationship of the Son and the Father. Both sections explore this relationship thoroughly. We notice also a similar feature to one we found in Luke's Gospel: Section 3 tells of the Jews' first attack upon Jesus, 'they sought . . . to kill him' (5. 18); Section 3' tells how they capture him (18. 1-9). It may be also that the shorter, 'I am' sayings, 6. 20 and 18. 5, v6 and v8, are significant in establishing sectional relationship.

Sections 4 and 4', likewise, appeared to follow what was looking like the standard sectional structure:

		Section 4:				Section 4'
I	1	6. 1-15		I	1	15. 1-8
	2	6. 16-21			2	15. 9-17
	3	6. 22-34			3	15. 18-16. 4a
I'	1	6. 35-46		I'	1	16. 4b-15
	2	6. 47-59			2	16. 16-24
	3	6. 60-71			3	16. 25-33.

All the parts of Section 4 would seem to sub-divide. 6. 1-15, the feeding of the five thousand, is introduced by 6. 1-4, it was the Feast of Passover: 6. 5-15 describes both the feast and Jesus' reasons for separating from the people. 6. 16-18 begins the evening sea-crossing: 6. 19-21 completes it. 6. 22-24 describes the next day's seeking after Jesus: 6. 25-34 tells of the discussions Jesus has with the people when they find him. These are the three parts that complete the first series. They adequately set the theme for the second series of three parts: Jesus is 'the bread of life', 'from heaven'. The teaching of Jesus provokes responses each time. The pairs of pieces are 6. 35-40: v41-46; 6. 47-51; v52-59 and 6. 60-65: v66-71.

The parts which Section 4' comprises likewise sub-divide. Consider 15. 1-4 ('I am the vine true [literally] . . . fruit') and v5-8 ('I am the vine . . . much fruit'); 15. 9-11 (commandments) and v12-17 (commandment); and 15. 18-27 (the hating of Jesus, so also his disciples) and 16. 1-4a (the sufferings of disciples). These are the three parts of the first series. The second series begins with the words, 'Now I did not say these things to you from the beginning, because I was with you. But now I am going . . .'. The emphasis of the teaching, for the second series, here changes. So begins the first part with the piece, 16. 4b-11. The balancing piece begins, 'I have yet many things to say to you . . .': it is 16. 12-15. The second part begins with the piece, 16. 16-19, 'A little while and you will see me no more . . .'. The balancing piece is 16. 20-24, 'Truly, I say to you, you will weep . . .'. The third part is 16. 25-33 and it sub-divides: 16. 25-28 ('figures'): v29-33 ('figures').

The systematic presentation of parts is maintained, in both sections. For arguments of sectional correspondence of 'bread' and 'the vine', see above.

Sections 5 and 5', the last sections to be examined, appeared from the very beginning, to follow a structural-design which was different from that used in Sections 1, 2, 3 and 4. It transpired that the scheme was the same as that used in Section C. At 153 verses and 122 verses respectively, these parallel sections appeared to be the largest of the Gospel: it did seem that the writer had more material to present than his standard structural method could cope with and as a consequence opted for the larger design.

Section 5:			Section 5'		
I	1	7. 1-13	I	1	11. 55-57
	2	7. 14-32		2	12. 1-11
	3	7. 33-36		3	12. 12-19
I'	1	7. 37-44	I'	1	12. 20-29
	2	7. 45-52		2	12. 30-36
	3	7. 53-8. 11		3	12. 37-50
I	1	8. 12-30	I	1	13. 1
	2	8. 31-47		2	13. 2-17
	3	8. 48-59		3	13. 18-30
I'	1	9. 1-12	I'	1	13. 31-38
	2	9. 13-34		2	14. 1-14
	3	9. 35-41		3	14. 15-31.

On the grounds that the most ancient manuscripts fail to present the passage 7. 53-8. 11, it was excluded at first from the analysis. It became apparent, however, that the structural scheme was incomplete without it. The significance of this needs to be weighed.

In outline, the first half of Section 5 presents Jesus' arrival in Jerusalem and the questions that focus upon him and his teaching at the Feast of Tabernacles. The two series in turn are concerned with what happens early in the Feast (7. 1-36) and on the last day of the Feast (7. 37-8. 11). In the second and balancing half, it is the teaching content of the first three parts (8. 12-59) which is confirmed in the second three parts (9. 1-41) by the sign of the healing of the blind man and the responses of the man himself and of the Pharisees. It is in the first parts of these two series that we are given the phrase, 'I am the light of the world' (8. 12 and 9.5).

In outline, Section 5' in 11. 55-12. 50, tells of Jesus' arrival in Jerusalem at the Passover, the questions that are asked (compare 7. 11 and 11. 56, looking for him: they ask will he come? also 7. 26, v41 and 12. 34 'the Christ'?) and Jesus' teachings on his death (12. 24, v27, v31-

33) and on 'light' (12. 35, v36; see especially 12. 46 'I, a light into the world . . .') and 'blindness' (12. 40, compare 9. 1ff). The balancing material, 13. 1-14. 31, begins with the supper scene and talk of betrayal. It is followed by Jesus' teaching about his 'going' and his instructing his disciples (note 14. 6, 'I am the way, the truth and the life').

Clearly, Sections 5 and 5' correspond at many points. Their common themes and details are numerous. One further example is given here: *nipto,* the Greek word for 'wash' finds usage in the Gospel only in these sections (see 9.7, v11, v15 and 13. 5, v6, v8, v10, v12, v14).

The parts themselves, in all the sections, are determined by changes in locations, by passages of time, by pieces of introduction or conclusion, by changes in subject matter and by identification of sequence and consequence. The identification of sub-parts and their balance, one with the other, perhaps more than anything else, does confirm the complete-ness of a part. Series, therefore, are defined as parts are discerned and defined: they are confirmed also by what they contain in their subject-matter by way of discernable emphases and by what might be termed a general drift in a presentation. Surprisingly, maybe, the analysis of all the sections provides evidence which does seem to demonstrate the activities of a writer whose handling of the pieces of his material was at once both consistent and systematic.

It did seem, therefore, that the structure and contents of the Gospel could be summarised as in the chart on the following page. For a time this scheme satisfied all further enquiry. What was most compelling, of course, was that there was now, for the first time since Griesbach, an arguably-definite new 'bridge' between the Synoptics and John (in the the employment of an eleven-part chiasm). Attractive too was the now likely reason for a re-structuring of an earlier Johannine Gospel, that it was made to conform to the same, presumably acceptable basic pattern of other Gospels (of Matthew and of Luke) as it was enlarged to include further written remembrances and teachings of John after his death (see 21. 24 and v20-23). But, eventually, the question was to be asked: Why should the three middle sections be designed to a duplication of the structures of all the other sections? It is noted above how the writer's handling of the pieces of his material was at all times consistent and systematic. The observation also was made that the sections each side of the central sections were even-numbered (that is, four). The possibility arose, therefore, that the Gospel was not an eleven-section chiasm (of varying sectional structures) but a seven-section chiasm of twelve parts per section throughout. By this stage in the process, it had been discovered that the Book of the Revelation to John constituted (within a framework of balancing Prologue and Epilogue) a systematically consist-ent seven-section chiasm in which all the sections presented themes in 'sevens'. Tradition has it that the Gospel and the Book of the Revelation come from the same writer . . .

'The Gospel of John': A summary of the above:

1	1. 1-2. 12 (63vs)	Prologue; John the Baptist's Testimony; Jesus' appearance; Peter's Call; sign 1: 'water into wine'; feast 1: 'marriage'; structure: 1, 2, 3: 1, 2, 3
2	2. 13-4. 54 (103vs)	Sacrifice and worship: Jesus' universal significance; sign 2: 'healing of official's son'; feast 2: 'Passover'; structure: 1, 2, 3: 1, 2, 3
3	5. 1-47 (47vs)	Part 1: 'Father and Son'; sign 3: 'healing of a paralysed man'; feast 3: 'a feast of the Jews'; structure: 1, 2, 3: 1, 2, 3
4	6. 1-71 (71vs)	Part 2: 'I am the bread of life'; sign 4: 'feeding of the five thousand'; feast 4: 'Passover'; structure: 1, 2, 3: 1, 2, 3
5	7. 1-9. 41 (153vs)	Part 3: 'I am the light of the world'; sign 5: 'healing of a blind man; feast 5: 'Tabernacles'; structure: (1, 2, 3: 1, 2, 3) : (1, 2, 3: 1, 2, 3)
C	10. 1-11. 54 (96v)	Part 4: 'I am the gate . . . the good shepherd', 'I am the resurrection and the life'; sign 6: 'the raising of Lazarus'; feast 6: 'Dedication'; structure: (1, 2, 3: 1, 2, 3) : (1, 2, 3: 1, 2, 3)
5'	11. 55-14. 31 (122vs)	Part 5: 'I am the way, the truth and the life'; feast: 'Passover', part 1: Entry into Jerusalem, Supper and Betrayal; structure: (1, 2, 3: 1, 2, 3) : (1, 2, 3: 1, 2, 3)
4'	15. 1-16. 33 (60vs)	Part 6: 'I am the true vine'; feast: 'Passover', part 2: parting discourses; structure: 1, 2, 3: 1, 2, 3
3'	17. 1-18. 27 (53vs)	Part 7: 'Father and Son'; feast: 'Passover', part 3: Jesus High-Priestly Prayer and Arrest; structure: 1, 2, 3: 1, 2, 3
2'	18. 28-19. 42 (55vs)	Jesus' Trials, Death and Burial; feast: 'Passover', part 4: Day of Preparation; structure: 1, 2, 3: 1, 2, 3
1'	20. 1-21. 25 (56vs)	Jesus' Resurrection and Appearances; Commissioning of Peter; Testimony of John the Apostle; the First Day of the Week (and following). structure: 1, 2, 3: 1, 2, 3

The following question was raised: was there good cause to add Sections 1 and 2 together, to add Sections 3 and 4 together, likewise also their parallels, 1' and 2', 3' and 4'? It was observed that the sectional sizes would show a greater consistency than before, they would be: I, 166 verses; II, 118 verses; III, 153 verses; C, 96 verses: III', 122 verses; II', 113 verses; and I', 111 verses. All the sectional parallels of themes and details as observed previously would apply as before: I with I', II with II' and so on. Because of the enlargement of the sections, new parallels would arise too, automatically.

The proposed Sections 1 and 2 are considered first. One modification might be made: 2. 12 might well be said to introduce the second half's content and, therefore, to perform as a linkage.

I	1	1. 1-18	I	1	2. 12-22
	2	1. 19-28		2	2. 23-3. 21
	3	1. 29-34		3	3. 22-36
I′	1	1. 35-42	I′	1	4. 1-26
	2	1. 43-51		2	4. 27-42
	3	2. 1-11		3	4. 43-54.

The two series of passages conclude in similar ways: compare 2. 11, 'This (the) beginning of the signs Jesus did . . . (literally) and 4. 54, 'This again a second sign Jesus did . . .'. We consider the 'rogue' passage, 3. 22-30, a displacement according to many scholars, which ought to follow 2. 12. Simply, because it continues and even concludes the teaching of the wedding feast, 2. 1-11, it links well the two series which were being viewed as separate sections. If they do belong together then the reference to Jesus' resurrection from the dead, in 2. 19-22, well parallels much content of the opposing new section, 18. 28-21. 25. Other sections, it is noted, also include the same.

Sections 1′ and 2′ are now considered. If these together comprise the concluding section of the Gospel then immediately parallels to the opening section are discerned in 18. 28, the first verse: consider 'ceremonial uncleanness' (compare 2. 6 and 3. 25, though the Greek is different) and the reference to Passover (see 2. 13 and v23) in juxtaposition.

I	1	18. 28-40	I	1	20. 1-18
	2	19. 1-12		2	20. 19-29
	3	19. 13-16a		3	20. 30, 31
I′	1	19. 16b-22	I′	1	21. 1-14
	2	19. 23-30		2	21. 15-23
	3	19. 31-42		3	21. 24, 25.

The concluding pieces again display parallelism of detail: compare 19. 35 and 21. 24, 'the truth' of 'the testimony' of John, whose reference is grammatically in the third person. The contents of 19. 31-42 and 20. 1-18 regarding the tomb in the garden do suggest an uninterrupted flow in narrative and hence that the two proposed sections are in fact two halves of the same section. We note how Matthew includes both Jesus' 'death' and 'resurrection' in his last section of his Gospel.

The proposed Sections 3 and 4 link in terms of subject matter on the theme of 'life'. Eight words on 'life' and 'living' are found in 5. 1-47: eighteen are found in 6. 1-71. The dominating passages on the theme are in the second series of parts of both halves, 5. 19-47 and 6. 35-71:

I	1	5. 1-9a		I	1	6. 1-15
	2	5. 9b-13			2	6. 16-21
	3	5. 14-18			3	6. 22-34
I'	1	5. 19-30		I'	1	6. 35-46
	2	5. 31-40			2	6. 47-59
	3	5. 41-47			3	6. 60-71.

The Section would conclude, therefore, with the first references in the Gospel to the 'betrayer' (see 6. 64 and v70, 71).

If the proposed Sections 3' and 4' did in fact constitute one section then the act itself of 'betrayal' would lie chiastically opposite the first telling of it. We consider:

I	1	15. 1-8		I	1	17. 1-5
	2	15. 9-17			2	17. 6-19
	3	15. 18-16. 4a			3	17. 20-26
I'	1	16. 4b-15		I'	1	18. 1-11
	2	16. 16-24			2	18. 12-18
	3	16. 25-33			3	18. 19-27.

The teachings of Jesus in the series of the first half touch the contents of the prayers in the first series of the second half (consider 'love', 'joy', 'sent . . .', 'in me'/'in us', 'the world', 'hate' . . .). The lack of a setting for the section continues till 18. 1. The continuity between 16. 33 and 17. 1 would seem assured. The first half of the Section, therefore, speaks of Jesus' pending separation from his disciples by way of Jesus' preparation of his friends: in the second half it is confirmed in the prayer (the first three parts) and takes place immediately following (in the second three parts).

The evidence would seem to support the conclusion that the structure of the Gospel of John is best described as a chiasm of seven sections (incorporating the Prologue and Epilogues), each section of which is constructed of twelve parts, in two series of two times three. The meanings of the numbers 'seven' (fulfilment, perfection and completion) and 'twelve' (symbolising the elective purposes of God) will have been know to the writer. They carry significance in the Gospel's total presentation. The number 'three' may well have been expressive of 'the trinity' even then, for in John's Gospel we find many references to 'Father', 'Son' and 'Spirit'.

The first stage in the presentation of the literary analysis of John's Gospel is now just about complete. Full justice, of course, cannot be done in such a few pages. What, it is hoped, is clear are the main arguments for describing the structure and contents of the Gospel in the following summary form:

'The Gospel of John'

I   SECTION 1: 1. 1-4. 54 (166 verses)

1. 1-2. 11: Integral Prologue; John the Baptist's Testimony; Jesus' appearance; Peter's call; Sign 1: 'water into wine'; Feast 1: 'marriage;

2. 12-4. 54: sacrifice and worship; Jesus' universal significance; Sign 2: 'healing of official's son'; Feast 2: 'Passover'

  II   SECTION 2: 5. 1-6. 71 (118 verses)

5. 1-47: Sign 3: 'healing of a paralysed man'; Feast 3: 'a feast of the Jews'; life;

6. 1-71: 'I AM THE BREAD OF LIFE'; Sign 4: 'feeding of the five thousand'; Feast 4: 'Passover'

    III   SECTION 3: 7. 1-9. 41 (153 verses)

7. 1-8. 11: Feast 5: 'Tabernacles'; 'Will he come . . .?; 'the Christ?'; 'a prophet?'; a 'practitioner of the law?'

8. 12-9. 41: 'I am the light of the world'; Sign 5: 'healing of a blind man'

      C   SECTION 4: 10. 1-11. 54 (96 verses)

10. 1-42: 'I am the door . . ./I am the Good Shepherd'; Feast 6: 'Dedication';

11. 1-54: 'I am the resurrection and the life'; Sign 6: 'the raising of Lazarus'

    III'   SECTION 5: 11. 55-14. 31 (122 verses)

11. 55-12. 50: Feast 7: 'Passover', part I; 'Will he come?'; 'the Christ?'; light and blindness;

13. 1-14. 31: 'I am the way, the truth and the life'; parting discourses, part I

  II'   SECTION 6: 15. 1-18. 27 (113 verses)

15. 1-16. 33: 'I AM THE TRUE VINE'; parting discourses, part II; 'in me . . . love . . . joy . . . the world . . . hates . . . sent. . .'

17. 1-18. 27: Jesus' High Priestly Prayer and arrest 'the world . . . hates . . . sent . . . love . . . joy . . . in us . . .'

I'   SECTION 7: 18. 28-21. 25 (111 verses)

18. 28-19. 42: 'Passover', part III; Jesus' Trials, Rejection, Death and Burial;

20. 1-21. 25: Jesus' resurrection appearances; disciples' (& Peter's) commissioning; John's testimony

NOTE: all the sections are made up of two series of two times three parts, that is twelve parts in all. The Gospel is arranged to a numerical scheme of 'seven times twelve'.

Johannine infra-structure, Part II:

Given the present chiastic arrangement of the Gospel and, given the evident dislocations/displacements of the text and the almost universal agreement that the last chapter is a later addition, the question, addressed many times in the past, can be posed again: in what 'shape' did the book previously exist?

What is immediately apparent from the earlier (unrevised) summary chart of the Gospel's structure is that the first six proposed 'sections' present systematically a series of 'signs' coupled with 'feasts'. What is also apparent is that the last five proposed 'sections' present material which could be given the title, 'the seventh sign at the seventh feast'. Plainly, the possibility is that the Gospel originally existed in a linear scheme of seven sections, a 'Book of Seven Signs'. This is discussed.

'Signs', 'feasts' and the 'I am' sayings are the chief 'signifiers' of structure, identified in Part I. The 'I am' sayings are considered here. Because they and the teaching attached to them are in chiastic arrangement in the Gospel, it is reasonable enough to suggest that they might have been added, or rather added to in number, during the representing of an earlier and shorter version of the Gospel, designed to a linear scheme. Supporting this possibility is the startling abruptness of introduction to two of these sayings passages in an otherwise smoothly-running presentation: see 10. 1 and 15. 1.

At 10. 1, we encounter a sudden change in theme: 'blindness' and 'guilt' (9. 41) are hardly the issues addressed in Jesus' teaching (10. 1-18). At best, the reference to Jesus' healing the blind man (10. 21) may suggest continuity of a kind, but this detail is repeated in the balancing sub-section (in 11. 36, 37), which suggests that the reference was intended to relate more to what is ahead, in the text, than to what is behind.

At 15. 1, we come across a still more obviously abrupt entry. The previous verse, 14. 31, ends, 'Rise, let us go hence'. Untypically, in the current version of the Gospel, there is no description of setting, or time, or circumstance in the following verse, 15. 1. This feature of the text has led, almost universally, to the deduction that the current version suffers displacement here. The suggestion is often made that chapters 15 and 16 (why, therefore, not chapter 17?) really belong before 13. 31-14. 31 (14. 31 attaches well to 18. 1b following). An equally valid alternative deduction is now possible: it is that the content of 15. 1-18. 1a, like that of chapter 21 (and others?) was added, at the time of a chiastic re-structuring of the Gospel, to create sectional correspondences.

The issues concerning 'displacements' and 'dislocations' are best considered here, because it is they that point clearly to the possibility of an earlier 'shape' to the Gospel. A summary of the ones generally mentioned are given below. Frequently, it is claimed that they would improve the flow of the narrative, make harmonisations with the other Gospels more easy and avoid abruptness.

1) 3. 22-30 should follow 2. 12, to improve itinerary and the flow from 3. 21 to
    3. 31 (it would satisfactorily (?) re-connect the teaching of 3. 31-36 with the
    mouth of Jesus);

2) chapter 6 should stand between chapters 4 and 5, to improve itinerary (but
    it does not improve chronology: in the presentation, one Passover would
    follow another);

3) 7. 15-24 should read after 5. 47 to continue the theme of chapter 5 and to
    restore the contact of 7. 14 with 7. 25 following;

4) 10. 19-29 should read after 9. 41 and 10. 30 would then more properly
    follow 10. 18 (I am happy with this so long as a break is introduced
    between 10. 21 and v22);

5) 12. 36b-43 should appear after 12. 50 to improve continuity;

6) chapters 15 and 16 should be inserted before 13. 31-14. 31 (see above for
    a brief discussion); and

7) 18. 13-24 should be re-ordered (see Part I, Section 3′ for a discussion).

Taking these, then, into account, also the above considerations of
the chief 'signifiers' of structure and further, the more cohesive arguments
for 'additional' contents, the following scheme was drawn up, for
examination:

'The Book of the Seven Signs'

Prologue:	The very beginning; the Gospel's synopsis; life, light, grace and truth; believing; 1. 1-5, v9-14, v16-18;
1st Section:	first feast: 'marriage'; first sign: 'water to wine'; 'John and Jesus'; 1. 19-2. 12, 3. 22-30;
2nd Section:	second feast: 'Passover'; second sign: 'healing of official's son'; 2. 13-3. 21, 3. 31-36, 4. 3-54;
3rd Section:	third feast: 'a feast of the Jews': third sign: 'healing of paralysed man'; 5. 1-47, 7. 15-24;
4th Section:	fourth feast: 'Passover'; fourth sign: 'feeding of the five thousand'; 6. 1-71;
5th Section:	fifth feast: 'Tabernacles'; fifth sign: 'healing of a blind man'; 7. 1-14, v25-52, 8. 12-9. 41;
6th Section:	sixth feast: 'Dedication'; sixth sign: 'raising of Lazarus'; 10. 22-29, 10. 1-18, 10. 30-11. 48, v53, 54;
7th Section:	seventh feast: 'Passover'; seventh sign: 'Jesus' death and resurrection'; 11. 55-12. 36a, v44-50, v36b-43, 13. 1-38, 15. 1-17. 26, 14. 1-31, 18. 1b-20. 29;
Epilogue:	Signs; belief and life; 20. 30, 31.

THE PROLOGUE, in such a first, independent setting, would not
have included references to John the Baptist (v6-8, v15): these would
have been required only when this introduction to the Gospel was being

incorporated into the first section, as the first part of three which were designed to contrast John and Jesus. It seems that, in this way, the earlier (original?) Prologue can be restored. This ammendment has been suggested before (4), but now for the first time we have a sound reason for it.

SECTION 1 clearly benefits from the inclusion of 3. 22-30 as its closing part. Speaking of 'baptising (v22, 23), 'purifying' (26) and the 'bride' and the 'bridegroom' (v29), content-wise, it well continues the themes and details in the earlier parts: further, it settles the issue of the priority of Jesus over John (an issue which runs through the first three parts). What appears to be significant, structurally, is the following comparison:

The first half of Section I:			Section 1 (as before):		
I	1	1. 1-18	I	1	1. 19-28
	2	1. 19-28		2	1. 29-34
	3	1. 29-34		3	1. 35-42
I'	1	1. 35-42	I'	1	1. 43-51
	2	1. 43-51		2	2. 1b-11, 12
	3	2. 1-11		3	3. 22-30.

In other words, the sub-structural scheme of the earlier version is carried over into the current one. (The same is possibly true of all the first six sections: the seventh, and last, is clearly a larger, composite scheme.) Each of the series is re-defined, very likely, by some editing of the parts: for example, will 2. 1 have read, 'On the third day . . .'? Chiasm and completion in the re-formation will have required this. Of the earlier version, the first series is about events in Bethany, beyond the Jordan: the second series, for the first two parts, is about events in Galilee; the third part tells of events in Judea.

SECTION 2 is not easily re-constructed: the following is tentatively proposed:

The second half of Section I:			Section 2 (as before):		
I	1	2. 12-22	I	1	2. 13, v23b-25
	2	2. 23-3. 21		2	2. 23a, 3. 1-21
	3	3. 22-36		3	3. 31-36
I'	1	4. 1-26	I'	1	4. 3b-26
	2	4. 27-42		2	4. 27-42
	3	4. 43-54		3	4. 43-54.

It is likely that the episode concerned with Jesus' clearing of the Temple (2. 14-22) is not original. It can be argued that it was added at the time of the re-shaping of the Gospel. It may have been part of John's previously unincluded reminiscences, or it may have come from one (or all) of the synoptic gospels. Interestingly, we can observe in Mark's Gospel how 'the clearing of the Temple' appears deliberately designed to lie opposite (in his seven-day chiastic structure of Jesus' Jerusalem Days) the telling of 'the Death of Jesus'. That the re-structurer of John's Gospel was doing something very similar is a distinct possibility. The first part to the first series, in this reconstruction, is well occupied by the contents and phraseology of 2. 13, v23b-25: consider 'he knew what was in a person' (2. 25) as it applies not only to Nicodemus but also to the Samaritan woman.

Minor changes to the beginning of the second series can be deemed to have been necessary: 4. 1, 2 was needed to establish continuity, in the new scheme, and to establish the balance of the first series with the second. Verse three might simply have read, 'After this, he left Jerusalem . . . .'. Minor changes also will have had to have been made to the introductory verses of each of the first three parts.

SECTION 3 seems restored, with the inclusion of 7. 15-24 (reference the law and the sabbath healing): it especially establishes the balance between the two series.

The first half of Section II:			Section 3 (as before):		
I	1	5. 1-9a	I	1	5. 1-9a
	2	5. 9b-13		2	5. 9b-13
	3	5. 14-18		3	5. 14-18
I'	1	5. 19-30	I'	1	5. 19-30
	2	5. 31-40		2	5. 31-40
	3	5. 41-47		3	5. 31-47, 7. 15-24

Parts 3 of both series, in the earlier section, would have balanced for the wish of the Jews 'to kill' Jesus.

SECTION 4, which includes the first 'I am' saying (notably) would appear to be unchanged, basically. It constitutes the second half of the present Section II.

SECTION 5 reads fluently without 7. 15-24 (see above). It could be argued that part two in the first series (see the presentation in Part I) is the only one which is changed: instead of 7. 14-32, it would have been 7. 14, v25-32. The reason for such a change could have been the improving of the balance of material in the first two series: according to J. Schneider (5) the material seems to fall into two cycles:

Jesus teaches	7. 15-24	7. 37-39
His teaching evokes speculation among the people	7. 25-31	7.40-44
The mission of the Jewish officials and its consequences	7. 32-36	7.45-52.

Hence, some teaching of Jesus could be deemed to have been in need of insertion.

It is argued by some that 10. 19-21 properly concludes the section: rather 9. 40, 41 seems not to require it. Further, 10. 21 has its sectional parallel in 11. 37. What is plainly striking about this section, in its present form, is that it is double the structure we might expect of an earlier, unrevised section. The balance of much argument leads to the following proposed reconstruction of Section 5:

I	1	7. 1-13		I	1	9. 1-12
	2	7. 14, v25-32			2	9. 13-34
	3	7. 37-44, 8. 12-20			3	9. 35-41

The clear inference is that it was expanded deliberately to maintain the usage of the new sectional structure of twelve parts and to establish chiastic correspondences with its new sectional counterpart.

SECTION 6 could have undergone much modification also:

Section C (as existing)				Section 6 (as before):	
I	1	10. 1-6	I	1	10. 22-30
	2	10. 7-18		2	10. 31-39
	3	10. 19-21		3	10. 40-42
	1	10. 22-30			
	2	10. 31-39			
	3	10. 40-42			
I'	1	11. 1-5	I'		11. 1-54
	2	11. 6-16			much reduced, but
	3	11. 17-37			in three parts?
	1	11. 38-44		1	(11. 1-16)
	2	11. 45-53		2	(11. 17-37)
	3	11. 54		3	(11. 38-54)

We might rightly deduce, by comparison with the previous sections, that, as Section 6, it would have included the reference to the 'feast' (of Dedication) and the content on the 'sign' (the raising of Lazarus). But, we ask, as Section 6, would it have contained three 'I am' sayings? And further, as Section 6, would it have enjoyed so many balances of detail? That which is presented in the right-hand column satisfies at least some of the criteria of re-construction.

SECTION 7 may have included all the pieces referenced above, in the table: though is not too likely. Clearly, structurally, the content of this section's 'feast' and 'sign' will have required a more complex structure than that of the preceding sections. It may be that it employed series of three parts. In which case, the concluding series might have been:

1	20. 1-18	Jesus' first resurrection appearance (to Mary);
2	20. 19-23	Jesus' second appearance (to his disciples);
3	20. 24-29	Jesus' third appearance (to his disciples, to Thomas).

The epilogue, 20. 30, 31, would have appeared independently after this.

The following suggestion of a reconstruction results from a balance of all the main arguments as they concern dislocations in the text and as they concern material (synoptic or Johannine) which has the appearance of later addition. Judgements on what has been added for the sake of new intra- and inter-sectional parallelism are particularly important. It is gauged that the passages 13. 1-14. 31c and 18. 1b-27, also 18. 28-19. 16a and 19. 16b-42, exhibit parallelisms of the original work. The passages, 11. 55-12. 43 and 20. 1-29, which introduce and conclude the section, consist of the familiar three-parts.

	1	11. 55-57		3	20. 24-29
	2	12. 1-8		2	20. 19-23
	3	12. 12, 17-19, 37-43		1	20. 1-18
		....			....
I	1	13. 1		3	19. 31-33, 38, 40-42
	2	13. 2, 21b-30		2	19. 23-30
	3	13. 31-33, 36-38; 14. 31c	I'	1	19. 16b-22.
I'	1	18. 1b-11		3	19. 13-16a
	2	18. 12-18		2	19. 1-12
	3	18. 19-27	I	1	18. 28-40.

THE EPILOGUE, 20. 30, 31, fulfils every requirement of an independent, concluding piece for a 'Book of Signs'. What is likely, at the stage of re-structuring, is that 20. 19-23 and 20. 24-29 became attached (the balancing parts are 20. 19-25 and 20. 26-29): we note that 20. 1-18 sub-divides into 20. 1-10 and v11-18. The epilogue (20. 30, 31) will have assumed the place of the third part as a consequence. The material of 21. 1-25 would have been incorporated, in the shaping of the balancing second series of three parts which the final section enjoys now.

To sum up, therefore, the proposition of Part II is that John's Gospel previously existed in the form of a smaller 'Book of Seven Signs', made up of a Prologue, Seven (linearly-arranged) Sections and an Epilogue. It follows that the intention behind such a work was to reveal the truths attaching to Jesus, by presenting a selection of his deeds ('signs'), coupled with his teachings ('the discourses'), within a meaningful framework of Jewish 'Feasts'. The structural-use of 'seven' is itself harmonious with the conclusion that the writer sought to present Jesus as the one in whom Jewish hopes and expectations were fulfilled. Religious history, its practice and observances, finds its true meaning and focus in Jesus, his person, his life, his teachings and his purpose. The book's principal aim was to promote belief in him who is the Christ, the Son of God: it is this belief which leads to life.

What attaches to this is the further proposition that the book we now enjoy is the result of a re-structuring of this earlier one. In the past, 'Signs Sources' and 'Discourse Sources' (6) and the Synoptic Gospels (particu-larly Mark's) (7) have been discussed with little reference to the likely compositional stages this Gospel will have passed through. The possibility is that the earlier version of the Gospel, for its content, drew from the same, early sources of Christian tradition as did the Synoptic Gospels: it may be that the later version, for its additional contents, drew in part from Luke's Gospel but in the main from John's own teachings, or that it drew from Mark's Gospel (for contents, and for numerical ordering, given the examples of seven-part chiasm) and/or Matthew's (for the 'twelves' or for chiasm) to supply Luke, eventually, with some of the contents for his Gospel. The question of 'priority' is clearly before us. The similarities of structure of the earlier and the later version of John's Gospel and the Revelation to John are not overlooked either: they are highly suggestive of a common influence, if not of a common authorship.

Our task today:

Clearly, these propositions and the possibilities which they suggest demand a very careful and detailed assessment. It may be that the variables, appropriate for determining the compositional stages through which the book has passed, are too numerous to allow any definite conclusion to be reached. Nevertheless, it would seem that these issues, raised as a result of this analysis, might yet promise much.

One outcome, of the research presented here, is that the 'shape' of the Gospel as we now have it would seem to be assured. It may indeed be considered to be 'simple in outline', though not as simple as others have suggested previously. It may indeed be considered to be less 'complicated in detail' that it was. As a result, the discovery of the present sectional arrangement would seem to suggest that we can now better understand many things about the Gospel. Of particular interest to many is the Johannine view of the Eucharist. It is fascinating that we find, in contrast to the synoptic tradition, no institution of the Eucharist at the final supper, and yet what we do now find are two chiastically-parallel allusions to it. The issue is raised afresh, for with these teachings the five central sections, which include the larger 'I am' sayings, begin and end. Some primacy, in disclosure-terms, is being expressed here, it seems.

It would seem that another, fresh opportunity is given us for enjoying Gospel-literature in the way it was enjoyed a very long time ago.

6 The Revelation to John

Different in kind from the first five of the six 'books' of the New Testament under structural-analysis, the Revelation to John, though unique in the New Testament, is but one of many apocalyptic works produced in the first centuries, B.C. and A.D. Considered to be the supreme Christian example, it is described by Turner (1) as 'a symphony in three movements:

1 1-3   Christ's message to the churches;
2 4-20   The Visions of judgement on the enemies of God and victory for the faithful;
3 21, 22   God's Kingdom on earth.'

He continues, 'It weakens the effect if we analyse any farther. Every commentary has its detailed analysis; and they are all different because the book was not constructed so meticulously.'

All commentaries may indeed differ but, of course, this is no sound reason in itself for concluding that the book does lack detailed organisation. Could it be that the sixth of the six New Testament 'books' differed in kind from the first five, not only in 'content and purpose' but also in 'structure' (for its lack of it)? Was not it more likely that its composition benefited from a deliberate design intention? The obvious sectional usages of 'sevens' (of 'churches', of 'seals', of 'trumpets' and of 'plagues'/'bowls') readily suggests the possibility of there being a book infra-structure here which consists of seven sections which themselves thematically incorporate 'sevens'.

The task of analysis so began. And the conclusion to which I have come is that the book comprises the following chiasm:

```
          1. 1-8        The Prologue;
I    Section 1   1. 9-3. 22     'Seven Churches' (messages to);   (63vs)
  II    Section 2   4. 1-8. 1      'Seven Seals';   (60vs)
    III   Section 3   8. 2-11. 18   'Seven Trumpets';   (62vs)
      C   Section 4   11. 19-15. 4   'Seven Visions';   (60vs)
    III'  Section 5   15. 5-16. 21   'Seven Plagues/Bowls';   (25vs)
  II'   Section 6   17. 1-19. 10   'Seven Words of Condemnation on Babylon';
                                    (52vs)
I'   Section 7   19. 11-22. 5   'Seven final visions';   (58vs)
          22. 6-21       The Epilogue.
```

109

It is the work of a dramatic literary artist! The geometric scheme of 'seven times seven' is emphatically indicative surely of a future 'completion' of the things presented: that is, they will come to pass as it is written. As has been noted above, in earlier chapters, the number 'seven' symbolised 'perfection', 'completion' and 'fulfilment'. It may be that the basic idea behind this stylised framework is the 'Harvest' celebration of the Feast of Weeks: 'Count off seven weeks from the time you begin to put the sickle to the standing corn . . .' (Deut. 16. 9). It may be that it is related to the counting of 'seven weeks of years, seven times seven years . . .' (Lev. 25. 8-12): what follows is the 'fiftieth year', the 'year of Jubilee', a year of liberty, a holy year. The first of these two possibilities is the more likely: the subject of 'harvest', more than 'Jubilee', is prevalent in the series of 'revelations'.

A brief survey of the book's parts follows below. At this stage, however, it might be asked how this scheme compares with others. One of the nearest to this which I have found is that of J. W. Bowman (2). He gives annotation in twelve parts, but significantly describes the main body of the work as consisting of a linear scheme of 'seven acts', each one of which includes 'seven parts'. We agree, however, only on three acts, Sections 1, 2 and 5. Like Farrer (3), independently, he says, he discovered the use to which certain Greek words were being put, meaning 'I saw', 'was seen', 'I will show you' and 'he showed me'. Farrer settles for a less formal scheme. They both exaggerate the consistency of such usages and overlook other signifiers of structure.

N. W. Lund (4) sees the possibility of a chiasm. But, like R. H. Charles (5), he resorts to considerable rearrangement of the materials found in the Book. His chiasm is of twelve parts, 1 to 6 and 6' to 1'. The main elements, 2 to 2', are grossly unequal in size. In linear terms only, the nearest scheme to that which I describe is found in the commentary of Michael Wilcock (6). He identifies eight sections. We agree significantly on nearly every point in the first five of the eight. In section six, we differ only a little. The main difference lies in our interpretations of the structure towards the end of the book. Section 7, in his scheme is 19. 11-21. 8 (seven visions: the Drama behind History); his Section 8 is 21. 9-22. 19 (seven final revelations: Jerusalem the Bride). Wilcock fails to discern the significance of the repeated 'And I saw' of the seventh section: to some extent because of this, he fails to discern the completeness of the final vision (the seventh).

THE PROLOGUE   1. 1-8, is presented in two parts: 1. 1-3 is the title and introduction; 1. 4-8 is the address and greeting.

I: SECTION 1   1. 9-3. 22, 'the Messages to the Seven Churches', is arranged as follows:

	1. 9-20	Introduction;
1	2. 1-7	the message to the church in Ephesus;
2	2. 8-11	in Smyrna;
3	2. 12-17	in Pergamum;
4	2. 18-29	in Thyatira;
5	3. 1-6	in Sardis;
6	3. 7-13	in Philadelphia;
7	3. 14-22	in Laodicea;

The introduction describes John's Spiritual vision of Christ, in the midst of seven golden lampstands and holding seven stars in his right hand. The letters themselves possibly enjoy the 'seven-beat rhythm' which Wilcock (7) has observed.

II: SECTION 2   4. 1-8. 1, 'the Seven Seals', is arranged as follows:

	4. 1-5. 14	Introduction
1	6. 1, 2	the opening of the first seal;
2	6. 3, 4	the second seal;
3	6. 5, 6	the third seal;
4	6. 7, 8	the fourth seal;
5	6. 9-11	the fifth seal;
6	6. 12-7. 17	the sixth seal;
7	8.1	the seventh seal.

The introduction is in two parts: the first, 4. 1-11 describes the throne of God; the second, 5. 1-14 describes a scroll with seven seals which 'the Lamb' alone is worthy to open. The seals are opened. In the case of seal six, 6. 12-17 leads to the question which is answered in 7. 1-17. Who will stand before the day of wrath? The elect will.

III: SECTION 3   8. 2-11. 18, 'the Seven Trumpets', is arranged as follows:

	8. 2-6	Introduction;
1	8. 7	the first trumpet is blown;
2	8. 8, 9	the second;
3	8. 10, 11	the third;
4	8. 12, 13	the fourth;
5	9. 1-12	the fifth; the first woe;
6	9. 13-21	the sixth; the second woe;
7	10. 1-11. 18	the seventh; the third woe.

The introduction describes seven angels receiving a trumpet each, and another angel . . .. The section describes their activities. It may be that 8. 13 attaches to 9. 1: it seems it can fix either to the fourth or to the fifth scenes.

C: SECTION 4   11. 19-15. 4, 'Seven Visions', is arranged as follows:

	11. 19-12. 18	Introduction;
1	13. 1-10	the first vision;
2	13. 11-18	the second;
3	14. 1-5	the third;
4	14. 6-13	the fourth;
5	14. 14-20	the fifth;
6	15. 1	the sixth;
7	15. 2-4	the seventh.

It will be noticed that the Greek opens each of the seven visions with the words, *kai eidon*, 'And I saw'. We encounter the same emphasis of presentation in Section 7. The introduction describes the incidents, particularly in heaven, which precede these happenings.

III': SECTION 5   15. 5-16. 21, 'the Seven Plagues/Bowls', is arranged as follows:

	15. 516. 1	Introduction;
1	16. 2	the first bowl's contents is poured on the earth;
2	16. 3	the second;
3	16. 4-7	the third;
4	16. 8, 9	the fourth;
5	16. 10, 11	the fifth;
6	16. 12-16	the sixth;
7	16. 17-21	the seventh.

The introduction tells that the seven angels are commanded to pour out the seven bowls of God's wrath upon the earth. Long observed by commentators on the Book have been the similarities between the sections concerning 'The Seven Trumpets' and 'The Seven Plagues (Bowls)'. Consider the following parallels: of 'land' (16. 2 with 8.7), 'sea' (16. 3 with 8. 8, 9), 'rivers and springs' (16. 4-7 with 8. 10, 11), 'sun' (16. 8, 9 with 8. 12, 13), 'agony' (16. 10, 11 with 9. 1-12), 'Euphrates' (16. 12-16 with 9. 13-21) and 'a loud voice', 'earthquake' and 'city' (16. 17-21 with 10. 1-11. 18). Sections 3 and 5 do appear to require the designation III and III': that is they are chiastically parallel around the centre section, Section 4, therefore Section C.

II': SECTION 6   17. 1-19. 10, 'Seven Words of Condemnation on Babylon', is arranged as follows:

	17. 1-6	Introduction;
1	17. 7-14	the first word;
2	17. 15-18	the second;
3	18. 1-3	the third;
4	18. 4-20	the fourth;
5	18. 21-24	the fifth;
6	19. 1-5	the sixth;
7	19. 6-10	the seventh.

The Section begins with what is shown to the visionary, concerning the judgement of the great harlot. The 'words' of condemnation follow in turn. Coupled with the last are two statements ('blessed are those invited to the marriage-supper of the Lamb'; these 'words' are 'true'): the response of the seer is also given.

What evidence is there for seeing Sections 2 and 6 as chiastically parallel? It is comparatively little when compared with Sections 3 and 5. It is parts 4, 5 and 6 which comprise material common to the two sections. In parts 4 (6. 7, 8 and 18. 4-20) consider 'plague', 'death' and 'famine'. In parts 5 (6. 9-11 and 18. 21-24) consider the parallel of 'slain souls' with 'the blood of the prophets and saints, all killed on earth'. In parts 6 (6. 12-7. 17 and 19. 1-5) consider, in both, the 'great multitudes in heaven' celebrating 'salvation' with songs.

I': SECTION 7   19. 11-22. 5, 'Seven Final Visions', is arranged as follows:

	19. 11-16	Introduction;
1	19. 17, 18	the first vision;
2	19. 19-21	the second;
3	20. 1-3	the third;
4	20. 4-10	the fourth;
5	20. 11	the fifth;
6	20. 12-15	the sixth;
7	21. 1-22. 5	the seventh (a new heaven, earth and city).

The introduction is that of a vision; it begins, 'And I saw heaven opened . . .'. It prefaces the following seven visions, which each begin, as in Section 4, with the words, *kai eidon*, 'And I saw'. Vision 7 is one complete vision.

Lund (8) saw the possible chiastic parallelism of the 'Seven Epistles' (2. 1-3. 22) and the 'Seven Angels' (17. 1-22. 5). I disagree with his limits but agree with his deduction of parallelism. Both sections speak of 'the new Jerusalem' (3. 12 and 21. 2) and its 'coming down out of heaven' and also of being saved from 'the second death' (2. 11, 20. 14 and 21. 8). References to 'Satan' are found in Sections I, C and I' and have the appearance of chiastic usage (cf. 2. 9, v13, v13, v24, 3.9; 12. 9; and 20. 2, v7). Many more details could be considered.

THE EPILOGUE   22. 6-21, sub-divides: the contents of 22. 6-15 are balanced by 22. 16-21. Consider:

v6 the Lord . . . has sent his angel . . . servants	v16 I, Jesus have sent my angel . . . for the churches
v7a . . . I am coming soon . . .	v17 . . . Come . . . Come . . .
v8-15 I, John . . . heard and saw . . . . . . the words of the prophecy of this book . . . . . . tree of life . . . enter the city . . . outside . . Behold, I am coming soon . . .	v18-21 . . . he who testifies . . . the words of the book of this prophecy . . . . . . tree of life . . . in the holy city . . . Surely, I am coming soon . . .

It is noticed that the Prologue and the Epilogue contain similar details: consider 'Amen', I am the Alpha and the Omega, 'Behold . . . coming', the sending of the angel to John, testimony, hearing and keeping, the words of the prophecy, churches . . . Together, therefore, these opening and closing pieces frame the seven sections.

Similarities, too, between some of the introductory verses to the sections themselves are observed:

I:	Section 1:	1. 9	'I, John . . .';
II:	Section 2:	4. 1	'. . . a door was opened in heaven . . .'
III:	Section 3:	8. 2, 3	'. . . the seven angels standing before God . . . the altar . . .';
C:	Section 4:	11. 19	'And the temple of God in heaven was opened . . .';
III':	Section 5:	15. 5	'. . . and the temple of the tabernacle of the testimony in heaven was opened . . .';
II':	Section 6:	17. 1	'. . . one of the seven angels . . .';
I':	Section 7:	19. 11	'And I saw heaven opened . . .'

What is seen clearly from the first table above is that Sections 1, 2, 3, 4, 6 and 7 are more or less equal in size. It looks as though Section 5 has lost some verses, but see 22. 19!

That the Revelation to John could be described as comprising a Prologue, Seven Sections and an Epilogue, set in chiasm, suggests a possible book comparability with the version of John's Gospel as we now have it. Is there any real significance in this? Examined alongside each other they would seem to bear no comparison at all, in respect of their themes and significant details. The relationship is unlike that of the Gospel of Luke and Acts of the Apostles. Simply, the similarity between these two books is that of basic, common structure.

One further note is required. As in the case of John's Gospel, the Book of the Revelation to John has been considered also to be the product of re-structuring (9). An examination of the proposed alterations leads, nevertheless, to the conclusion that the overall scheme as presented above is basically unaffected: the exchanges of pieces proposed are small in comparison with the dislocations of John's Gospel. Plainly, the book can be considered to be very nearly, at least, in its original form.

It would seem that this book, the sixth 'book' of the New Testament, because of this discovery of its systematic, thematic presentation, can be enjoyed again as the author first intended. At its very least it is a literary art work of the highest quality.

7 Conclusion

Summary charts of the six books' structures appear in PART B.

Outlined in PART A in the Introduction and presented in the ensuing Chapters, these discoveries of book-structures would appear to lay to rest many of the erstwhile, difficult issues of New Testament enquiry. Though it is only one element in the study of literary criticism and one branch only of 'rhetorical criticism', 'structuralism' is plainly a focus of interest which promises a wide influence. The discoveries affect considerations of 'sources' and of 'tradition', the study of textual and translational problems, matters of editorial presentation, the tasks of communicating book contents, our understanding of the theologies of the different writers, the debate concerning history and story in the New Testament, the matter of lectionary-systems, questions of authorship and even the dating of the letters. These claims are startling but, it seems, they are wholly justified. The agenda that these discoveries set is described briefly below.

1. Structuralism and literary criticism:

The interest to date in structuralism, in New Testament study, has been less than general: the lack of sound, meaningful results has been the reason for this. Much structuralist analysis has been carried out already with regard to the 'letters': but how reliably has this work been done? It needs gathering up and evaluating. Similarly, also, the work to date on the Old Testament ought to be re-examined. That use has been made of acrostic as a literary-form (see Psalm 119, for example) is already beyond doubt. That use has been made of chiasm and simple-parallelism in Old Testament books is also beyond doubt. But to what extent are they employed? Do they govern the complete layout of books? Is, for example, the 'mysterious' arrangement of the pieces of the Book of Isaiah to be explained in this way? It may well be the case: the material of this book has clearly undergone a stage or two of re-structuring. Do any of the Old Testament books contain numerical listings of parts, such as are found in the Gospel of Matthew? Are any of them created to a scheme of 'seven' for example?'

What is most clearly the case is that rules of literary-structural criticism are required. Some are suggested in the above presentations. They might be considered to be contributions to this thinking, in draft form.

Structuralism emphasises the roles of 'wholes' and 'parts'. The parts which make up the wholes are examinable only in their fullest contexts. Not to do so may be to interpret inappropriately (and possibly perilously) the intended teachings. One Lucan Section which demonstrates this is the Gospel's Section 4: without the framing passages of Jesus' calling sinners and his work of forgiving, cleansing and healing, the Sermon on the Plain *could* convince a listener/reader that she/he can earn the status of 'disciple', for her/himself.

Other structuralists have written about 'deep structures' as 'codes' of communication. Might this now seem to be entirely proper? The discussion is introduced above regarding the purposes of the Evangelists in presenting their works, to numerical schemes (3, 4, 7, 10, 12, 14, some compounds of the same and also 1-5, C, 5'-1'), to schemes of 'days' or 'Jewish feasts', or in the paralleling of one book with another. We noted Luke's various applications of the scheme, 1-5, C, 5'-1', to the two books, to the central sub-section of the Gospel and to his genealogy of Jesus. Because the genealogy can be interpreted to mean that, with Jesus, begins the era of the 'twelfth seven' ('the perfect period of election'?), are we to deduce that the books themselves, of Matthew and of Luke, so introduce this 'perfect period of election'? It would seem a reasonable deduction.

The literature we are handling is clearly 'disclosure-literature': it is not only the pieces themselves, but also the sub-structures and the whole-structures (the 'infra-structures;') which communicate the truths as they focus on the good news of Jesus. The literary forms of chiasm, simple-parallelism and numerical-listings and also compounds of the same . . . all these have been employed most skilfully and with great effect. It would seem that our definition, of what a 'Gospel' is, will need to take all these things into account.

2. Textual criticism:

The advantages to the textual critic, of these discoveries of order, can be considered. Where a variant reading might introduce additional parallels of detail, within or between sub-structures, it may be considered to be original. For example, Lk. 9. 55, 56, 'for the Son of man came not to destroy men's lives but to save them', may well be the original counterpart to Lk. 19. 10, 'For the Son of man came to seek and to save the lost'. They fall opposite each other in the structure of the Central Section of the Gospel. Clearly, the force of the arguments, for and against, will need to be weighed carefully in each case. If a manuscript contains several such variants, against the witness of others, it may be that its value will have to be re-assessed.

3. Translation:

Translators could help present-day readers to discover for themselves the many balances of detail that lie hidden in current editions of these books. Consistent translation of Greek words, phrases and constructions would assist greatly. For example, in the Revelation to John, *kai eidon*, 'And I saw' is variously translated, 'Then I saw', and, 'And I looked'. In the Gospel of Luke, in the RSV, *polis* is translated 'town' in Lk. 10. 8-12 and 'city' in Lk. 19. 17-19. It may be that some difficulties in translation will be capable of resolution by reference to an opposing piece.

4. Editorial arrangement (and lectionary schemes):

The editorial arrangement of these books will need to reflect the major and minor sub-divisions that the writers intended. Revisions to the titling of sections and passages will be necessary also if present day readers of these scriptures are to be given the help they need. At the same time, current lectionary schemes will need to be revised in order that justice be done to the writers' intentions. It would seem that readings which are cut short, begun or ended improperly have misled congregations and preachers alike for much too long. Lectionary systems are discussed more fully below.

5. Communicating the contents of the books:

Those whose responsibility is to communicate the contents of these books, whether in Church, or Sunday School, or School, or College, will find that, in following the sectional-divisions of the books, their work is greatly simplified. The systems of disclosure employed would seem to be chosen with this purpose in mind. The arrangements of the contents assist the memorising of them as well as the grasping of their meanings. It is the structures of the books that, above everything else, give clarity to what they intend to reveal. No greater assistance, it seems, could be given the expositor.

These discoveries are not least important to all commentators.

6. Source considerations:

Previously, the differences between the three synoptic gospels have led more to conclusions about the sources themselves, available to the writers, than to discussions about the purposes, literary or otherwise, of the different writers. We have been asking why we find episodes of Jesus' life and ministry presented in different orders, in different settings, or in different details.

Why is the story of the woman who anoints Jesus found early in Luke's Gospel and late in Matthew's and Mark's? And why is its detail and main drift so clearly different in Luke's Gospel? We have answered these questions simply by suggesting Luke enjoyed a different source from the others. Why has Luke placed the genealogy where he has, and why is it different from Matthew's? That he had another source has answered the second part of the question, at least. Why are the temptations of Jesus, in the wilderness, presented in the Gospels of Matthew and Luke in different orders? What can account for the differences in the Beatitudes, or the Lord's Prayer in the two books? Ordinarily, the answers to these questions are that the writers had different sources to hand. No alternative and satisfactory reason could be entertained: it could not be that these things were deliberately re-written.

We have been faced with another series of questions. Why has Luke, who otherwise follows Mark, omitted major sections, most notably Mk. 6. 45-8. 26? What can account for Luke's use of Mark in three large blocks (Lk. 3. 1-6. 19; 8. 4-9. 50; 18. 15-24. 11) and for Luke's 'small' and 'large' insertions between them? It is the discovery of the literary frameworks to the three books which leads to the solutions of such problems. It is they that furnish us with the necessary evidence. The writers are to be considered as arrangers and authors in their own right: they achieved their ordered presentations by re-working the sources available to them.

The generally-accepted two-document hypothesis, that Matthew and Luke (independently of each other) drew from Mark's Gospel and a second source 'Q', is no longer viable. The basic case for 'Q' was that there was serious objection to the possibility that Luke knew and made use of Matthew's Gospel (or vice versa). Infancy narratives, reports of the Sermons (on the Mount/on the Plain), post-resurrection accounts, such passages as these, added to those already stated above, which differ greatly in the two Gospels, were assumed to demonstrate no traces of mutual knowledge. But now, Luke's use of Matthew's Gospel is 'intelligible' (Farrer [1]): we can be rid of 'Q'.

The priority of Mark's Gospel is assured. The second priority of Matthew's Gospel is most likely. Comparisons of the genealogies, the 'sermons' and much of the detailed content of the Gospels of Matthew and Luke would appear to warrant this conclusion. It makes much more sense to argue Luke's re-working of Matthew's Gospel than the other way about. The innovation for Gospel usage of the 1-5, C, 5'-1' scheme would, therefore, seem to be Matthew's.

Did it then find usage in Luke's two-book work or did it first influence the re-writing of John's Gospel? The issue here is that of the priority of the Gospels of Luke and John. We enter territory which has been, relatively speaking, little-traversed. Clearly, the issue of sources now broadens from that of the synoptics alone. Considerations of the sources of the Gospel of John can be separated no longer. Possible schemes of Gospel source-relationships can be drawn up. It would seem likely that the Gospel of Mark and the first version of John's Gospel came from the same traditions, but independently of each other. Subsequent developments of the Gospels likely drew, at each stage, from special sources available to the writers but in the main from the Gospels which preceded them.

7. History and story:

The discovery of the literary structures of the first five of the books under analysis provides a new and most persuasive line of argument for those whose study is Midrash and Historiography, History and Myth. It is an interest which no one now can ignore. The quest for the 'historical Jesus' ended some time ago. It is a quest that will not be tackled again, without true recognition of the fundamental difficulties.

Comparing book with book, we discern sacrifice of chronology, of history (*viz.* Matthew's genealogy), of exactness of detail and of theological interpretation, in favour of each author's own literary and didactic purposes. It is most assuredly the case that the Gospel writers create, as well as re-create, gospel 'pieces', for the purpose of sectional balances. Even the tradition behind Mark's Gospel declares that he 'adapted his teachings to the needs of the moment' and presented the contents to his own order. The tradition would seem to be reliable: the discovery of the structure of his Gospel supports these statements.

Eternal truth, rather than historically factual truth, it would seem, is the more important to the writers. Story is no less a vehicle of eternal truth that history: simply, it is interpreted history. And history itself, it is to be understood, is an interpretation only of available 'historical' data. The dividing-line between history and story is imagined commonly to be much thicker than it really is.

8. The theological endeavours of the Evangelists:

Clearly, the structural-schemes the Evangelists use, for their numberings and arrangements of their sections and parts, provide evidence of their different intentions as regards theological disclosure.

We might argue that Mark's endeavour is simply to tell about 'Days in the Life of Jesus', in four series of seven. By this, it might be said that he 'earths' Jesus, that he presents the incarnate Christ. There is no possible denial of this reality. It is the life, mission and, particularly, the death of 'a person' and not a matter of disembodied teachings, which is at the heart of the Good News. It is the right identity of 'this person' which is paramount. It might be argued that the very structure of the Gospel further emphasises focus on the 'Day of the Lord', which is yet to come.

Matthew's scheme displays, perhaps at first, less a theological-outlook, more a didactic endeavour. The five teaching blocks, nevertheless, are most firmly set within Jesus' life-story: in the eleven sections, they occupy alternating positions. And they point to Jesus' proper identification with Moses: by Jesus, entry into the Kingdom (the promised land) is assured; by Jesus, is the new law given. These teachings and the episodes of the story, for their many direct references and allusions to Old Testament scriptures (which Matthew, himself, supplies) point clearly to a developed, scriptural and theological understanding of Jesus' person and purpose.

Luke, by paralleling 'stories of Jesus', in his first book, and 'stories of the Church', in his second, gives indication of the way his theological-mind was working. The life of Jesus is lived again in the life of the Church, it is a life and a mission which the Spirit brings to birth and sustains. The thesis, that Luke wrote a historical scheme to replace a primitive eschatology (2), would seem in need of revision.

Luke's use of fewer, direct references to the Old Testament scriptures (compare Matthew's Gospel) is more than made up for by his greater use of allusion to them. Features like this, which can be compared with Matthew's Gospel, appear to point to the growing sophistication, that was being enjoyed in the Church, in theological understanding.

With John's Gospel, in both its versions, the theological expositions of the 'signs', in the contexts of Jewish 'feasts', present Jesus in his indisputably-true divinity as the one who is completing the religious laws, hopes and practices of the Jews. It may be that the earlier version of the Gospel, in its seven, linearly-arranged sections, revealed more clearly these theological truths than does the current version. The present structure, with its chiastically-arranged allusions to the institution of the eucharist, seems to demonstrate again a later, and more sophisticated, maturing in theological reflection. Clearly, the scheme of 'seven times twelve' has to be meaningful in terms of theological disclosure. The 'perfect' age of 'election' has its focus in/on Jesus.

The Revelation to John, for its chiastic scheme of 'seven sevens', is emphatic in its presentation that that which is revealed will come to completion: everything that is written will happen eventually.

These introductions to future discussions link with those above, under the heading of Structuralism and Literary Criticism. The study of literary structures and of theological disclosure is really one and the same. The issue of 'sources' connects firmly too.

It has often been noted in the past that Mark's Gospel begins its account of Jesus with his baptism, that Matthew's begins with the genealogy, demonstrating Jesus' descent from Abraham, that Luke's genealogy of Jesus goes back to Adam and to God, and that John's Prologue takes us all the way back to the very beginning of creation. Each writer would seem to have chosen their own basic point of theological reference. Were they persuaded of an alternative, each in turn, as they read the work of the one before them? At variance with this possibility is the finding that the Prologue of John existed prior to the period of major re-structuring.

9. Lectionary systems:

Were the Books created for lectionary-purposes? Were any of them designed to reflect the contents of a Jewish lectionary system? These questions have been addressed by, principally, Carrington (3) and Goulder (4). Does the discovery of the literary structures of these six books contribute anything to this discussion?

There is little doubt that these books lend themselves to serialised readings in Christian assemblies. But were they designed for daily readings, for weekly readings in an annual scheme, or simply, loosely for both? The evidence has to be considered.

Evidence exists in most early manuscripts which suggests that the books were read in a systematic fashion: titles and numbers in the margins associated with additional margin divisions are found. It is observed, however, that these divisions vary between manuscripts: further, they differ a great deal from those established by the analyses in this book. We can conclude only that the structural divisions, that the writers themselves intended, were lost before these notes were added. Further, if the books were written as lectionary systems, they were not being read as they were designed to be read.

It follows that the books are not being read publicly, in the assemblies of Christians today, as they were intended. Many of the currently-used lectionary-systems invite the public reading of passages with most inappropriate limits.

That the books themselves are reflective of Jewish lectionary systems (and their contents) and that they are so designed as alternative, Christian lectionaries is supported by patchy evidence only. In the first place, the details of Jewish and Christian practices in the first century have to be re-created by a reading-back of the practices of the third and fourth centuries. And in the second place, a significant number of contrary direct-quotations disrupt the correspondences between the gospels and their proposed, Jewish lectionary counterparts. Significant parallels between the Gospels and some of the Old Testament scriptures do exist: the Journey to Jerusalem, at the centre of Luke's Gospel, most assuredly connects, at many points, with the Book of Deuteronomy (to Goulder's and Drury's (5), I would add others). But, the reasons for such are other than lectionary ones, it seems.

The lack of hard evidence for an early dating of Christian feasts would appear to limit all investigation into the possible lectionary-purposes of the writers of these six books. Easter is the oldest feast. It may be that the gospels were designed to be read in the period leading up to it, but when would the readings have begun? In the case of Mark's Gospel the occasion, in the Eastern Church, might have been that of Epiphany, when a celebration of Jesus' baptism was held. In the case of Matthew's and Luke's Gospels, the season of Advent might have occasioned the beginning of the reading of one, or both, of these books. But, the earliest evidence for an observance of Epiphany (in the East) is that of the third century and the earliest observance of Advent (in the West) is that of the sixth century. What seems most likely is that it was the reading of the books themselves, to imposed lectionary systems, that gave rise to the fixings of the Christian feast days of Epiphany and Advent. It cannot be satisfactorily argued, on the evidence we possess, that it was the other way about.

Some currently-used lectionaries include readings from Luke's Gospel between Advent and Easter and readings from the Acts of the Apostles between Easter and Advent. We can see how Luke's two-book work could be read as an annual scheme, but no evidence of content and no evidence of history exists which categorically proves this was his purpose. Likewise, we cannot prove that Mark's Gospel was composed deliberately to be read in a calendar month. The seventh days of each of the series, however, might be considered appropriate for reading on the 'first day of the week': series 1 and 4 conclude with resurrection accounts and series 2 and 3 conclude with considerations of blindness and physical/spiritual sight.

Literary-ordering of the six books, not lectionary-ordering, is what available evidence supports. And this evidence is that of the contents and the arrangements of the contents. We note that each of the six books can be read, without too much physical discomfort, in one sitting. We can only assume that, if they were written that they might form the bases for exposition, the books were tackled in the early Christian assemblies 'slice by slice' (section by section and sub-section by sub-section).

10. Authorship:

Questions of authorship can be raised afresh. The discovery of the framework to Mark's Gospel would appear to justify acknowledgement of the reliability, in its greater part at least, of the tradition passed down through Papias (see the conclusion to chapter 2). It witnesses to the Gospel, to the author and to his working-method.

The discovery of the structures of the 'first book' of the New Testament supports the view that it is a 'handbook for teaching' (6): does this tell us more about Matthew? Because the purposes of all the writers can be understood more clearly now, it would seem to be the case.

The authorship of the traditionally styled 'two-book work' of Luke can be re-assessed. A present-day argument is that, as the Gospel of Luke is theologically far superior to that of the Acts of the Apostles, they could not both have been written by the same person. It is most certainly possible that another writer could have taken the Gospel and written a book on the Church in parallel to it, but would he have had such a similar command of literary-styles? We might argue that the Gospel's theology is more sophisticated than that of the Acts of the Apostles simply because several presentations already existed before Luke began his work. In contrast to this, it would appear likely that Luke was the first to write about the Church. It would seem to be the case that the Church was more interested in developing its theological understanding of Jesus, in the first place, than it was in developing its understanding about itself. Indeed, the latter could not have been achieved either without or before the former.

The traditional, apostolic origin of the fourth Gospel could be considered to be reinforced by the discovery of its present and earlier structures. It is unlikely, however, that the writer of the first version is the one who re-structured it and added material, to form the second. The passage, 21. 20-24, does seem to suggest that this was carried out after John's death. The possible connections with Luke's Gospel, at the stage of its re-presentation, can be considered further, as also the likelihood that much of the additional material was what John himself taught in his church-setting.

The similarity of the structures of the Gospel of John (both earlier and later versions) and the Revelation to John might fire fresh speculation regarding the traditional apostolic authorship of this apocalypse. Did John leave two books, both structured basically in the same way . . . just as Luke did?

11. The dating of the letters:

The dating of the New Testament Letters has relied, in the past, very heavily upon the evidence of the Acts of the Apostles. This evidence will need re-assessing. The book's literary arrangement may have necessitated some changes in the chronological ordering of Paul's journeyings.

12. Symbolism: literature, art and artefact:

The study of symbolism in art and in architecture is one which has fascinated every serious enquirer. What now has to be examined is the possibility of a relationship existing between the infra-structural designs of First Century faith-literature and Judaeo-Christian art and artefact of temple, synagogue, catacomb and home.

The question is really an obvious one. Art and literature are stable mates. Both have been employed by great civilisations and peoples throughout the ages to record history and tell story, myth and legend.

Pictorial or symbolical art, whether in stone, timber, plaster or canvas, is structured and stylised. Literary art is no different. The 'missing link' is well found in an example of Ethiopian, Coptic art which tells the story of the 'Line of the Lion of Judah': its form is of four series of eleven, framed pictures, in oils on a single canvas. Writing most certainly, generally-speaking, eclipsed pictorial story telling. Did it learn from its stable mate? Did it employ 'designs' it found in the world of art and artefacts? Here, we begin to examine this whole subject, by way of illustration and introduction only, with reference to the symbolisms of lamp and lampstand.

The multi-branched lampstand, one of the most common of all Jewish symbols and technically termed the 'menorah', is fully described in Exodus 25. 31-40 and 37. 17-24. It is considered to be symbolic of the 'tree of life'. It has a base, a stand and branches which number seven in all. The central branch is a straight extension of the stand. The three branches each side are paired: each pair, of increasing radius, is a continuous, semi circular piece concentric with the top of the central branch (developments later introduced straights and angles).

The 'menorah' of this description might be reflected in the structure of John's Gospel. Its seven-section chiasm can be described as three pairs of balancing sections about a central section. Both this Gospel and the lamp(stand) clearly indicate 'light and life'. It might be argued that four of these lampstands are reflected in the structure of Mark's Gospel, of four series of 'seven days'.

Each of the seven lamps atop the lampstand of Zechariah's vision are described as having seven spouts (Zech. 4. 2). Compare, therefore, this design with that of the seven times seven chiastic structure of the Revelation to John. Can this be coincidence, only?

Additionally, it is noted that whilst the 'menorah' commonly comprised seven branches it did exist also, in the First Century, in five-, nine- and eleven-branched versions. The latter, suggestive of 1-5, C, 5'-1', is particulary stimulating . . . (see chapters 3 and 4 for the designs of the Gospels of Matthew and Luke and the Acts of the Apostles).

It would appear that the genre of these six New Testament books might warrant the technical definition of 'menorahic literature'. It might be judged also that the 'menorah' itself is deserving of a greater Christian significance and a place in cathedral, church and home.

PART B

Index of Summary Charts

The Gospel of Mark:
'Days in the Life of Jesus/The Day of the Lord'

Introduction: 1. 1-20 (20 verses):
'The Beginning of the Gospel of Jesus Christ':
Four Parts: First: 1. 1   The Title
              Second: 1. 2-8   John's Ministry
              Third: 1. 9-13   Jesus' Baptism and days in the wilderness
              Fourth: 1. 14-20 The beginning of Jesus' Ministry

The First Series of Seven Days (Series 1):   1. 21-5. 43 (172 verses):
'Jesus' First Days of Ministry confined to Galilee and the Sea Region':
              Day One: 1. 21-38   Capernaum and other Cities
              Day Two: 1. 39-45
              Day Three: 2. 1-22
              Day Four: 2. 23-3. 6
              Day Five: 3. 7-4. 41
              Day Six: 5. 1-20
              Day Seven: 5. 21-43   The Raising of a Dead Child

The Second Series of Seven Days (Series C1):   6. 1-8. 26 (119 verses):
'Days of Increase in the Ministry of Jesus':
              Day One: 6. 1-29   Jesus' Identity is Questioned
              Day Two: 6. 30-52
              Day Three: 6. 53-7. 23
              Day Four: 7. 24-30
              Day Five: 7. 31-37
              Day Six: 8. 1-21
              Day Seven: 8. 22-26   A Blind Man is Healed

The Third Series of Seven Days (Series C1'):   8. 27-10.52 (114 verses):
'The Days of Jesus' Journeying to the Cross and Glory':
              Day One: 8. 27-9. 1   Jesus' Identity is Questioned
              Day Two: 9. 2-29
              Day Three: 9. 30-50
              Day Four: 10. 1-16
              Day Five: 10. 17-31
              Day Six: 10. 32-45
              Day Seven: 10. 46-52   A Blind Beggar is Healed

The Fourth Series of Seven Days (Series 1'):   11. 1-16. 8 (241 verses):
'Jesus' Passion and Resurrection: the Jerusalem Days':
              Day One: 11. 1-11.   Jerusalem
              Day Two: 11. 12-19
              Day Three: 11. 20-13. 37
              Day Four: 14. 1-11
              Day Five: 14. 12-72
              Day Six: 15. 1-47
              Day Seven: 16. 1-8   Jesus: 'He Has Risen!'

Conclusion: 16. 9-20 (12 verses):
'The Story Continues'
Four parts: First: 16. 9-11   Jesus' first appearance: disbelief
              Second: 16. 12, 13   Jesus' second appearance: disbelief
              Third: 16. 14-18   Jesus' third appearance: belief
              Fourth: 16. 19, 20   Jesus' ascension and continuing work

The Gospel of Matthew:

Section 1:   1. 1-4. 24 (89 verses):   7:7 parts:
Genealogy; Jesus' Birth and Early Years, Baptism, Temptations & Purpose:
1. 1-17; 18. 25; 2. 1-6; v7-12; v13-15; v16-18; v19-23
3. 1-3; v4-12; v13-17; 4. 1-11; v12-17; v18-22; v23, 24

Link: 4. 25/5. 1, 2

Section 2:   5. 3-7. 27 (107 verses):   12:10:12 parts:
Blessings: The Law, Prophets, Religion, Coming Kingdom & Jesus:
5. 3; v4; v5; v6; v7; v8; v9; v10; v11, 12; v13; v14-16; v17-20
   5. 21-26; v27-32; v33-37; v38-42; v43-48; 6. 1; v2-4; v5, 6; v7-15; v16-18
6. 19-21; v22, 23; v24; v25-34; 7. 1-5; v6; v7-11; v12; v13, 14; v15-20; v21-23; v24-27

Link: 7. 28, 29/8. 1

Section 3:   8. 2-9. 35 (68 verses)   12 parts:
Jesus' Galiliean Ministry, Person & Purpose:
8. 2-4; v5-13; v14-17; v18-27; v28-9. 1; v2-8; v9-13; v14-17; v18-26; v27-31; v32-34, v35

Link: 9. 36/v37, 38

Section 4:   10. 1-42 (42 verses):   12 parts:
The Mission of the Twelve and Jesus' Mission Instructions:
10. 1-4; v5-10; v11-15; v16; v17-20; v21, 22; v23; v24, 25; v26-31; v32, 33; v34-39; v40-42

Link: 11. 1/v2-6

Section 5:   11. 7-12. 45 (69 verses):   12 parts:
Disclosures of Jesus' Identity: The Response of Belief and Unbelief:
11. 7-15; v16-19; v20-24; v25-27; v28-30; 12. 1-8; v9-14; v15-21; v22-32; v33-37; v38-42; v43-45

Link: 12. 46-50/13. 1, 2

Section C: 13. 3-52 (50 verses)   12 parts:
Parables of the Kingdom:
13. 3-9; v10-17; v18-23; v24-30; v31, 32; v33; v34, 35; v36-43; v44; v45, 46; v47-50; v51, 52

Link: 13. 53/v54-58

Section 5':   14. 1-16. 12   (87 verses)   12 parts:
Disclosures of Jesus' Identity: The Response of Belief and Unbelief:
14. 1-12; v13, 14; v15-21; v22-33; v34-36; 15. 1-9; v10-20; v21-28; v29-31; v32-39; 16. 1-4; v5-12

Link: 16. 13-17/v18-20

Section 4':   16. 21-18. 35 (70 verses)   12 parts:
The Church and Jesus' Instructions to His Disciples:
16. 21-23; v24-28; 17. 1-13; v14-21; v22, 23; v24-27; 18. 1-4; v5, 6; v7-9; v10-14; v15-20; v21-35

Link: 19. 1/v2

Section 3':   19. 3-21. 16 (78 verses)   12 parts:
Jesus' Judean Ministry (Journeying to Jerusalem), Person & Purpose:
19. 3-9; v10-12; v13-15; v16-22; v23-26; v27-30; 20. 1-16; v17-19; v20-28; v29-34; 21. 1-11; v12-16

Link: 21. 17/v18-22

Section 2':   21. 23-25. 46 (206 verses):   12:10:12 parts:
Woes; The Law, Prophets, Religion, Coming Kingdom & Jesus:
21. 23-27; v28-31a; v31b, 32; v33-41; v42-44; v45, 46; 22. 1-10; v11-14; v15-22; v23-33; v34-40; v41-46
   23. 1-12; v13; (v14); v15; v16-22; v23, 24; v25, 26; v27, 28; v29-36; v37-39
   24. 1, 2; v3-8; v9-14; v15-22; v23-28; v29-31; v32-35; v36-44; v45-51; 25. 1-13; v14-30; v31-46

Link: 26. 1, 2/v3-5

Section 1':   26. 6-28. 20 (156 verses):   7:7 parts:
Jesus' Death and Resurrection; The Disciples' Purpose:
26. 6-13; v14-16; v17-30; v31-35; v36-56; v57-75; 27. 1-10
27. 11-26; v27-56; v57-61; v62-66; 28. 1-10; v11-15; v16-20.

The Gospel of Luke (The First of Two Books):

Prologue: 1. 1-4 (4 verses): parts in simple parallelism:
The Purpose of Luke's Writing:
2 parts: 1. 1, 2; v3, 4 (each part comprising three further parts)

Section 1:   1. 5-80 (76 verses):   parts in simple parallelism:
Angel's Announcements of Promises of Births: Belief/Disbelief:
2 parts: 1. 5-38; 1. 39-80 (each part is in simple parallelism: 1. 5-25;
1. 26-38 and 1. 39-56; 1. 57-80: each of these parts is chiastic)

> **Section 2:**   2. 1-52 (52 verses):   parts in chiasm:
> Jesus' Birth: Salvation:
> 3 parts: 2. 1-20 (s.p.); 2. 21-40 (ch.); 2. 41-52 (s.p.)

> > **Section 3:**   3. 1-4. 44 (82 verses)   parts in chiasm:
> > Jesus' Baptism, Three Trials (God's Son, Christ, King) and Rejection:
> > 3 parts: 3. 1-20; 3. 21-4. 30; 4. 31-44 (each chiastic)

> > > **Section 4:**   5. 1-8. 21 (159 verses):   parts in chiasm:
> > > Sinners to Disciples:
> > > 3 parts: 5. 1-6. 19 (s.p.); 6. 20-49 (ch.); 7. 1-8. 21 (s.p.)

> > > > **Section 5:**   8. 22-9. 43a (77½ verses):   parts in chiasm:
> > > > Jesus' Identity, 'The Christ', His Death, Glorious Return as Judge, His
> > > > Transfiguration, The Disciples' Purpose:
> > > > 3 parts: 8. 22-56; 9. 1-27; 9. 28-43a (each part in simple parallelism)

> > > > > **Section C:**   9. 43b-19. 46 (434½ verses):   parts in chiasm:
> > > > > Jesus' Journey to Jerusalem: His Teaching on the Way:
> > > > > 3 parts: 9. 43b-10. 24; 10. 25-18. 30; 18. 31-19. 46 (each chiastic)

> > > > **Section 5':**   19. 47-21. 38   (87 verses):   parts in chiasm
> > > > Jesus' Teaching in the Temple: His Death, The Christ, Apocalypse and
> > > > Return as Judge, in Glory, the Disciples' Purpose:
> > > > 3 parts: 19. 47-20. 26; 20. 27-21. 4; 21. 5-38 (each: simple parallelism)

> > > **Section 4':**   22. 1-53 (51 verses):   parts in chiasm:
> > > Disciples to Sinners: Jesus' Arrest:
> > > 3 parts: 22. 1-13 (s.p.); 22. 14-30 (ch.); 22. 31-53 (s.p.)

> > **Section 3':**   22. 54-23. 25 (42 verses):   parts in chiasm:
> > Jesus' Three Trials (The Christ, God's Son, King), and Rejections:
> > 3 parts: 22. 54-62; 22. 63-23. 12; 23. 13-25 (each chiastic)

> **Section 2':**   23. 26-53 (28 verses):   parts in chiasm:
> Jesus' Death: Salvation:
> 3 parts: 23. 26-31 (s.p.); 23. 32-46 (ch.); 23. 47-53 (s.p.)

Section 1':   23. 54-24. 53 (55 verses):   parts in simple parallelism:
Angels Announce, 'Jesus Is Risen!'; Belief/Disbelief, a New Promise:
2 parts: 23. 54-24. 11; 24. 13-53 (each part is in simple parallelism: 23. 54-56; 24.
1-11 and 24. 13-32; 24. 33-53: each of these parts is chiastic).

Notes on structure:
The scheme, 1-5, C, 5'-1', is repeated in the central sub-section, 10. 25-18. 30, and
also in the genealogy, 3. 23e-38.
The same scheme is also repeated in Luke's second book, which parallels the first
book, section for section, in many of its themes and much of its detail.

The Acts of the Apostles (The Second of Two Books by Luke):

Section 1:   1. 1-26 (26 verses): parts in chiasm:
Integral Prologue: The Purpose of the Book: Continuity with the First
(1. 1-5: 2 parts in simple parallelism: 1. 1, 2; v3-5, each part comprising three further
parts) and the Pre-Pentecost Days in Jerusalem:
2 parts: 1. 1-11; 1. 12-26 (each part, in simple parallelism)

  Section 2:   2. 1-42 (42 verses):   parts in chiasm:
The Birth of the Church's Mission:
3 parts: 2. 1-13 (s.p.); 2. 14-36 (ch.); 2. 37-42 (s.p.)

    Section 3:   2. 43-5. 42 (110 verses)   parts in simple parallelism:
The Developing Church in Jerusalem: Arrests, Trials and Judgements:
2 parts: 2. 43-4. 31; 4. 32-5. 42 (each part is chiastic: 2. 43-3. 26; 4. 1-4; 4. 5-31
and 4. 32-5. 13; 5. 14-18; 5. 19-42: each of these are simple parallelisms)

      Section 4:   6. 1-9. 31 (146 verses):   parts in simple parallelism:
The Jerusalem Church: Persecution and Scattering; Saul's Conversion;
2 parts: 6. 1-8. 3; 8. 4-9. 31 (each part is chiastic: 6. 1-7; 6. 8-8. 1a; 8. 1b-3 and
8. 4-40; 9. 1-22; 9. 23-31: all these parts are chiastic too)

        Section 5:   9. 32-11. 26 (86 verses):   parts in chiasm:
Peter, On Mission: The Role of Vision and Spirit: Jesus Is Judge:
3 parts: 9. 32-43; 10. 1-11. 18; 11. 19-26 (each in simple parallelism)

          Section C: 11. 27-15. 35 (144 verses):   parts in chiasm:
Three Journeys of Saul and Barnabas, From Antioch:
3 parts: 11. 27-12. 25; 13. 1-14. 28; 15. 1-35 (each chiastic)

        Section 5':   15. 36-18. 23   (103 verses):   parts in chiasm:
Paul, On Mission: The Role of Vision and Spirit: Jesus Is Judge:
3 parts: 15. 36-16. 10; 16. 11-18. 8; 18. 9-23 (each: simple parallelism)

      Section 4':   18. 24-22. 29 (153 verses)   parts in simple parallelism:
In Ephesus and Jerusalem: Uproar; Paul's Arrest:
2 parts: 18. 24-20. 16; 20. 17-22. 29 (each part is chiastic: 18. 24-19. 22; 19.
23-41; 20. 1-16 and 20. 17-38; 21. 1-30; 21. 31-22. 29: all these parts are
chiastic too)

    Section 3':   22. 30-26. 33 (122 verses)   parts in simple parallelism:
Paul's Trials: The Judgements and His Appeal to Caesar:
2 parts: 22. 30-24. 27; 25. 1-26. 32 (each part is chiastic: 22. 30-23. 22; 23.
23-35; 24. 1-27 and 25. 1-21; 25. 22; 25. 23-26. 32: each of these parts are
simple parallelisms)

  Section 2':   27. 1-28. 15 (59 verses):   parts in chiasm:
Paul's Eventful Journey to Italy and Rome:
3 parts: 27. 1-12 (s.p.); 27. 13-44 (ch.); 28. 1-15 (s.p.)

Section 1':   28. 16-31 (15 verses):   parts in chiasm:
In Rome, Paul's Work Continues:
2 parts: 28. 16-22; 28. 23-31 (each part, in simple parallelism)

LUKE'S STORY OF THE CHURCH, sectionally in its themes and many details, very
much repeats HIS STORY OF JESUS. The life of Jesus, Luke's two-book
structural-scheme would seem to suggest, is lived again in the life of the Church: it is a
life and, therefore, a mission which the Spirit brings to birth and sustains.

Luke's Gospel Section 1 (1. 5-80): Angel's Announcements of Promises of Births: Belief and Disbelief:

Sub-section I, 1. 5-38:   Angel's Announcements of Promised Births: Zechariah's Disbelief; Mary's Belief:

1,   1. 5-25: The Promise of the Birth of John:

    (i)   .i   A dating; Zechariah and Elizabeth, old and barren, blameless before the law (1. 5-7);

        .i'   Zechariah enters the temple: seeing an angel, he is frightened (1. 8-12);

      (c) .i   the angel announces news of a son and of his purpose (1. 13-17);

         .i' Zechariah questions: the angel judges his disbelief (1. 18-20);

    (i') .i   Zechariah (dumb) leaves the temple and goes home (1. 21-23);

        .i'   Elizabeth conceives (1. 24, 25).

1',   1. 26-38:   The Promise of the Birth of Jesus:

    (i)   .i   The angel visits Mary (a young virgin) betrothed to Joseph (1. 26, 27);

        .i'   The angel says she is 'favoured'; rather, Mary is frightened (1. 28, 29);

      (c) .i   the angel announces news of a son and of his purpose (1. 30-33);

         .i' Mary questions but believes: the angel explains about the 'power of the Most High' . . . (1. 34-37);

    (i') .i   Mary accepts her role (1. 38a);

        .i'   the angel departs from her (1. 38b).

Sub-section I', 1. 39-80:   Further Announcements: Exultations:

1,   1. 39-56: Greetings and Exultations: Elizabeth and Mary:

    (i)   .i   Mary goes with haste to a city of Judah (1. 39);

        .i'   she enters Zechariah's house and greets Elizabeth (1. 40);

      (c) .i   Elizabeth and John (in utero) exult (1. 41-45);

         .i' Mary exults (1. 46-55);

    (i') .i   Mary stays three months (1. 56a);

        .i'   and returns to her home (1. 56b).

1',   1. 57-80:   The Birth and Naming of John: Zechariah's Exultations:

    (i)   .i   A son is born to Elizabeth (1. 57);

        .i'   neighbours rejoice (1. 58);

      (c) .i   the boy is named John by Zechariah, who's dumbness goes; all wondered what the child would be (1. 59-66);

         .i' Zechariah (filled with the Holy Spirit) exults and speaks of the role of his son (1. 67-79);

    (i') .i   the child grew and became strong in spirit (1. 80a);

        .i'   he was in the desert until his ministry began (1. 80b).

Luke's Gospel Section 1′ (23. 54-24. 53): Angels Announce that Jesus Is Risen: Belief and Disbelief: Jesus Announces a New Promise:

Sub-section I, 23. 54-24. 11:   Angels Announce, 'Jesus Is Risen': The Women's Report to the Men Is Not Believed:

1,   23. 54-56: The Tomb: Women See How Jesus' Body Is Laid:
   (i)   .i   The day of Preparation (23. 54a);
          .i′   the sabbath was beginning (23. 54b);
      (c) .i   women follow and see the tomb and Jesus' body (23. 55);
           .i′ they return to prepare spices and ointments (23. 56a);
   (i′)   .i   on the sabbath they rested (23. 56b);
          .i′   according to the commandment (23. 56c).

1′,   24. 1-11:   The Tomb Is Empty: Angels Announce, 'He Is Risen'
   (i)   .i   They go to the tomb with prepared spices (24. 1);
          .i′   they find no body (24. 2, 3);
      (c) .i   they see angels and are frightened (24. 4-6a);
           .i′ the angels explain (24. 6b, 7);
   (i′)   .i   the women return from the tomb and tell the eleven and the rest (24. 8, 9);
          .i′   Mary Magdalene, Joanna and Mary (James' mother) tell the apostles: they are not believed (24. 10, 11).

Sub-section I′, 24. 13-53:   Jesus' Appearances Result in Belief: He Makes a New Promise:

1,   24. 13-32: Jesus Appears to Two Disciples:
   (i)   .i   Two disciples journey to Emmaus (24. 13, 14);
          .i′   Jesus, unrecognised, joins them (24. 15, 16);
      (c) .i   the disciples speak of their sadness and bewilderment concerning Jesus (24. 17-24);
           .i′ the 'stranger' chastises their disbelief and speaks of Jesus, beginning with Moses and the prophets (24. 25-27);
   (i′)   .i   reaching Emmaus, they invite the 'stranger' to stay with them (24. 28, 29);
          .i′   they recognise Jesus as he breaks bread: he vanishes (24. 30-32).

1′,   24. 33-53:   Jesus Appears to Them All and Makes a New Promise:
   (i)   .i   The two disciples return to Jerusalem and find the eleven and others; 'the Lord has risen indeed' (24. 33-35);
          .i′   Jesus appears as they speak: he gives proof of his resurrection state (24. 36-43);
      (c) .i   he explains about himself from Moses, the prophets and the psalms (24. 44);
           .i′ applying the scriptures, he commissions them and promises 'power from on high' (24. 45-49);
   (i′)   .i   going to Bethany, he blesses them and ascends (24. 50, 51);
          .i′   returning to Jerusalem, in the temple they bless God (24. 52, 53).

Luke's Gospel Section 2 (2. 1-52): The Birth of Jesus: Salvation:

Sub-section I, 2. 1-20:   Keeping to roman Law Results in Jesus Being Born in Bethlehem: Shepherds Are Told and Find Jesus:

1: (i)   A dating; a census: the census requirement (2. 1, 2: v3);
    (i')   Joseph and Mary travel to Bethlehem: while there she gives birth (2. 4, 5: v6, 7);
1': (i)   an angel announces the news to shepherds: more angels appear (2. 8-12: v13, 14);
    (i')   the shepherds seek Jesus: they report what they were told; Mary keeps these things in her heart (2. 15-17: v18-20)

Sub-section C, 2. 21-40:   They Go to Jerusalem to Fulfil the Requirements of the Law:

1:   (i)   Jesus' circumcision and naming (2. 21a: v21b);
     (i')   to Jerusalem for the purification and presentation according to the law (2. 22: v23, 24);
  C: (i)   the person and witness of Simeon who was looking for the consolation of Israel (2. 25-32: v33-35);
     (i')   the person and witness of Anna to those who were looking for the redemption of Jerusalem (2. 36, 37: v38);
1': (i)   all is completed according to the law: they return to Galilee (2. 39a: v39b);
     (i')   the child grew and became strong . . .: the favour of God was upon him (2. 40a: v40b)

Sub-section I', 2. 41-52:   Jesus (at Twelve Years) Accompanies His Parents To Go to Jerusalem at the Time of the Passover: He Separates from Them, But Is Found in the Temple:

1: (i)   to Jerusalem annually at the Passover: when Jesus was twelve (2. 41: v42);
    (i')   returning, Jesus stays, unknown to his parents: then they seek him and return to Jerusalem (2. 43: v44, 45);
1': (i)   after three days they find him in the temple: his response to his parents' challenge is not understood (2. 46, 47: v48-50);
    (i')   Jesus returns with them to Nazareth; his mother keeps these things in her heart: Jesus grows in wisdom . . . (2. 51: v52).

Luke's Gospel Section 2' (23. 26-53): The Death of Jesus: Salvation:

Sub-section I, 23. 26-31 Jesus Is Led Away

1:   (i)   Jesus is led away: Simon of Cyrene is seized to carry the cross (23. 26a: v26b);

    (i')   a crowd follows: women also, who are weeping for Jesus (23. 27a: 27b);

1':   (i)   Jesus tells them to weep for themselves and their children: he explains (23. 28: v29);

    (i')   he foretells grief: he explains (23. 30: v31);

Sub-section C, 23. 32-46:   Jesus Is Crucified: He Dies:

1:   (i)   two others are to be put to death with Jesus: at the place of the Skull, they are crucified (23. 32: v33);

    (i')   'Father, forgive them . . .,' Jesus prays: they cast lots to divide his garments (23. 34a: v34b);

  C: (i)   rulers scoff: 'save . . . Christ': soldiers mock: 'King of the Jews . . . save yourself' (23. 35: v36-38);

    (i')   one of the criminals rails: 'Christ . . . save . . .' the other says to Jesus, 'Remember me . . . kingdom' (23. 39-41: v42, 43);

1':   (i)   darkness came: the curtain of the temple is torn in two (23. 44: v45);

    (i')   'Father, into thy hands . . .,' Jesus prays: he breathes his last (23. 46a: v46b);

Sub-section I', 23. 47-53:   Jesus Is Buried:

1:   (i)   the centurion witnesses Jesus' innocence: all the crowd returns home beating their breasts (23. 47: v48);

    (i')   his acquaintances and the women stand at a distance: they see everything (23. 49ab: v49c);

1':   (i)   Joseph of Arimathea, looking for the kingdom of God: he goes to Pilate and asks for the body of Jesus (23. 50, 51: v52);

    (i')   he takes it down from the cross and wraps it in linen: he places it in a new tomb (23. 53a: v53b).

Luke's Gospel Section 3 (3. 1-4. 44): Jesus' Baptism: Three Trials: God's Son, The Christ and King: His Rejection:

Sub-section I, 3. 1-20:   John's Ministry: Three Questions:

1:   A dating and John's call (in the desert, fulfilling Isaianic prophecy): crowds go out to him (3. 1-6: v7-9);

  C: Three questions (and answers) (chiasm: 3. 10, 11: v12, 13: v14);

1':   John is not 'the Christ' . . .: he preaches good news, he is imprisoned (3. 15-17: v18-20)

    Sub-section C, 3. 21-4. 30:   Jesus' Ministry Begins: His Baptism, His Three Trials, His Sonship:

    1:   At Jesus' baptism, the Holy Spirit descends on him and he is announced (God's) beloved Son: he is supposed the son of Joseph, he is the Son of God (3. 21, 22: v23-38, an eleven part chiasm, seven names per part);

      C: Jesus' three trials in the desert: 'If you are the Son of God . . .'; authority over kingdoms of the world . . .; 'If you are the Son of God . . .' (chiasm: 4. 1-4: v5-8: v9-15);

    1':   In Nazareth, Jesus reads Isaianic prophecy; the Spirit of the Lord is upon him: his sonship of Joseph is queried and he is rejected as a prophet (4. 16-21: v22-30)

Sub-section I', 4. 31-44:   Jesus' Ministry: The First Reports: Three Rebukings:

1:   In Capernaum, a city of Galilee, Jesus is teaching on the sabbath: the people are astonished at the authority of his teaching (4. 31: v32);

  C: Three rebukings: of a demon which recognises Jesus as 'the Holy One of God'; of a fever Simon's mother-in-law suffered; and of more demons who also knew Jesus to be 'the Son of God' and 'the Christ' (chiasm: 4. 33-37: v38, 39: v40, 41);

1':   In a desert place, crowds come to him to keep him with them: but he is to preach in other cities and goes into Judea (4. 42: v43, 44).

Luke's Gospel Section 3′ (22. 54-23. 25): Jesus' Three Trials (The Christ, God's Son and King); Rejections:

Sub-section I, 22. 54-62:   Peter's Three Denials of Jesus:

1:    The setting is described: the first denial (22. 54, 55: v56, 57);

  C: a little later, the second denial: challenge and retort (*cf,* the first and third: note the brevity: 22. 58a: v58b);

1′:   The third denial: Peter's sorrow (22. 59, 60: v61, v62).

Sub-section C, 22. 63-23. 12: Jesus' Three Trials:

  1:    Jesus is mocked: Jesus before the council . . . 'the Christ'? 'the Son of God'? (22. 63-65: v66-71);

    C: Jesus is accused before Pilate; Pilate asks him, 'Are you the King of the Jews?'; Pilate finds 'no crime' in him amid further accusations (chiasm: 23. 1, 2: v3: v4, 5);

  1′:   Jesus is sent to Herod who looks for a sign from Jesus: Jesus is again mocked and returned to Pilate (23. 6-10: v11, 12).

Sub-section I′, 23. 13-25:   The Crowd's Three Rejections of Jesus:

1:    Pilate addresses the chief priests, the rulers and the people: they reject Jesus (for the first time) (23. 13-16: v18, 19);

  C: Pilate addresses them again: (for the second time) they reject Jesus (*cf,* the first and third: note the brevity: 23. 20: v21);

1′:   For a third time, Pilate addresses the crowd, himself wishing to free Jesus: again they reject him and Pilate passes sentence (23. 22, 23: v24, 25).

Luke's Gospel Section 4 (5. 1-8. 21): Sinners to Disciples:

Sub-section I, 5. 1-6. 19:   Jesus' Ministry to Sinners: Ref. 'The Law':

1:   (i)   The call of Simon . . . 'a sinful man': the cleansing of a leper (ref. Moses) (5. 1-11: v12-16);

   (i')   a healing/forgiving of sins (blasphemy charge): the call of Levi, . . . tax collectors and sinners (5. 17-26: v27-39);

1':   (i)   Sabbath law (6. 1-5: v6-11);

   (i')   the choosing of twelve (incl. a betrayer) on the mountain: down from the mountain — healings (6. 12-16: v17-19)

Sub-section C, 6. 20-49:   Jesus' 'Sermon on the Plain': A Sermon on Discipleship: (Sinners and Disciples: the Law and the Prophets):

1:   Prophetic Teaching:
Four Blessings and Woes (6. 20-26):
(Blessings: '. . . poor; . . . hunger; . . . weep; . . . hate you' 6. 20-23;
Woes: '. . . rich; . . . well fed; . . . laugh; . . . speak well' 6. 24-26)

   C: Paraenetic Teaching:
   (i)   Eight Straightforward Commands (6. 27-30): ('love . . ., do good . . ., bless . . ., pray . . ., if . . ., if . . ., give . . ., and if . . .')
      (c)   Four Statements: a Summary Command and three supporting arguments (Sinners and Disciples; cf. Mt. 7. 12: 'Law and Prophets') (6. 31-34) ('love . . ., do good . . ., lend . . .')
   (i')   Eight Commands (with Reasons) (6. 35-38): ('love . . ., do good . . ., lend . . ., be merciful . . ., do not judge . . ., do not condemn . . ., forgive . . ., give . . .')

1':   Parabolic Teaching:
Four Illustrations of Blessing and Woe (6. 39-49): (Blind Man: 6. 39, 40; Speck of sawdust: 6. 41, 42; Tree/its Fruit: 6. 43-45; House-builders: 6. 46-49)

Sub-section I', 7. 1-8. 21:   Jesus' Ministry to Sinners: Ref. 'The Prophets':

1:   (i)   Healing of slave of 'unworthy' centurion: widow's son raised by a 'great prophet' (7. 1-10: v11-17);

   (i')   Isaianic prophecy is fulfilled: someone greater than John (himself, greater than a prophet) is here, a friend of tax collectors and sinners . . . (7. 18-23: v24-35)

1'   (i)   In Simon's house, the 'prophet' forgives sins: the twelve and women travel with Jesus (7. 36-50: 8. 1-3):

   (i')   a parable and its teaching: disciples 'hear and do' (8. 4-15: v16-21).

Luke's Gospel Section 4′ (22. 1-53): Disciples to Sinners:

Sub-section I, 22. 1-13:   The Plot to Betray Jesus Is Prepared: The Passover Is Prepared Also:

1:    (i)   The Feast of Unleavened Bread ('the Passover') approaches; the chief priests and scribes plot against Jesus (22. 1: v2);

    (i′)   Satan enters Judas who plots with the chief priests and officers to betray Jesus 'away from the multitude' (22. 3, 4: v5, 6);

1′:   (i′)   The day of Unleavened Bread arrives; Jesus sends Peter and John to prepare 'the passover' (22. 7, 8: v9);

    (i′)   Jesus' instructions, the details regarding the place for the preparation of the passover (22. 10-12: v13)

Sub-section C, 22. 14-30: The Last Supper: The Passover Meal:

1:    At table: Jesus speaks about himself and the kingdom (22. 14-20):

   (i)   his not eating and drinking: kingdom related (22. 14-18);

   (i′)   his identification with the bread and the cup (22. 19, 20)

      C: The betrayer is present at the table (22. 21-23):

         (i)   the betrayer is present (22. 21);

           (c)   Jesus 'goes' as it is determined (.i):
              but the betrayer will reap woe (.i′) (22. 22);

         (i′)   who is the betrayer? (22. 23)

1′:   Settling an argument, Jesus speaks about himself and the kingdom (22. 24-30):

   (i)   the argument over 'the greatest': Jesus serves (22. 24-27);

   (i′)   the disciples will eat and drink 'at my table in my kingdom' . . . (22. 28-30)

Sub-section I′, 22. 31-53:   Preparations for the Betrayal: The Betrayal Itself:

1:    (i)   Simon and Satan: Simon is ready . . . (22. 31, 32: v33, 34);

    (i′)   Preparations, swords: scripture to be fulfilled, 'reckoned with transgressors' (22. 35, 36: v37, 38)

1′:   (i)   At the Mount of Olives, prayerful preparations, against temptation (22. 39, 40: v41-46);

    (i′)   Judas' betrayal of Jesus and healing of sword-wound: chief priests, officers and elders arrest Jesus as a 'criminal' (22. 47-51: v52, 53).

Luke's Gospel Section 5 (8. 22-9. 43a): Jesus' Identity; His Authority; The Christ; His Death; His Glorious Return as Judge; His Transfiguration; The Disciples' Purpose:

Sub-section I, 8. 22-56:   A Journey across the Lake and Back:

1:    (i)   They set out across the lake, a storm breaks: Jesus stills it; 'Who is this?' they wonder (8. 22, 23: v24, 25);

    (i')   they arrive and Jesus ministers freedom to a demoniac; the people ask Jesus to leave so he returns across the lake (8. 26-33: v34-39);

1':   (i)   They return and Jesus is called to Jairus' house and his only daughter: on the way, a woman with an issue of blood is healed; she is commended for her 'faith' (8. 40-42a: v42b-48);

    (i')   Jesus is told Jairus' daughter is dead: arriving at the house, he enters with Peter, James and John and raises her, to the amazement of her parents (8. 49, 50: v51-56)

Sub-section C, 9. 1-27: The Disciples Are Sent Out: They Return:

1:    (i)   Instructed by Jesus, the disciples are sent out (with instructions to take minimum provisions) to preach the kingdom of God and to heal (9. 1-5: v6);

    (i')   Herod hears about what they do and wonders who Jesus is . . . John raised from the dead, Elijah, one of the old prophets risen (9. 7, 8: v9);

1':   (i)   The disciples return to Jesus who speaks of the kingdom of God to the crowd and heals: five thousand are miraculously fed from minimum provisions (9. 10, 11: v12-17);

    (i')   Jesus asks the disciples, 'Who do the people say that I am?' John the Baptist, Elijah, one of the old prophets risen. Peter supplies the true identity, 'the Christ' and Jesus speaks of his suffering, death and resurrection. He speaks of the costs and the rewards of following him, his parousia and the kingdom of God (9. 18-22: v23-27)

Sub-section I', 9. 28-43a: An Ascent and Descent of a Mountain:

1:    (i)   Jesus takes Peter, James and John up on a mountain where he is transfigured: Moses and Elijah appear (9. 28, 29: v30, 31);

    (i')   Peter and his companions see this and Peter comments: a cloud overshadows them and they hear a voice saying, 'This is my Son, my chosen, listen to him.' (9. 32, 33: v34-36);

1':   (i)   They come down from the mountain and a man asks Jesus to heal his only son: Jesus rebukes their 'faithlessness' (9. 37-40: v41);

    (i')   The boy convulses but Jesus rebukes the unclean spirit, heals him and gives him back to his father. All were astonished at the majesty of God (9. 42: v43a).

Luke's Gospel Section 5' (19. 47-21. 38): Jesus' Teaching in the Temple: His Authority; His Death; The Christ; The Apocalypse and His Return as Judge, in Glory; The Disciples' Purpose:

Sub-section I, 19. 47-20. 26: Jesus Is Questioned by the Chief Priests, Scribes and Elders:

1: (i) Jesus was teaching daily in the temple: the chief priests, scribes and principal men seek to destroy him; all the people 'hung upon his words' (19. 47a: v47b, 48);

(i') the chief priests, scribes and elders question Jesus on his authority: they fail to answer Jesus' question (afraid of the people) (20. 1-4: v5-8).

1': (i) Jesus tells a parable (about wicked tenants): he supports its meaning with reference to a scripture (20. 9-16a: v16b-18);

(i') perceiving he had told the parable against them, the scribes and the chief priests try to trap him: they question him on tribute to Caesar (20. 19, 20: v21-26)

Sub-section C, 20. 27-21. 4: Jesus Is Questioned by Sadducees: Scribes Commend Him for His Answer:

1: (i) Sadducees question Jesus on the resurrection and Moses' law: they give an example of a widow (20. 27, 28: v29-33);

(i') Jesus replies on marriage and heaven: he then interprets Moses' understanding of resurrection (20. 34-36: v37, 38);

1': (i) Scribes commend Jesus for his answer: he then questions them about 'the Christ' as David's son (20. 39, 40: v41-44);

(i') Jesus warns the people concerning the scribes who receive the greater condemnation: in contrast, he commends a poor widow (20. 45-47: 21. 1-4).

Sub-section I', 21. 5-38: Jesus Is Questioned by His Disciples:

1: (i) Jesus speaks of the destruction of the temple: his disciples question him about the date and about the signs preceeding it (21. 5, 6: v7);

(i') Jesus answers, warning (1) of others coming . . .; (2) of upheavals on earth and signs in heaven; (C1) of a time of persecution . . .; (C1') of a time of vengeance . . .; (2') of signs in heaven and distress on earth . . .; and (1') of *his* parousia (a six part chiasm: 21. 8, 9; v10, 11; v12-19; v20-24; v25, 26; v27, 28).

1': (i') He tells a parable (of the fig tree) and gives the explanation to it: Jesus then gives final warning (21. 29-33: 34-36);

(i') daily he teaches in the temple, but at night stays on Mount Olivet: early each morning, the people gather to hear him in the temple (21. 37: v38).

Luke's Gospel Section C (9. 43b-19. 46): 'Jesus' Journey to Jerusalem: His Teaching on the Way':

Sub-section I, 9. 43b-10. 24:   Setting Out for Jerusalem   (43½ verses):

1:   Jesus' Fate, disciples (know, concealed) (7½ verses) (9. 43b-45: v46-50);

  2:   Messengers are sent ahead, Son of Man came to save
     (6 verses) (9. 51-53: v54-56);

    C: Three 'Would-be' disciples and the Kingdom of God
      (6 verses) (chiasm: 9. 57, 58: v59, 60: v61, 62);

  2':   Seventy are sent ahead (20 verses) (10. 1-16: v17-20);

1':   Blessedness of disciples (hidden, know) (4 verses) (10. 21, 22: v23, 24);

Sub-section C, 10. 25-18. 30:   Jesus' Teaching on the Way   (331 verses):

1:   Inheriting Eternal Life: law and love (18 verses) (10. 25-37: v38-42);

  2:   Prayer: persistence; the Holy Spirit is given (13 verses) (11. 1-4: v5-13);

    3:   The Kingdom of God: what is internal is of importance
      (53 verses) (11. 14-36: v37-12. 12);

      4:   Earthly & Heavenly Riches; the coming of the son of man (36 verses)
        (12. 13-34: v35-48);

        5:   Divisions; warning and prudence; repentance of sinners (20 verses)
          (12. 49-59: 13. 1-9);

          C: Sabbath Law: Kingdom and entry; Jerusalem: Jesus to be killed:
            (50 verses) (chiasm: 13. 10-30: v31-35: 14. 1-24);

        5':   Divisions; warning and prudence; repentance of sinners (43 verses)
          (14. 25-35: 15. 1-32);

      4':   Earthly & Heavenly Riches; judgement: reward and punishment (41
        verses) (16. 1-31: 17. 1-10);

    3':   The Kingdom of God is within, not coming with signs (27 verses) (17.
      11-19: v20-37);

  2':   Prayer: persistence; receiving the Kingdom (17 verses) (18. 1-14: v15-17);

1'   Inheriting Eternal Life: law and love (13 verses) (18. 18-27: v28-30);

Sub-section I', 18. 31-19. 46: Arriving in Jerusalem (59 verses):

1:   Jesus' fate, disciples do not understand (4 verses) (18. 31-33: v34);

  2:   Son of David, son of man came to seek, to save (19 verses) (18. 35-43: 19.
    1-10);

    C: Parable on discipleship and the Kingdom of God (18 verses) (chiasm: 19.
      11-15: v16-23: v24-28);

  2'   Davidic blessing; entry into Jerusalem (12 verses) (19. 29-36: v37-40);

1'   Jerusalem's fate (do not know, hidden) (6 verses) (19. 41-44: v45, 46).

The Acts of the Apostles, Section C (11. 27-15. 35): 'Three Journeys of Saul (Paul) and Barnabas, from Antioch:

Sub-section I, 11. 27-12. 25:   Saul and Barnabas Go to Jerusalem (They Take Famine Relief):

1:   A famine is foretold: relief is to be sent to Judea by Barnabas and Saul (11. 27, 28: v29, 30);

  2 :   Herod kills James: it pleases the Jews, so he arrests Peter and puts him in prison (12. 1, 2: v3, 4);

    C: the church prays; Peter is freed from prison by an angel: the praying company are slow to believe he is free (12. 5-10: v11-17);

  2':   Herod orders the sentries be put to death: Tyre and Sidon seek peace with Herod; an angel smites him (12. 18, 19: v20-23);

1':   Barnabas and Saul return from Jerusalem having fulfilled their mission (12. 24: v25);

Sub-section C, 13. 1-14. 28: Barnabas and Saul (Paul) Go on a Mission:

1:   The church in Antioch; Barnabas and Saul are set apart for a mission: after fasting and praying, they go (13. 1, 2: v3);

  2:   John (Mark) accompanies them: a Jewish magician and a (Gentile) proconsul are ministered to: John Mark leaves them (a 3-part chiasm: 13. 4, 5: v6-12: v13);

    C: (i)   the first sabbath in Antioch of Psidia (13. 14-43):
        .i   invitation is given to them to speak (13. 14: v15);
         .ci   'the law, kingship, the one coming (13. 16-25);
         .ci'   'Jesus, not the law, brings freedom' (13. 26-41);
        .i'   invitation is given to them to speak on the next Sabbath: Jews and converts . . . (13. 42: v43);
      (i')   the next sabbath (13. 44-52):
        .i   the Jews are jealous and revile Paul (13. 44: v45);
         .ci   they judge they are 'unworthy of eternal life'; Paul and Barnabas 'turn to Gentiles' (13. 46, 47);
         .ci'   the Gentiles are glad; those ordained to eternal life believe (13. 48, 49);
        .i'   the Jews incite trouble; Paul and Barnabas have to leave (13. 50: v51, 52);

  2':   Jews and Greeks believe but Jews stir up Gentiles to stone Paul: a cripple is healed: Paul is stoned; by tribulation they 'enter the kingdom' (a 3-part chiasm: 14. 1-7: v8-18: v19-22);

1':   elders are appointed with fasting and prayer and they journey back to Antioch: arriving, they report (14. 23-26: v27, 28);

Sub-section I', 15. 1-35:   Paul and Barnabas Go to Jerusalem Concerning the Law and the Gentiles:

1:   Dissension arose over the law and Gentiles: Paul and Barnabas are sent to Jerusalem: they are welcomed on arrival; the issue is raised (15. 1-3: v4-5);

  2:   the apostles and elders are gathered: after much debate, Peter speaks (15. 6: v7-11);

    C: all the assembly keeps silence: they then listen to Barnabas and Saul tell about the Gentiles (15. 12a: v12b);

  2':   James speaks, refering to what Peter has said: he gives his judgement (15. 13-18: v19-21);

1':   plans are made, a letter is written: Paul and Barnabas return to Antioch and stay there (15. 22-29: v30-35).

144

The Acts of the Apostles, Section 5 (9. 32-11. 26): Peter, on Mission: The Role of Vision and Spirit; Jesus Is Judge:
Sub-section I: 9. 32-43: Peter's Ministry Leads to Many Turning to the Lord:
1: (i) Peter goes to Lydda (9. 32);
    (i') a healing leads people to 'turn to the Lord' (9. 33, 34: v35);
1': (i) in Joppa, Tabitha dies (9. 36, 37);
    (i') Peter is called from Lydda; his raising of Tabitha leads to many who 'believed in the Lord' (9. 38-41: v42, 43);

Sub-section C: 10. 1-11. 18: The Conversion and Baptism of Cornelius and His Household (Gentiles) Under Peter's Ministry: His Giving Account of His Mission in Jerusalem (The Role of Vision and the Spirit):
1: The Conversion of Cornelius and his household (10. 1-48):
    (i) at Caesarea, Cornelius is instructed in a vision: at Joppa, Peter has a vision: (10. 1-8: v9-16);
      (c) the Spirit advises Peter of Cornelius' messengers' arrival and of his need to accompany them: Peter goes down to them and questions them (10. 17-20: v21-23a);
    (i') on meeting, both Peter and Cornelius explain about their visions: Peter speaks of Jesus (. . . the judge) and the Holy Spirit falls on all who are listening (10. 23a-33: v34-48);
1': Peter's report, in Jerusalem: Gentiles have 'life' (11. 1-18):
    (i) the apostles hear that Gentiles have received the word of God: in Jerusalem, Peter is criticised (11. 1: v2, 3);
      (c) Peter gives a full report, firstly of his vision; and secondly of the events which followed on from it (11. 4-10: v11-17);
    (i') those who are critical are silenced: they then glorify God that Gentiles too are 'granted repentance unto life' (11. 18a: v18b);

Sub-section I': 11. 19-26: In Antioch, Greeks Too Turn to the Lord: Barnabas Calls Saul to Help Teach the 'Christians' There:
1: (i) the ministry of the scattered church was to Jews only (11. 19);
    (i') but in Antioch, Greeks too were spoken to: 'a great number that believed turned to the Lord' (11. 20: v21)
1': (i) the Church in Jerusalem hears about this and sends Barnabas to them: under his ministry, many 'were added to the Lord' (11. 22: v23, 24);
    (i') Barnabas seeks out Saul and takes him to Antioch: they teach; it is there, disciples are first called 'Christians' (11. 25, 26a: v26b, c).

The Acts of the Apostles, Section 5′ (15. 36-18. 23): Paul, on Mission: The Role of Vision and Spirit; Jesus Is Judge:

Sub-section I: 15. 36-16. 10:   Paul and His Travelling Companions: The Role of Vision and Spirit: His Strengthening of the Churches:

1:   (i) Paul plans to revisit cities of his earlier mission with Barnabas: they separate; Paul chooses Silas and travels through Syria . . . strengthening the churches (15. 36-38: v39-41);

      (i′) he chooses Timothy (son of a Greek father) to accompany him: the churches are strengthened (16. 1-3: v4, 5);

1′: (i) They travel through Phrygia and Galatia; the Spirit prevents them from going into Asia: at Mysia, the Spirit again prevents them going somewhere, so they arrive at Troas (16. 6: v7, 8);

      (i′) in the night, Paul has a vision of a Macedonian asking for help in his country: it is concluded that God is calling Paul to preach the gospel there (16. 9: v10);

Sub-section C: 16. 11-18. 8:   Believers and Households Are Baptised Under Paul's Ministry: Paul Encounters Troubles with Jews and Turns to the Gentiles:

1:   Paul in Philippi: an exorcism gets him into trouble and prison:

      (i) Lydia, a worshipper of God, and her household are baptised; she offers Paul hospitality: an exorcism lands Paul in prison (16. 11-15: v16-24);

          (c) an earthquake shakes the prison doors open: the jailer is stopped from killing himself (16. 25, 26: v27,28);

      (i′) the jailer tends Paul's wounds; he and his household believe and are baptised: day breaks; after an apology, and farewell to Lydia, they leave the city (16. 29-34: v35-40);

1′: Paul in Thessalonica, Beroea, Athens and Corinth:

      (i) Paul in the synagogue teaching, 'Jesus is the Christ'; trouble ensues: Paul is sent away; more trouble follows him; he is sent to Athens (Silas and Timothy stay in Beroea) (17. 1-9: v10-15);

          (c) Paul sees the idols, he is mocked for preaching Jesus and the resurrection; he is taken to the Areopagus: there he speaks (judgement) and is mocked for speaking of the resurrection (17. 16-21: v22-34);

      (i′) Paul again argues in the synagogue: Silas and Timothy arrive as he teaches 'Christ was Jesus'; he turns to the Gentiles; he stays with a worshipper of God; the ruler of the synagogue and his household believe; many are baptised (18. 1-4: v5-8);

Sub-section I′: 18. 9-23:   Paul (and Companions) According to Vision and God's Guidance Minister Where They Are Called: Disciples Are Strengthened:

1:   (i) In a night vision, Paul is directed to stay in Corinth; no harm will come to him: he stays (18. 9, 10: v11);

      (i′) Paul is attacked and brought before the tribunal: the synagogue ruler is beaten (18. 12-15: v16, 17);

1′: (i) Paul travels to Syria with companions and parts from them in Ephesus where he speaks in the synagogue: they ask him to stay; he will return 'if God wills' (18. 18, 19: v20, 21);

      (i′) at Caesarea, he greeted the church and then went to Antioch: after some time there, he goes through Galatia and Phrygia strengthening all the disciples (18. 22: v23).

The Acts of the Apostles, Section 4 (6. 1-9. 31): The Jerusalem Church: Persecution and Scattering; Saul's Conversion:

Sub-section I, 6. 1-8. 3:   The Church in Jerusalem: The Events Leading Up to Its Persecution:

1:   In Jerusalem, the church grows: the 'seven' are chosen (6. 1-7):
    (i)   The church grows: Hellenists argue with Hebrews (6. 1);
       (c)   the twelve ask for seven to help: seven (notably Stephen) are chosen (6. 2-4: v5, 6);
    (i')   the church continues to grow in Jerusalem (6. 7);
    C: Stephen's Ministry and Martyrdom (6. 8-8. 1a):
       (i)   Stephen is challenged: he is seized and charged (6. 8-10: v11-15);
          (c)   Stephen's speech (7. 1: v2-53);
            .i   the law: history (7. 2-34)
                       Stephen's judgements (7. 35-40);
            .i'   the prophets: history (7. 41-50)
                       Stephen's judgements (7. 51-53);
       (i')   Stephen is stoned: he dies (Saul approves) (7. 54-58: v59-8. 1a);
1':   The Church in Jerusalem suffers persecution (8. 1b-3):
    (i)   the church is scattered; the apostles alone stay (8. 1bc);
       (c)   Stephen is buried (8. 2);
    (i')   the church suffers much imprisonment (8. 3);

Sub-section I', 8. 4-9. 31: The Scattered Church: The Events Which Follow Its Initial Persecution:

1:   The ministry of Philip (and the apostles from Jerusalem) (8. 4-40):
    (i)   Philip's success in Samaria: Simon believes (8. 4-8: v9-13);
       (c)   apostles in Jerusalem hear and send Peter and John; through them Samaria receives the Spirit: Simon observes how; he wants the power to do the same and is judged; the apostles return to Jerusalem (8. 14-17: v18-25);
    (i')   Philip ministers to an Ethiopian, who believes (8. 26-31: v32-40);
    C: Saul's call and purpose (9. 1-22):
       (i)   Saul goes to Damascus for letters: he would imprison followers of the Way in Jerusalem (9. 1, 2a: v2b);
          (c)   on the road to Damascus, he is blinded: in Damascus, he is given his sight and told of his mission (to the Gentiles) (9. 3-9: v10-19a);
       (i')   Saul proclaims Jesus in Damascus: he confounds the Jews (9. 19b-21: v22);
1':   Saul and the apostles in Jerusalem (9. 23-31):
    (i)   a Jewish plot against Saul is exposed: he escapes with help (9. 23, 24a: v24b, 25);
       (c)   in Jerusalem, the disciples are afraid of Saul until Barnabas supports him: in Jerusalem, Saul preaches in the name of the Lord (9. 26, 27: v28);
    (i')   he argues with Hellenists who seek to kill him; he is sent to Tarsus: the church enjoys peace; it grows (9. 29, 30: v31).

The Acts of the Apostles, Section 4' (18. 24-22. 29): In Ephesus, Uproar; and in Jerusalem, Uproar and Paul's Arrest:

Sub-section I, 18. 24-20. 16:   Paul's Ministry and Troubles in Ephesus: to Jerusalem:

1:   In Ephesus, Apollos, then Paul, ministers; in the Spirit, Paul resolves to go to Jerusalem (and Rome) (18. 24-19. 22):
   (i) Apollos is instructed in the Way, he confounds Jews: through Paul, twelve believers receive the Spirit (18. 24-28: 19. 1-7);
     (c) Paul's preaching — all Asia hears: Paul's miracles — all Ephesus hears (19. 8-10: v11-17);
   (i') believers give up old practices: in the Spirit, Paul resolves to go through Macedonia to Jerusalem (19. 18-20: v21, 22);
   C: Paul causes an uproar in Ephesus (19. 23-41):
     (i) Demetrius and craftsmen have a charge against Paul: Artemis is threatened (19. 23, 24: v25-27);
       (c) Uproar in Ephesus (a basic, three-part chiasm: 19. 28; v29: 19. 30; v31: 19. 32, 33; v34);
     (i') in speaking of Artemis, the town clerk advises Demetrius and craftsmen to use the court (19. 35-40: v41);
1':   Paul's continuing ministry, travelling and making for Jerusalem (20. 1-16):
   (i) Paul goes to Macedonia . . . and returns: companions go ahead to Troas (Unleavened Bread) (20. 1-3: v4-6);
     (c) met to break bread, Paul speaks . . . Eutychus falls out of the window; he is raised up: bread is broken, the boy is fine (20. 7-10: v11, 12);
   (i') Paul separates again from companions for a time: he hopes to reach Jerusalem for Pentecost (20. 13-15: v16);

Sub-section I', 20. 17-22. 29:   Paul's Farewell to Ephesian Elders and Others: His Arriving in Jerusalem Leads to Trouble and His Arrest:

1:   Paul's farewell speech to Ephesian elders (20. 17-38):
   (i) Ephesian elders are called: they arrive (20. 17: v18a);
     (c) Paul's speech concerning his ministry and future (a four-part chiasm: 20. 18b-21: v22-24: v25-31: v32-35);
   (i') they pray, kiss and separate (20. 36: v37, 38);
   C: Paul is warned not to go to Jerusalem: he goes there, causes an uproar and is attacked (21. 1-30):
     (i) in Tyre, Paul is warned not to go to Jerusalem: in Caesarea with Philip (of the 'seven'), he is warned (21. 1-6: v7-14);
       (c) Paul goes to Jerusalem: he is welcomed (21. 15, 16: v17);
     (i') in the company of apostles, Paul is warned and action is taken: but in the temple he is set upon (21. 18-26: v27-30);
1':   Paul is held, but delivers a speech in Jerusalem (21. 31- 22. 29):
   (i) the crowd cry, 'Away with him': the tribune mistakes Paul's identity and citizenship (21. 31-36: v37-40);
     (c) Paul's speech concerning his call and purpose (a four-part chiasm: 22. 1-5: v6-11: v12-16: v17-21); .
   (i') they cry, 'Away with (him) . . .': the tribune learns of Paul's citizenship (22. 22-24: v25-29).

The Acts of the Apostles, Section 3 (2. 43-5. 42): The Developing Church in Jerusalem: Arrests, Trials and Judgements:

Sub-section I, 2. 43-4. 31:   An Episode Concerning Two Apostles:

1:   (i)   Wonders and signs, the church sharing (2. 43-45: v46, 47);
     (i') a healing leads to preaching in Solomon's Portico (3. 1-10: v11-26);

  C: (i)   Peter and John are arrested for preaching about Jesus and the resurrection (4. 1, 2: v3);
       (i') the church grows (4. 4a: v4b);

1':   (i)   tried by the council, they are charged not to preach (4. 5-12: v13-22);
      (i') on release, they report . . ., signs and wonders (4. 23-28: v29-31).

Sub-section I', 4. 32-5. 42:   An Episode Concerning All The Apostles:

1:   (i)   The church sharing (4. 32-35: v36-37);
     (i') two deaths; signs and wonders; together in Solomon's Portico (5. 1-11: v12-16);

  C: (i)   their arrest, because of jealousies (5. 17: v18);
       (i') miraculous escape and command (5. 19, 20: v21a);

1':   (i)   re-taken, they are presented before the Sanhedrin (5. 21b-26: v27-32);
      (i') they are charged with teaching in the name of Jesus: beaten, they are released (5. 33-39b: v39c-42).

The Acts of the Apostles, Section 3' (22. 30-26. 32): Paul's Trials: The Judgements and His Appeal to Caesar:

Sub-section I, 22. 30-24. 27:   Paul Before the Tribune and the Council: His Transfer to Caesarea and before the Governor, Felix:

1:   (i)   Paul before the Sanhedrin and the tribune (22. 30-23. 5: v6-11);
      (i') a plot against Paul (23. 12-15: v16-22);
   C: (i)   Paul's transfer to Caesarea planned (23. 23-24: v25-30);
        (i') Paul's transfer carried out (23. 31-33: v34, 35);
1': (i)   Paul's before Felix (24. 1-9: v10-21);
      (i') Felix and Drusilla see Paul privately: Felix reaches his limit; he leaves Paul in prison (24. 22, 23: v24-27).

Sub-section I', 25. 1-26. 32:   Paul before Governor Festus: His Appeal to Caesar: Paul before King Agrippa:

1:   (i)   Festus is informed about Paul; Jews plot again: before Festus, Paul appeals to Caesar (25. 1-5: v6-12);
      (i') Festus informs Agrippa about these things (25. 13-16: v17-21);
   C: (i)   Agrippa makes a request to hear Paul (25. 22a);
        (i') Festus responds, 'Tomorrow . . .' (25. 22b);
1': (i)   Paul before Agrippa: the introduction is by Festus; account is given by Paul (25. 23-27: 26. 1-23);
      (i') Festus interrupts; Paul challenges Agrippa, who reacts: Agrippa and Bernice rise, Paul's doing nothing deserving death: he would have been freed if he had not appealed to Caesar (26. 24-29: v30-32).

The Acts of the Apostles, Section 2 (2. 1-42): The Day of Pentecost: The Birth of the Church's Mission:

Sub-section I, 2. 1-13:   The Spirit Is Given: The People's Initial Response:

1:    The Holy Spirit is given (2. 1, 2: v3, 4);

1':   God-fearing Jews 'from every nation under heaven' are amazed and perplexed (2. 5, 6: v7-13);

Sub-section C, 2. 14-36:   Peter's Speech:

1:    The Holy Spirit's outpouring is the fulfilment of Joel's prophecy . . . (2. 14-16: v17-21);

C: Jesus whom they killed and God raised is witnessed to by David (2. 22-24: v25-28);

1':   the Holy Spirit's outpouring is the assurance of Jesus' exaltation (2. 29-31: v32-36);

Sub-section I', 2. 37-42:   The People's Considered Response:

1:    those who were amazed earlier now ask what they should do: Peter tells them (2. 37: v38, 39);

1':   Peter exhorts them further: three thousand respond that day and devote themselves to the apostles' teaching . . . (2. 40: v41, 42).

The Acts of the Apostles, Section 2' (27. 1-28. 15): Paul's Eventful Journey to Italy and Rome:

Sub-section I, 27. 1-12:   Setting Out for Italy:

1:    Paul and others are handed over to the centurion and put on board ship: they set sail, the centurion shows kindness; they encounter difficulties on the voyage (27. 1, 2: v3-8);

1':   Paul's warning: it is unheeded (27. 9, 10: v11, 12);

Sub-section C, 27. 13-44:   Storms and Shipwreck:

1:    Storms; hope of being saved goes: Paul gives encouragement and foretells their running aground (27. 13-20: v21-26);

C: trouble heightens: Paul's advice is acted upon (27. 27-29: v30-32);

1':   Paul again encourages the company; no one will lose their life: they run aground and the ship is wrecked (27. 33-38: v39-44);

Sub-section I', 28. 1-15:   Arrival in Rome (After Stay on Malta):

1:    the Maltese show kindness; they are amazed Paul does not die: Paul heals; supplies are given them (28. 1-6: v7-10);

1':   they set sail, with no report of problems: they arrive in Rome and are greeted (28. 11-13a: v13b-15).

The Acts of the Apostles, Section 1 (1. 1-26): Integral Prologue; Convincing Proofs; The Promise of the Spirit; The Pre-Pentecost Days in Jerusalem:

Sub-section I, 1. 1-11:   A 'Replacement' for Jesus:

1:    Prologue: the story up to Jesus' ascension, proofs of Jesus' resurrection; his speaking of the kingdom; his command: 'stay in Jerusalem' . . . the promise of the Holy Spirit (ref. John's baptism) (1. 1, 2: v3-5);

1':   the final meeting; the promise of the Spirit; the apostles are to be witnesses in Jerusalem, Judea . . .; Jesus' ascension and the angels' announcements (1. 6-8: v9-11);

Sub-section I', 1. 12-26:   A 'Replacement' for Judas:

1:    returning to Jerusalem, they stay together: the eleven and others, the women, Mary (Jesus' mother) and his brothers, in prayer (1. 12, 13a: v13b, 14);

1':   Judas Iscariot: the Psalms' fulfilment and his replacement; a witness from John's baptism to Jesus' ascension, a witness of his resurrection; the proposal of two names: the lot falls on Matthias who is added to the eleven (1. 15-22: v23-26).

The Acts of the Apostles, Section 1' (28. 16-31): In Rome, Paul's Work Continues; Belief and Disbelief:

Sub-section I, 28. 16-22:   Paul, Under House Arrest: A First Meeting:

1:    In Rome, Paul stays by himself with a soldier guarding him (28. 16a: v16b);

1':   he seeks to be heard by leading Jews and explains his situation, because of the hope of Israel (28. 17-20: v21, 22);

Sub-section I', 28. 23-31: Paul's Ministry in His House: A Later Meeting:

1:    they come to him in large numbers; he instructs them in the scriptures: some are convinced, others disbelieve; '. . . the Gentiles will listen . . .' (28. 23: v24-28);

1':   for two years, Paul lives there; he preaches the kingdom of God and teaches about Jesus (28. 30: v31).

The Gospel of John:

I   **Section 1:** 1. 1-4. 54 (166 verses):
Integral Prologue; John the Baptist's Testimony; Jesus' Appearance; Peter's Call:
Sign One: Water Into Wine; Feast One: Marriage:
1. 1-34 (3 parts v1-18; v19-28; v29-34); 1. 35-2. 11 (3 parts: v35-42; v43-51; 2. 1-11):
Sacrifice and Worship: Jesus' Universal Significance: Sign Two: Healing of
Official's Son; Feast Two: Passover:
2. 12-3. 36 (3 parts: 2. 12-22; v23-3. 21; v22-36); 4. 1-54 (3 parts: v1-26; v27-42;
v43-54).

II   **Section 2:** 5. 1-6. 71 (118 verses):
Sign Three: Healing of a Paralysed Man; Feast Three: A Jewish Feast:
5. 1-18 (3 parts: v1-9a; v9b-13; v14-18); 5. 19-47 (3 parts: v19-30; v31-40;
v41-47):
'I Am the Bread of Life'; Sign Four: Feeding of Five Thousand; Feast Four:
Passover:
6. 1-34 (3 parts: v1-15; v16-21; v22-34); 6. 35-71 (3 parts: v35-46; v47-59; v60-71).

III   **Section 3:** 7. 1-9. 41 (153 verses):
Feast Five: Tabernacles; The Christ?
7. 1-36 (3 parts: v1-13; v14-32; v33-36); 7. 37-8. 11 (3 parts: v37-44;
v45-52; v53-8. 11):
'I Am the Light of the World'; Sign Five: Healing of Blind Man:
8. 12-59 (3 parts: v12-30; v31-47; v48-59); 9. 1-41 (3 parts: v1-12; v13-34;
v35-41).

C   **Section 4:** 10. 1-11. 54 (96 verses):
'I Am the Door/the Good Shepherd'; Feast Six: Dedication:
10. 1-21 (3 parts: v1-6; v7-18; v19-21); 10. 22-42 (3 parts: v22-30; v31-39;
v40-42):
'I Am the Resurrection and the Life'; Sign Six: The Raising of Lazarus:
11. 1-37 (3 parts: v1-5; v6-16; v17-37); 11. 38-54 (3 parts: v38-44; v45-53;
v54).

III′   **Section 5:** 11. 55-14. 31 (122 verses):
Feast Seven: Passover, Part I; The Christ?
11. 55-12. 19 (3 parts: v55-57; 12. 1-11; v12-19); 12. 20-50 (3 parts: v20-29;
v30-36; v37-50):
'I Am the Way, the Truth and the Life'; Parting Discourses:
13. 1-30 (3 parts: v1; v2-17; v18-30); 13. 31-14. 31 (3 parts: 13. 31-38; 14.
1-14; v15-31).

II′   **Section 6:** 15. 1-18. 27 (113 verses):
'I Am the True Vine': Parting Discourses, Part II:
15. 1-16. 4a (3 parts: v1-8; v9-17; v18-16. 4a); 16. 4b-33 (3 parts: v4b-15;
v16-24; 25-33):
Jesus' High Priestly Prayer and Arrest:
17. 1-26 (3 parts: v1-5; v6-19; v20-26); 18. 1-27 (3 parts: v1-11; v12-18; v19-27).

I′   **Section 7:** 18. 28-21. 25 (111 verses):
Passover, Part III: Jesus' Trials, Death and Burial:
18. 28-19. 16a (3 parts: 18. 28-40; 19. 1-12; v13-16a); 19. 16b-42 (3 parts:
v16b-22; v23-30; v31-42):
Resurrection Appearances; Peter's Commissioning; John's Testimony:
20. 1-31 (3 parts: v1-18; v19-29; v30, 31); 21. 1-25 (3 parts: v1-14; v15-23; v24,
25).

Note: the central positionings of the extended 'I am . . .' sayings and in paricular the
oppositions of 'bread' and 'vine'.

Note: all seven sections divide into twelve parts (two times two times three).

The Gospel of John: The Earlier Version: A Reconstruction:

Taking into account (i) the discovery of the present structure, (ii) evident displacements in the current text and (iii) some of the more commonly agreed redactional arguments, the following is proposed:

'The Book of the Seven Signs':

Independent Prologue: 1. 1-5, v9-14, v16-18: (14 verses): The Very Beginning; The Gospel's Synopsis: Life, Light, Grace and Truth; Believing:
3 parts: 1. 1-5; v9-13; v14, 16-18.

Section 1: 1. 19-2. 12, 3. 22-30: (53 verses):
Feast One: Marriage; Sign One: Water to Wine: John and Jesus:
1. 19-42 (3 parts: v19-28; v29-34; v35-42); 1. 43-3. 30 (3 parts:
1. 43-51; 2. 1-12; 3. 22-30).

Section 2: 2. 23-3. 15, v31-36, v16-21, 4. 3-54 (82 verses):
Feast Two: Passover; Sign Two: Healing of Official's Son:
2. 23-3. 21 (3 parts: 2. 23-25; 3. 1-15; 3. 31-36, 16-21); 4. 3-54 (3 parts: v3-26;
v27-42; v43-54).

Section 3: 5. 1-47, 7. 15-24 (57 verses):
Feast Three: A Feast of the Jews; Sign Three: Healing of Paralysed Man:
5. 1-18 (3 parts: v1-9a; v9b-13; v14-18); 5. 19-47 & 7. 15-24 (3 parts: 5. 19-30;
v31-40; v41-47, 7. 15-24).

Section 4: 6. 1-71 (71 verses):
Feast Four: Passover; Sign Four: Feeding of the Five Thousand:
6. 1-34 (3 parts: v1-15; v16-21; v22-34); 6. 35-71 (3 parts: v35-46; v47-59; v60-71).

Section 5: 7. 1-14, v25-32, v37-44, 8. 12-20, 9. 1-41: (79 verses):
Feast Five: Tabernacles; Sign Five: Healing of a Blind Man:
7. 1-8. 12 (3 parts: 7. 1-13; v14, v25-32; v37-44, 8. 12-20); 9. 1-41 (3 parts: 9. 1-12;
v13-34; v35-41).

Section 6: 10. 22-42, 11. 1-54: (maximum 75 verses):
Feast Six: Dedication; Sign Six: Raising of Lazarus:
10. 22-42 (3 parts: 10. 22-30; v31-39; v40-42); 11. 1-54 (3 parts from: 11. 1-16;
v17-37; v38-54).

Section 7: 11. 55-12. 43, 13. 1-38, 14. 1-31, 18. 1b-20. 29: (maximum 145 verses):
Feast Seven: Passover; Sign Seven: Jesus' Death and Resurrection:
11. 55-12. 43 (3 parts: 11. 55-57; 12. 1-8; v12, 17-19, 37-43);
13. 1-18. 27 (13. 1-14. 31 [3 parts: 13. 1; v2, 21b-30; v31-33, 36-38, 14. 31c];
               18. 1b-27 [3 parts: 18. 1b-11; v12-18; v19-27]);
18. 28-19. 42 (18. 28-19. 16a [3 parts: 18. 28-40; 19. 1-12; v13-16a];
                19. 16b-42 [3 parts: 19. 16b-22; v23-30; v31-33, 38, (40), 41, 42]);
20. 1-29 (3 parts: 20. 1-18; v19-23; v24-29).

Epilogue: 20. 30, 31: (2 verses):
Other Signs/These Signs: Belief and Life (20. 30; v31).

Note: Sections 1 to 6 each divide into two series of three parts. Section 7 divides into an introductory series of three parts, two series of three parts followed by another two series of three parts, and an ending of a further series of three parts.

The Revelation to John:

Prologue: 1. 1-8: (8 verses): parts in simple parallelism:
The Title; Address and Greeting: 'Jesus Is Coming':
1. 1-3; v4-8.

I   **Section 1:** 1. 9-3. 22: (63 verses):
The Messages to the Seven Churches:
Introduction: 1. 9-20;
Seven Churches: 2. 1-7; v8-11; v12-17; v18-29; 3. 1-6; v7-13; v14-22.

   II   **Section 2:** 4. 1-8. 1: (60 verses):
The Seven Seals:
Introduction: 4. 1-5. 14;
Seven Seals: 6. 1, 2; v3, 4; v5, 6; v7, 8; v9-11; v12-7. 17; 8. 1.

      III   **Section 3:** 8. 2-11. 18: (62 verses):
The Seven Trumpets:
Introduction: 8. 2-6;
Seven Trumpets: 8. 7; v8, 9; v10, 11; v12, 13; 9. 1-12; v13-21; 10. 1-11. 18.

         C   **Section 4:** 11. 19-15. 4: (60 verses):
Seven Visions:
Introduction: 11. 19-12. 18;
Seven Visions: 13. 1-10; v11-18; 14. 1-5; v6-13; v14-20; 15. 1; v2-4.

      III'   **Section 5:** 15. 5-16. 21: (25 verses):
The Seven Plagues (Bowls):
Introduction: 15. 5-16. 1;
Seven Plagues: 16. 2; v3; v4-7; v8, 9; v10, 11; v12-16; v17-21.

   II'   **Section 6:** 17. 1-19. 10: (52 verses):
Seven Words of Condemnation on Babylon:
Introduction: 17. 1-6;
Seven Words: 17. 7-14; v15-18; 18. 1-3; v4-20; v21-24; 19. 1-5; v6-10.

I'   **Section 7:** 19. 11-22. 5: (58 verses):
Seven Final Visions:
Introduction: 19. 11-16;
Seven Visions: 19. 17, 18; v19-21; 20. 1-3; v4-10; v11; v12-15; 21. 1-22. 5.

Epilogue: 22. 6-21: (16 verses): parts in simple parallelism:
The Concluding Testimony: 'Jesus Is Coming':
22. 6-15; v16-21.

Note: Compare the seven-section structure of this book with those of the two versions of John's Gospel.

Note: All Sections, bar Section 5, are of similar length. Have some verses been removed from Section 5? (But, see 22. 19).

REFERENCES

Chapter 1, Introduction

1 M. D. Goulder:
'The Evangelists' Calendar: A Lectionary Explanation of the Development of Scripture', *SPCK 1978, p75;*

2 K. E. Bailey:
'Poet and Peasant: A Literary Cultural Approach to the Parables in Luke', *Eerdmans 1976, p45;*

3 M. D. Goulder:
'The Chiastic Structure of the Lucan Journey', *Texte Untersuchungen Vol. 87, 1963, p195;*

4 Bailey: *op. cit. p47;*

5 C. H. Talbert:
'Literary Patterns, Theological Themes and the Genre of Luke-Acts', *Soc. Bibl. Lit./Scholars Press 1974, pp85, 87;*

6 D. R. Miesner:
'The Missionary Journeys' Narrative: Patterns and Implications'; *C. H. Talbert (ed.):* 'Perspectives on Luke-Acts', *T. & T. Clark Ltd, 1978, p201;*

7 Talbert: *op. cit. p83;*

8 *ibid. pp67-70;*

Chapter 2, Mark's Gospel:

1 W. G. Kummel:
'Introduction to the New Testament', *SCM 1975, pp 85, 86;*

2 Henry Bettenson:
'Documents of the Christian Church', *Oxford University Press 1963, p27;* and
R. McL. Wilson:
'Mark'; *Matthew Black and H. H. Rowley (eds.):* 'Peake's Commentary on the Bible', *Nelson 1977, p799.*

Chapter 3, Matthew's Gospel:

1 B. W. Bacon:
'Studies in Matthew', *1930;*

2 F. C. Grant:
'The Gospel of Matthew', *The Interpreter's Dictionary of the Bible, Abingdon, Nashville 1962, p304;*

3 R. G. Hamerton-Kelly:
'The Gospel of Matthew', *The Int. Dict. of the Bible, Suppl. Vol., Abingdon, Nashville 1981, p582;*

4 J. D. Kingsbury:
'Form and Message of Matthew', *Int., XXIX (1975) pp13-23,* and the 'Structure of Matthew's Gospel and his concept of Salvation-History', *CBQ XXXV (1973), pp451-474;*

5 F. W. Green:
'The Gospel according to Saint Matthew', in 'The Clarendon Bible', *Oxford 1936;*

6 J. C. Fenton:
'The Gospel of St Matthew', *The Pelican New Testament Commentaries, Penguin Books 1963;*

7 *ibid. p16;*

8 *ibid. p14;*

9 *ibid. p16;*

10 Nestle-Aland:
'Novum Testamentum Graece', *Deutsche Bibelstiftung, Stuttgart 1981;*

11 Fenton: *op. cit. p119;*

12 Eduard Schweizer:
'The Good News according to Matthew', *translated by David E. Green, John Knox Press, Atlanta 1975, pp 218-222;*

13 Fenton: *op. cit. p315;*

14 *ibid. p16;*

15 ibid. p16;

16 Hubert J. Richards:
'The First Christmas: What Really Happened?', *Collins Fontana Books 1973, p73.*

Chapter 4, The Gospel of Luke and the Acts of the Apostles:

1 Talbert: 'Literary Patterns . . .' *op. cit. p80;*

2 I. Howard Marshall:
'Commentary on Luke', *NIGTC, Eerdmans 1978, p40;*

3 Goulder: 'The Evangelists' Calendar' *op. cit. p9;*

4 Robert Maddox:
'The Purpose of Luke-Acts', *T. & T. Clark, Edinburgh 1982, p12;*

5 Nestle-Kilpatrick:
'H KAINH ΔIAΘHKH', *Second Edition, British and Foreign Bible Society, 1954;*

6 Nestle-Aland: *op. cit.;*

7 Talbert: 'Literary Patterns . . .' *op. cit.;*

8 *ibid. p23;*

9 David Gooding:
'According to Luke: A new exposition of the Third Gospel', *IVP 1987;*

10 Eduard Schweizer:
'The Good News according to Luke', *London SPCK 1984;*

11 Goulder: 'The Chiastic Structure . . .' *op. cit. pp195-202;*

12 Bailey: *op. cit.;*

13 Talbert; 'Literary Patterns . . .' *op. cit.;*
        'Perspectives . . .' *op. cit.;*

14 Marshall: *op. cit.;*

15 Goulder: 'The Chiastic Structure . . .' *op. cit.;*

16 *ibid. p195;*

17 Bailey: *op. cit. pp82, 83;*

18 Craigh Blomberg:
'Midrash, Chiasmus, and the Outline of Luke's Central Section', *pp217-259, Gospel Perspectives (Studies in Midrash & Historiography) Vol. III, ed. France & Wenham, JSOT Press 1983;*

19 Miesner: *op. cit. pp199-214;*

20 A. M. Farrer:
'On Dispensing with Q', *Nineham:* 'Studies in the Gospels', *Blackwell 1955, p66;*

21 V. Martin & R. Kasser (eds.):
'Papyrus Bodmer XIV', *Cologny-Geneve 1961;*

22 John Drury:
    'Tradition and Design in Luke's Gospel', *Darton, Longman & Todd, London, 1976, pp122-127.*

Chapter 5, John's Gospel:

1 W. G. Kummel:
   'The New Testament: The History of the Investigations of its Problems', *SCM Press Ltd.*, *1973, pp74, 75;*
2 C. K. Barrett:
   'The Gospel according to St John', *The Westminster Press, Philadelphia, Second Edition 1978, pp11, 12;*
3 Maxwell Staniforth (translator):
   'The Didache': 'Early Christian Writings', *The Penguin Classics 1968, p231;*
4 W. F. Howard:
   'The Fourth Gospel in Recent Criticism and Interpretation', *revised C. K. Barrett, 1955, p299;*
5 Barrett: *op. cit. p316;*
6 *ibid. pp18-21;*
7 *ibid. pp15-18;* also,
   John Marsh:
   'The Gospel of St John', *Pelican New Testament Commentaries, Penguin Books 1968, pp44-46.*

Chapter 6, The Revelation to John:

1 N. Turner:
   'Revelation'; *Matthew Black and H. H. Rowley (eds.):* 'Peake's Commentary on the Bible', *Nelson 1977, p1043;*
2 J. W. Bowman:
   'Revelation, Book of'; *The Interpreter's Dictionary of the Bible, Abingdon, Nashville 1981, pp64, 65;*
3 A. Farrer:
   'The Revelation of St John the Divine', *Oxford University Press, 1964;*
4 N. W. Lund:
   'Chiasmus in the New Testament: A Study in Formgeschichte', *Chapel Hill, N. C.; University of North Carolina Press, 1942;*
5 R. H. Charles:
   'Revelation', *ICC (Edinburgh: T. & T. Clark), 1920;*
6 Michael Wilcock:
   'I Saw Heaven Opened: the Message of Revelation', *The Bible Speaks Today Series, Inter-Varsity Press, 1975;*
7 *ibid. p37;*
8 Lund:*op. cit.;*
9 Turner: *op. cit. pp1060, 1061;*

Chapter 7, Conclusion:

1 Farrer: *op. cit.;*
2 Hans Conzelmann:
   'The Theology of St Luke', *Faber and Faber, London, 1960;*

3 P. Carrington:
   'The Primitive Christian Calendar', *Cambridge 1952;*

4 M. D. Goulder:
   'Midrash and Lection in Matthew', *1974, London;* also,
   Goulder:
   'The Evangelists' Calendar', *op. cit.;*

5 Drury: *op. cit.;*

6 K. Stendahl:
   'The School of St Matthew and its Use of the O. T.', *1954:* also,
   K. Stendahl:
   'Matthew'; 'Peake's Commentary . . .' *op. cit. p769.*